I0795648

IMAGES
of America

NORTH SMITHFIELD

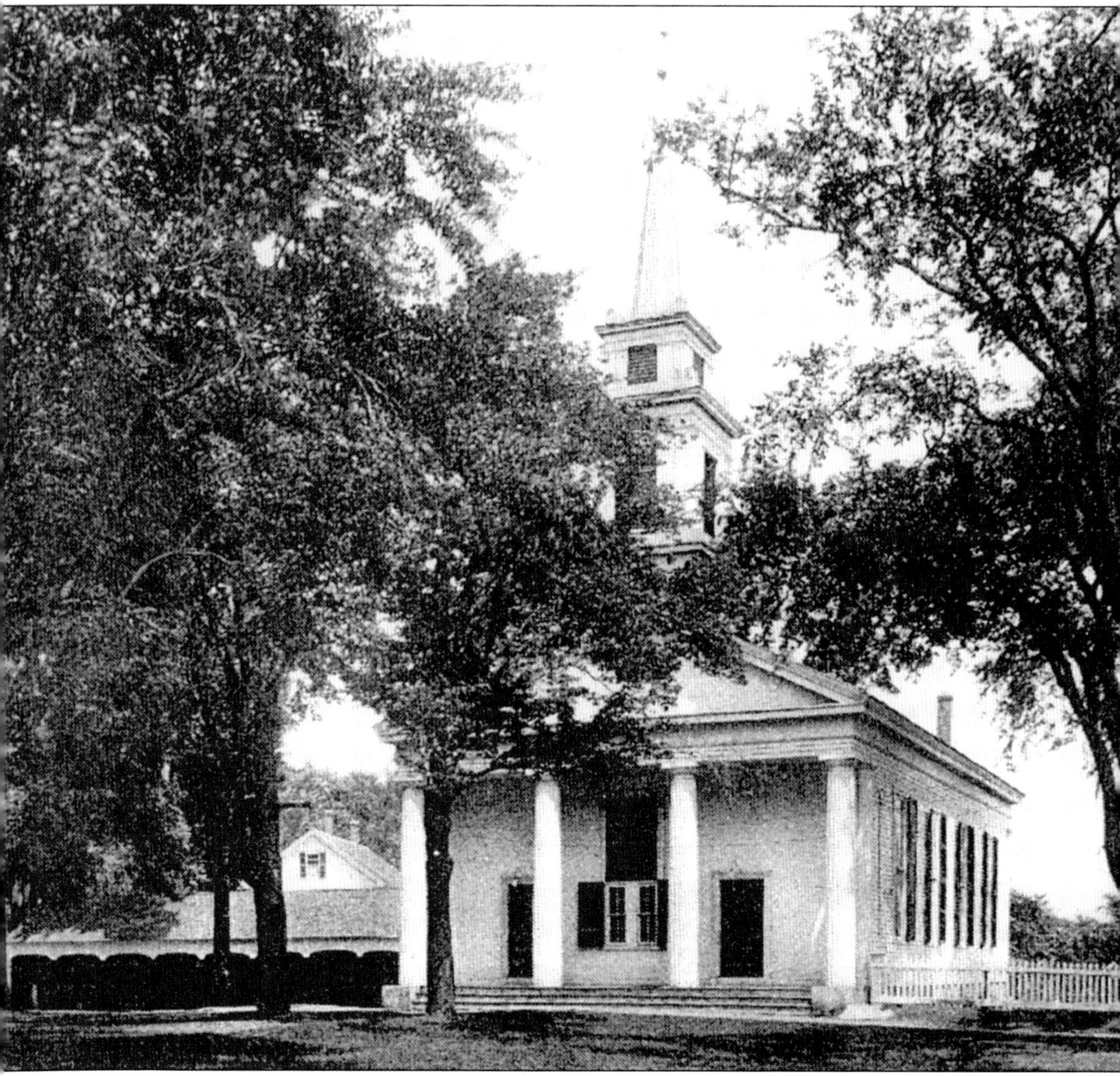

The Slatersville Congregational Church was built in 1832 by the John Slater family to serve the needs of a growing mill village. The church provided one of the area's first Sunday schools, organized by Ruth Slater, who believed that the mill children, who worked during the week, should receive some education in morals and basic academics. The church and the common it faces are well-known landmarks throughout Rhode Island.

IMAGES
of America

NORTH SMITHFIELD

North Smithfield Heritage Association

ARCADIA
PUBLISHING

ISBN 978-0-7385-1145-0

Published by Arcadia Publishing
Charleston, South Carolina

Printed in the United States of America

Library of Congress Catalog Card Number: 2002112250

For all general information, contact Arcadia Publishing:
Telephone 843-853-2070
Fax 843-853-0044
E-mail sales@arcadiapublishing.com
For customer service and orders:
Toll-free 1-888-313-2665

Visit us on the Internet at www.arcadiapublishing.com.

The North Smithfield Heritage Association logo pictures the plow, representing the agricultural origins of the town, and the loom, a feature of the textile industry, which provided the economic basis for later development.

Contents

ACKNOWLEDGMENTS

The North Smithfield Heritage Association is indebted to the following people and organizations for providing the photographs used in this volume: Claire Allard (CA), Ernest Allard (EA), Ray Auclair (RA), Sue Branchaud (SB), Betty Cesario (EC), Wally Dumais (WD), Doris Green (DG), Alan and Cornelia Hurd (Hurd), Harold Kilmer (HK), Doris Mowry (DPM), Thomas Mundy (TM), Irene Nebiker (IGN), Walter Nebiker (WAN), Chris and Sue North (CSN), the archives of the North Smithfield Heritage Association (NSHA), Ruth Pacheco (RP), Harriet Peloquin (HP), Shirley Reichenberg (SR), Garcie Robertson (GR), Walter Sawyer (WS), the Slatersville Congregational Church (SCC), George Smith (GS), Irene Souza (IS), Wallace Stone (WSt), the Tabor family (Tabor), Mary Titherington (MT), Lawrence Walter (LW), the Woonsocket High School Social Studies Department (WHS-SSD), and anyone we may have inadvertently left out. We thank you one and all.

Digital photographic restoration was done by Lew Place of Slatersville.

This volume was compiled by members of the North Smithfield Heritage Association: Moe Bourget, Wally Dumais, Mary Fagan, Irene Nebiker, Ruth Pacheco, and Louise Vanhouwe.

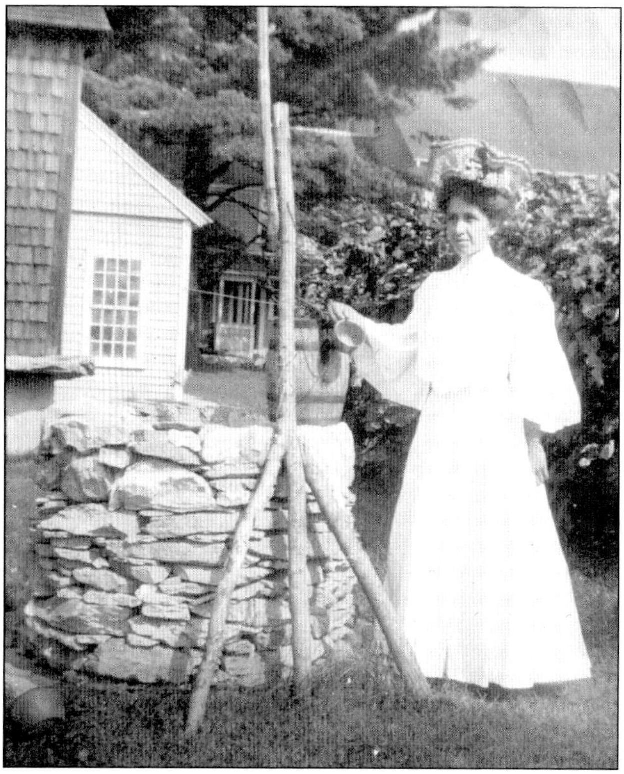

Veronica Lincoln dips water from an old oaken bucket on the rim of a well in Union Village in the late 19th century.

INTRODUCTION

Colonial settlement in what is now North Smithfield began within a generation of Roger Williams's founding of Providence in 1636. By 1660, John and Nathaniel Mowry and Edward Inman had begun negotiations with a band of Wampanoags who had control over the lands around Woonsocket Hill. During the next 50 years, their families and others, such as the Arnolds, Comstocks, Smiths, Sayles, and Paines, established their homestead farms about the landscape as part of the early westward expansion of the Providence colony. The Mowry settlers on Sayles Hill survived King Philip's War, but what, if any, homes survived is unknown. The Mowrys and Inmans stayed. By 1731, the area was included in the town of Smithfield. In 1871, the boundaries of the present town were set, first as the town of Slater and, less than two weeks later, as the town of North Smithfield.

Agriculture was the backbone of the economy throughout the 17th and 18th centuries, with small saw-, grist-, and fulling mills and scythe stone operations developing along streams, such as the Branch River and Crookfall Brook, in the latter 1700s. A strong Quaker ethic influenced politics and economics.

In 1806, Samuel Slater sent his brother John to find a site for a new cotton manufactory beyond Pawtucket. Selecting the falls on the Branch River near the location of an old fulling mill, John Slater developed what became the first planned mill village, with housing for single workers and families on the height above the mill. Slatersville grew to be a thriving community during the 1800s. The Congregational church, the first Sunday school, a library, and civic organizations were active. Prominent residents played a part in Rhode Island's constitutional crisis known as the Dorr Rebellion in 1842.

Just downstream on the Branch River, a scythe factory was expanded to produce sabers for the Union army during the Civil War, and a cotton mill was established on the site in the 1840s. The mills and the accompanying housing were the nucleus of Forestdale.

Farther down the Branch River, a small late-18th-century scythe works and a 19th-century cotton mill were sufficient to be the heart of a settlement called Branch Village.

The influx of Irish immigrants to the factories developing near the confluence of the Branch and Blackstone Rivers spread over a fluid state line from Blackstone, Massachusetts, into Rhode Island and helped name this village Waterford.

Where the highway from Connecticut met the old road from Providence to Mendon, and the road to Woonsocket Falls, another small village developed based on transportation and services for travelers. Union Village boasted the town's first bank (established in 1803) and a widely respected academy before midcentury.

Beyond the villages, the poor glacial soils were worked by persevering farmers, who raised much of the food that supplied village residents. As the soils gave out, some families went to work in the local mills or in the city of Woonsocket. Transportation routes connected various parts of the town, first by stagecoach and later by railroad and highway. North Smithfield's water from the Crookfall Brook became Woonsocket's most important water supply.

Throughout the 20th century, North Smithfield evolved from an agricultural and industrial community into what is today a suburban residential area in which modern housing is replacing the features of the past landscape, some images of which we hope to preserve in this book.

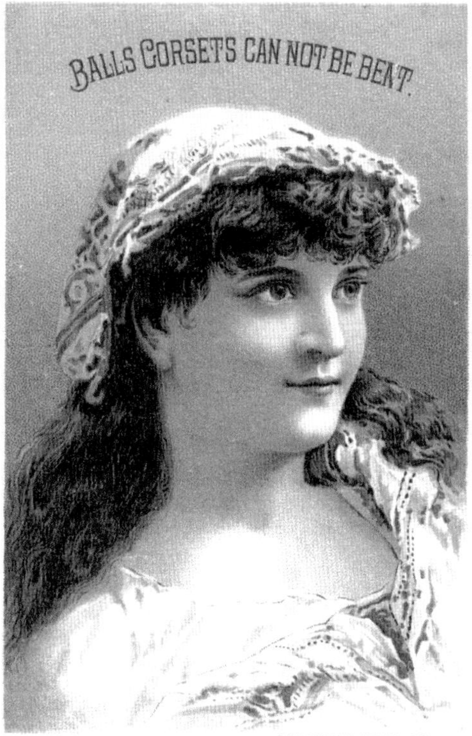

Early in the 20th century, local businesses varied greatly in the products they offered.

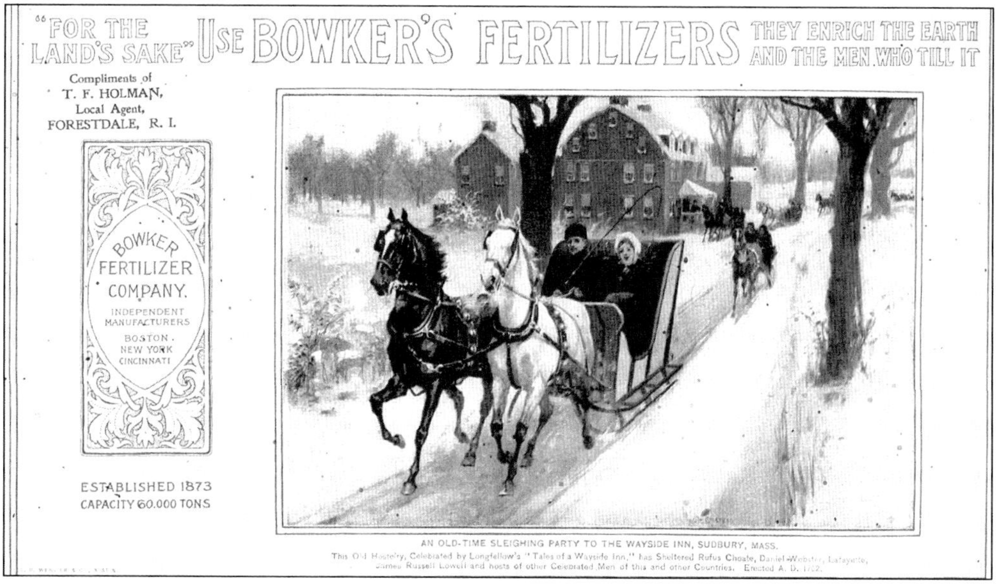

One

The Earliest Years 1650–1700

In the 1650s, Nathaniel Mowry and Edward Inman of Providence began negotiations with a band of Wampanoag Indians for a vast land tract of 2,500 acres, extending southward from Woonsocket Hill. Their settlement began on Sayles Hill, spreading north and west. Other men and families moved southward from Massachusetts to take up land north of the Inman-Mowry grant.

The evidence from these early years was still clear 50 years ago, but rapidly increasing development as the 20th century ended altered the landscape radically. Many of the dwelling houses succumbed to age and vandalism; family burying grounds were bulldozed or buried; mill sites on small streams were swept away. Yet there remain some sturdy relics of these years, some of which have been restored and well maintained.

A number of the houses of this early period are presented here. They are where the action took place—the handwork, the meetings, and the education that made this town viable through the Indian wars and the Revolution.

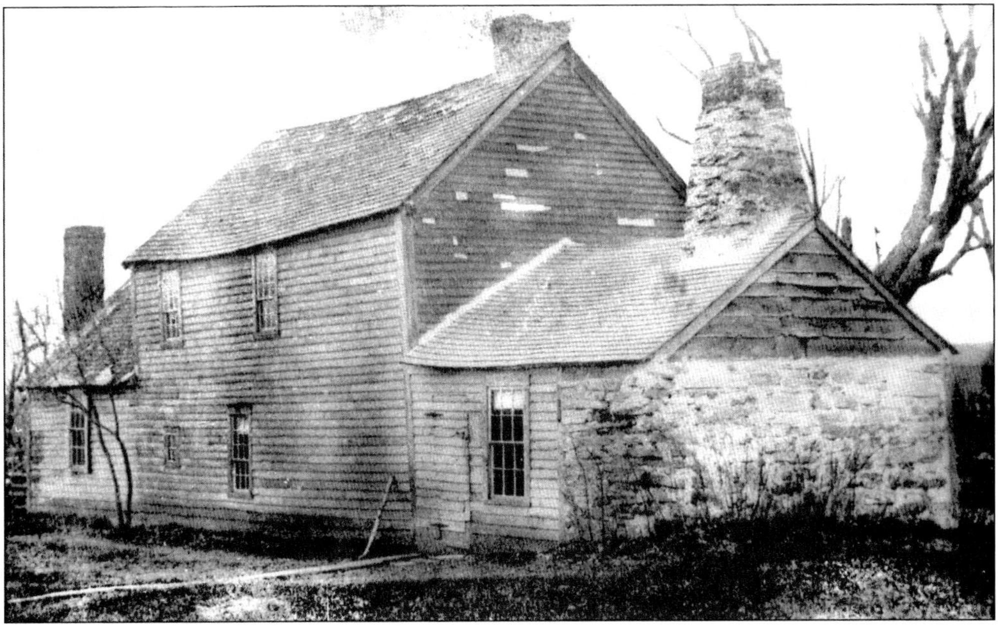

The John Mowry-Inman-Sayles homestead, one of the earliest to be photographed, is shown as it was in 1915. The square center section had a kitchen ell at each end, the western one having a huge stone fireplace and chimney, the eastern one having a small corner fireplace. No longer standing, this house was located at the corner of Sayles Hill and Iron Mine Hill Roads and is dated *c.* 1690.

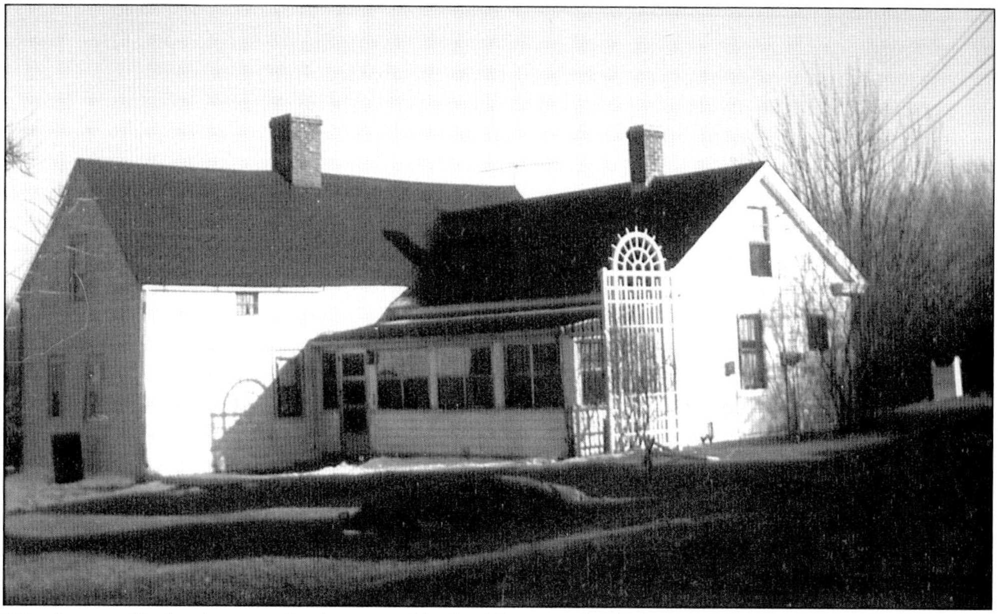

The Inman-Sayles house, the larger gable building to the left in this photograph, was said to have been the home of Edward Inman. Its interior features dated to 1700 or earlier. Located on Iron Mine Hill Road near the junction with Sayles Hill Road, the house burned in the 1970s. (HK.)

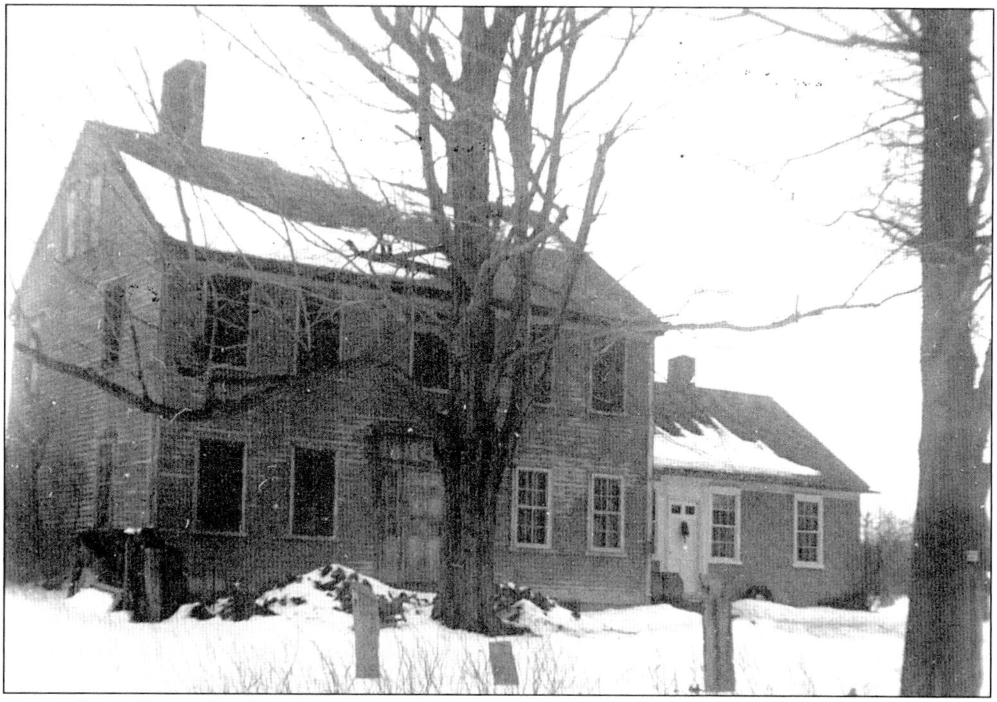

On Sayles Hill Road to the west of the Inman and Mowry houses is the Nathaniel Mowry house, the ell of which dates possibly to 1690. At this house, Mowry and his wife, Joanna Inman, raised 11 children, whose homes represented the second generation of houses in North Smithfield. The house has been restored in recent years. (HK.)

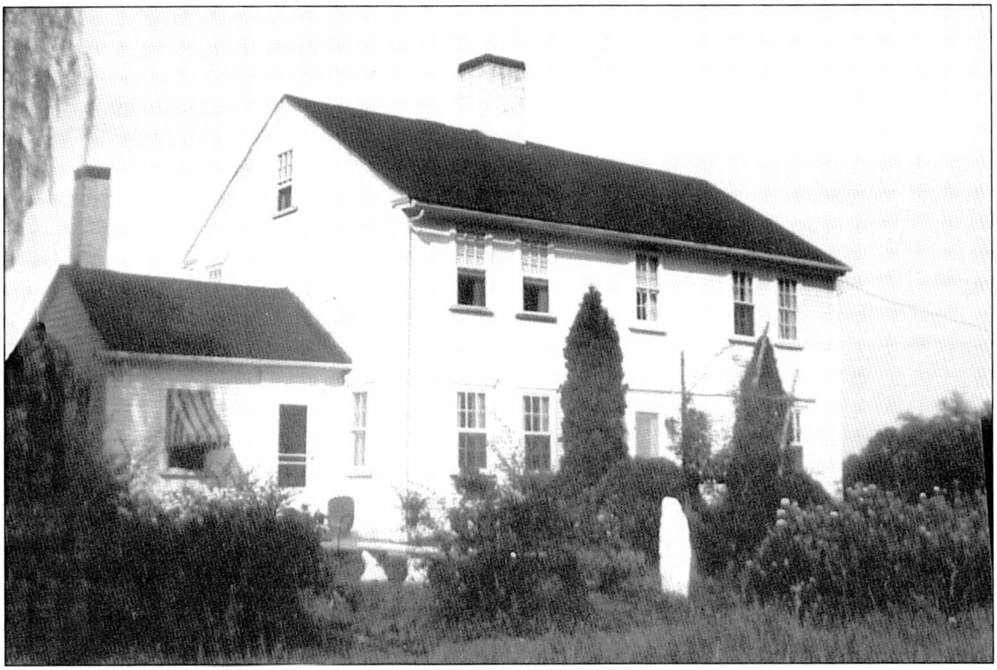

The Clifford house, atop Sayles Hill, is shown as it appeared in the 1950s. It was restored when occupied by the Arcand family in the 1960s. Rose Arcand was the first woman representative to the state legislature. The house is associated with the Inmans and Mowrys.

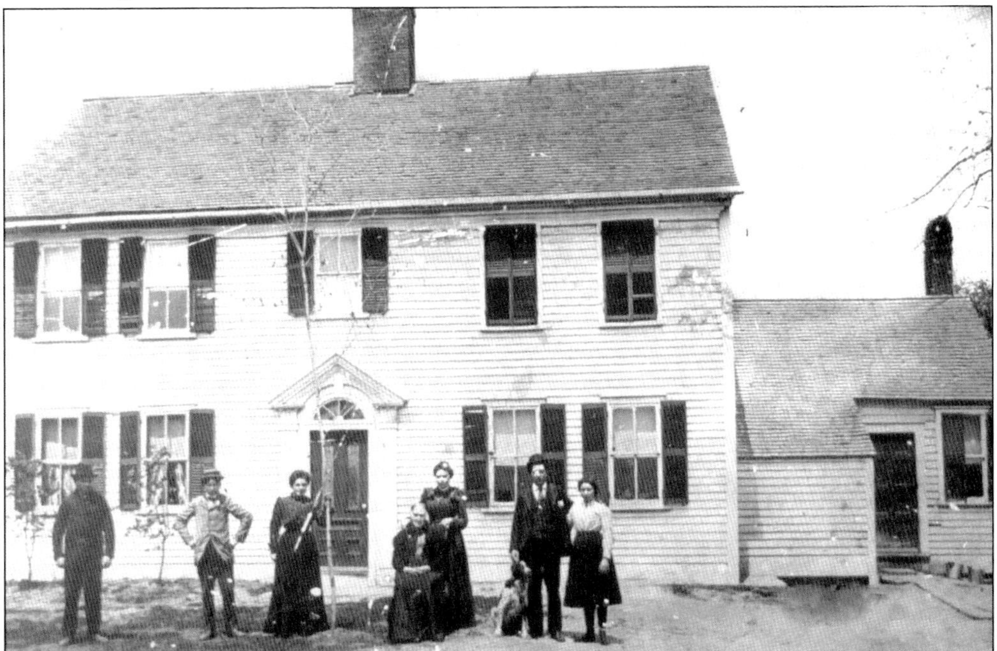

Across Sayles Hill from the Clifford house is the Connolly house, occupied by Milton West and family (Connolly descendants) in the mid-1900s. In the fields behind the house were the graves of John and Mary Mowry, who died of smallpox in 1690. This house also has early Mowry associations.

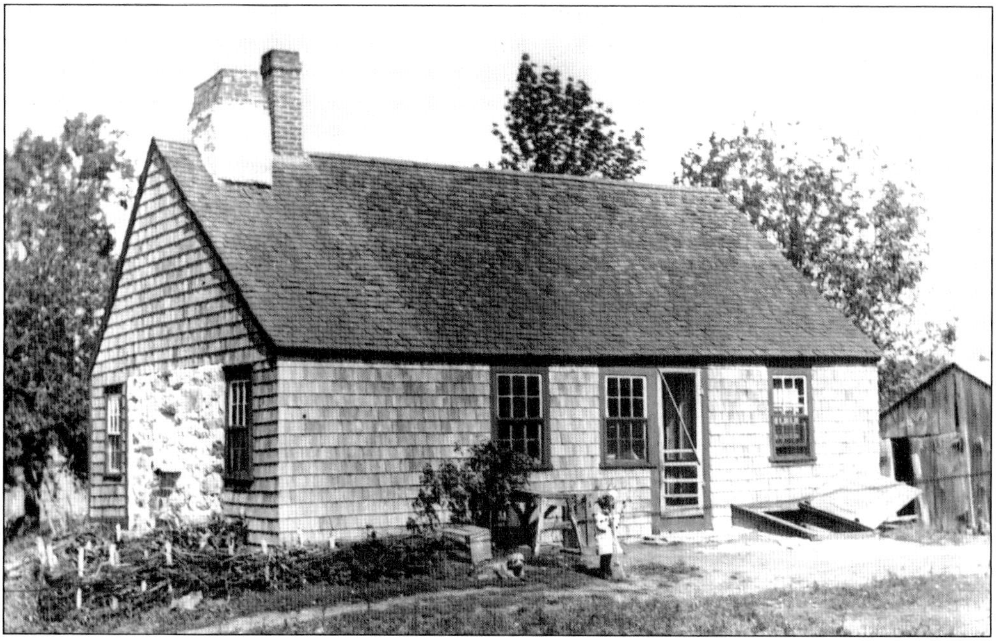

The similarity of the stone end and chimney on this house to that of the Mowry-Sayles-Inman house suggests a date c. 1700. Notes on this 1915 photograph date the house to 1746. Definitely associated with Caleb Mowry, the house is on the southwestern side of Sayles Hill. It was most recently in the Czarny family. (DPM.)

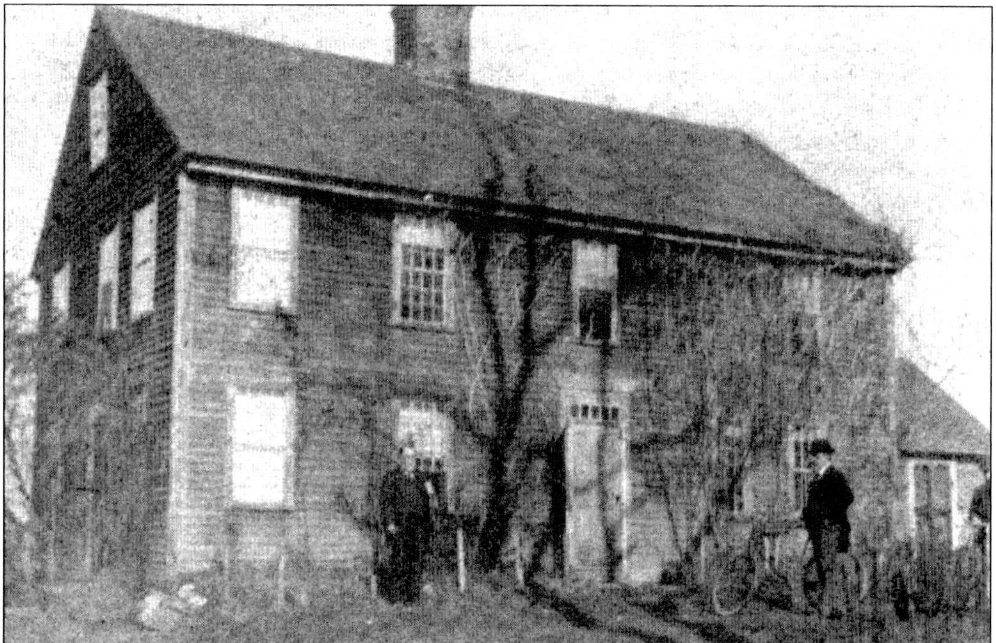

Adjoining the Caleb Mowry farm to the southwest on Grange Road is the John Malavery house, dating to c. 1720. Malavery's wife was Experience Mowry, daughter of Nathaniel Mowry. The house was in the Mowry family for more than 200 years. In this early-1900s photograph, trumpet vines cover the front of the house. (DPM.)

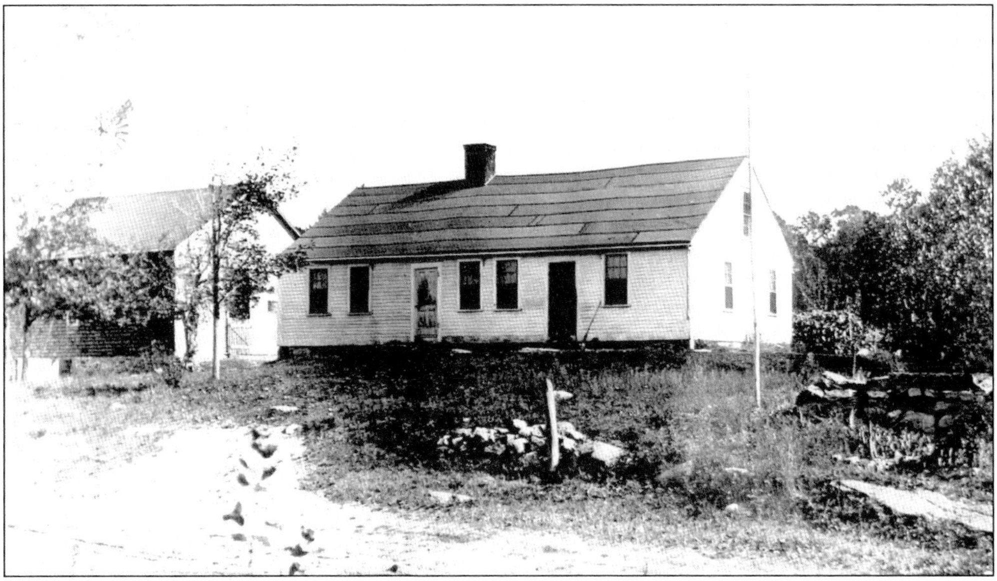

The Blackmar-Wing house, on Providence Pike, was built in several sections, the earliest dating to *c.* 1690, when James Blackmar rebuilt his home after King Philip's War. It has been in the Mowry family for many years. Note the windmill at the far left in this *c.* 1915 photograph. (DPM.)

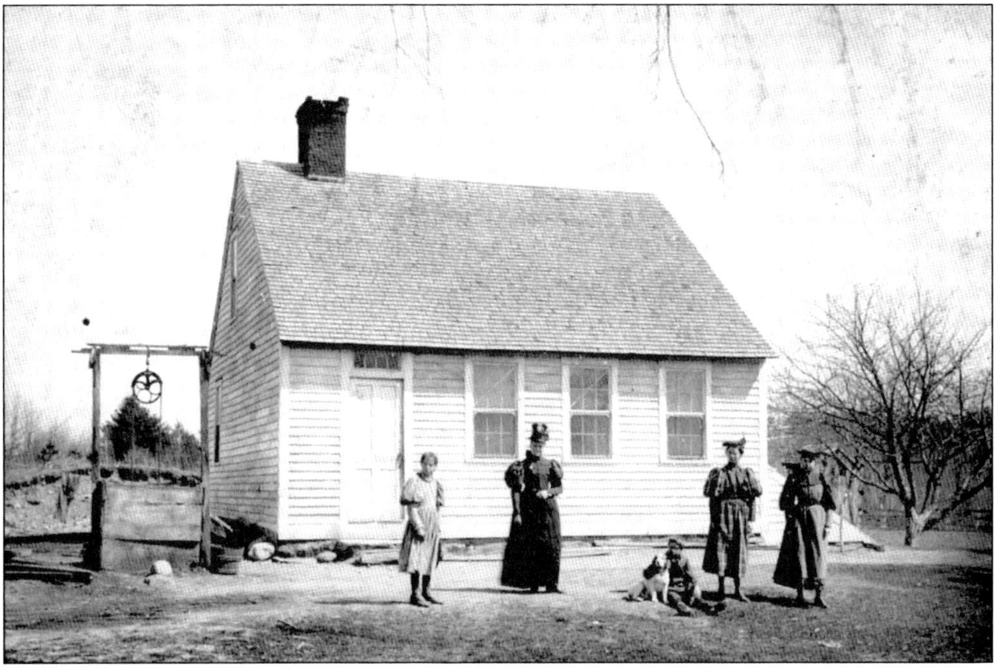

The Florence Mowry house, on Douglas Pike, is often called a "half-house" because the chimney at one end could be adapted for an extra fireplace as the house was expanded. It is characteristic of early-18th-century houses. (Hurd.)

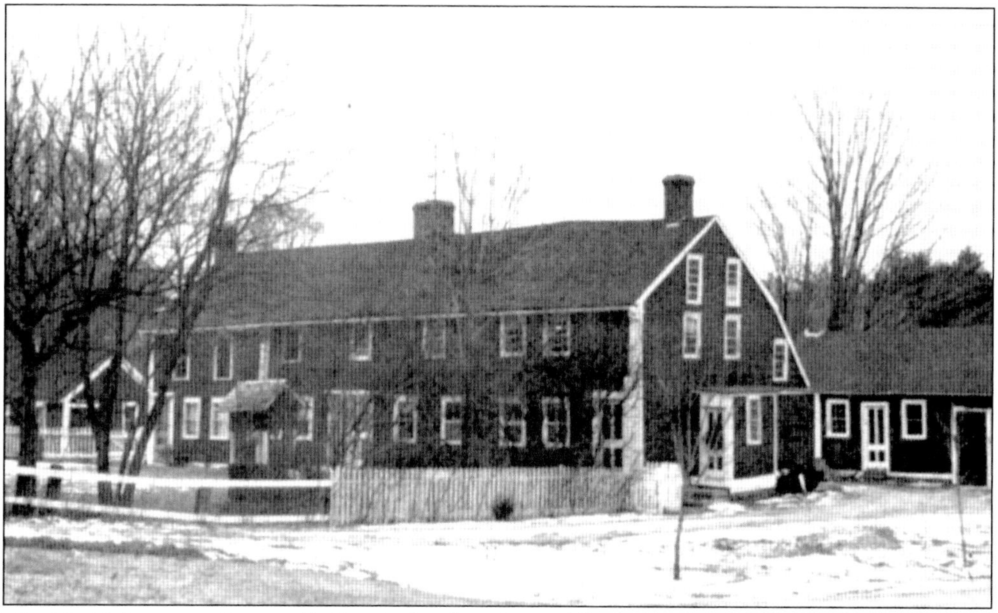

The Todd farm, on Greenville Road, developed as additions were made on either side of the center-chimney house built *c.* 1740. Once operated as a dairy, the farm was often the site of Woonsocket Fine Arts Society outings, at which local artists painted the varied farm scenery.

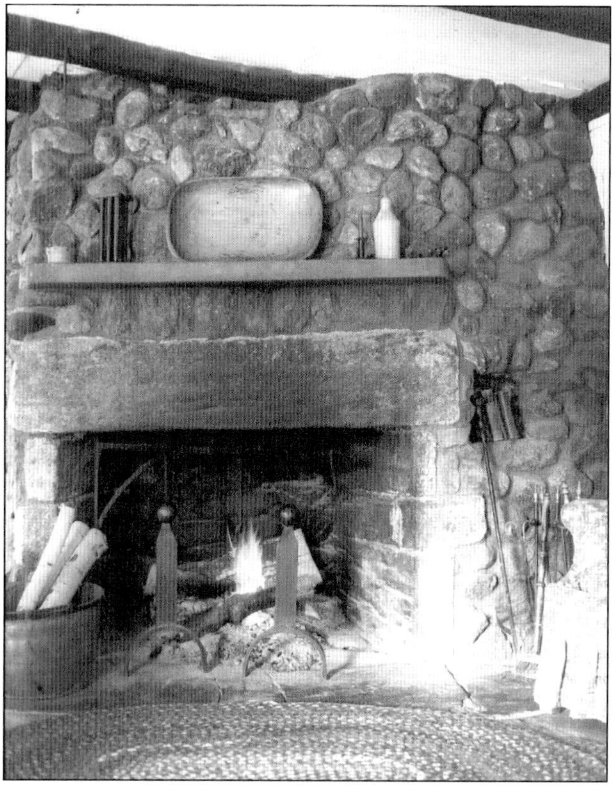

This fireplace in the keeping room of the Tisdell house is one of three—one square and two angled so that the center chimney could heat three rooms. The fireboxes are of cut stone blocks, and the chimney face is fieldstone. Now part of the Audubon Fort preserve, the one-and-a-half-story house and ell are dated *c.* 1731.

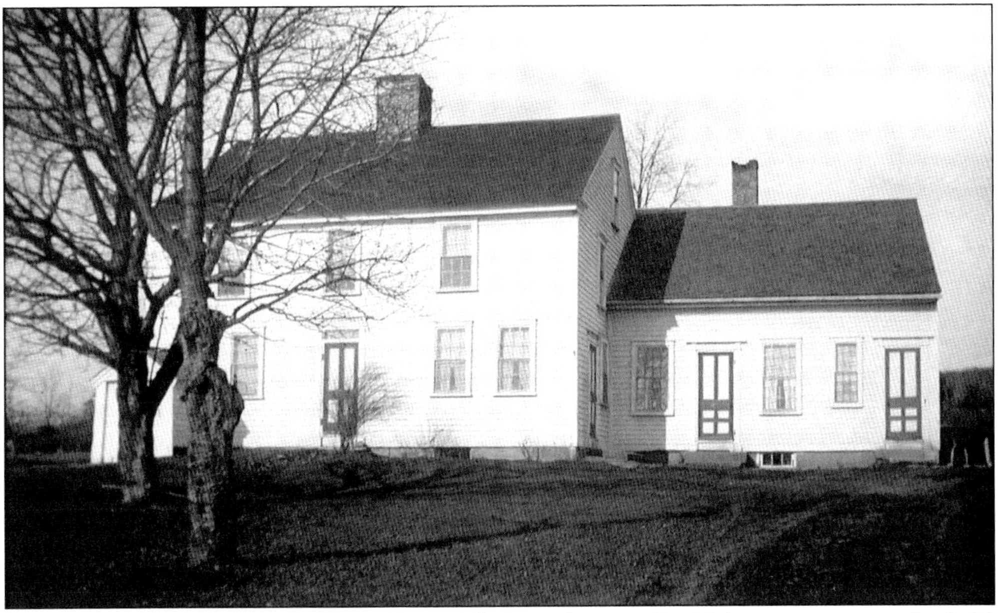

Typical of the second and third generation of Mowry homes, the 18th-century two-and-a-half-story "King" David Mowry house has a large ell at one end. It is located at a bend on Providence Pike near Quinn's Transmissions. (SR.)

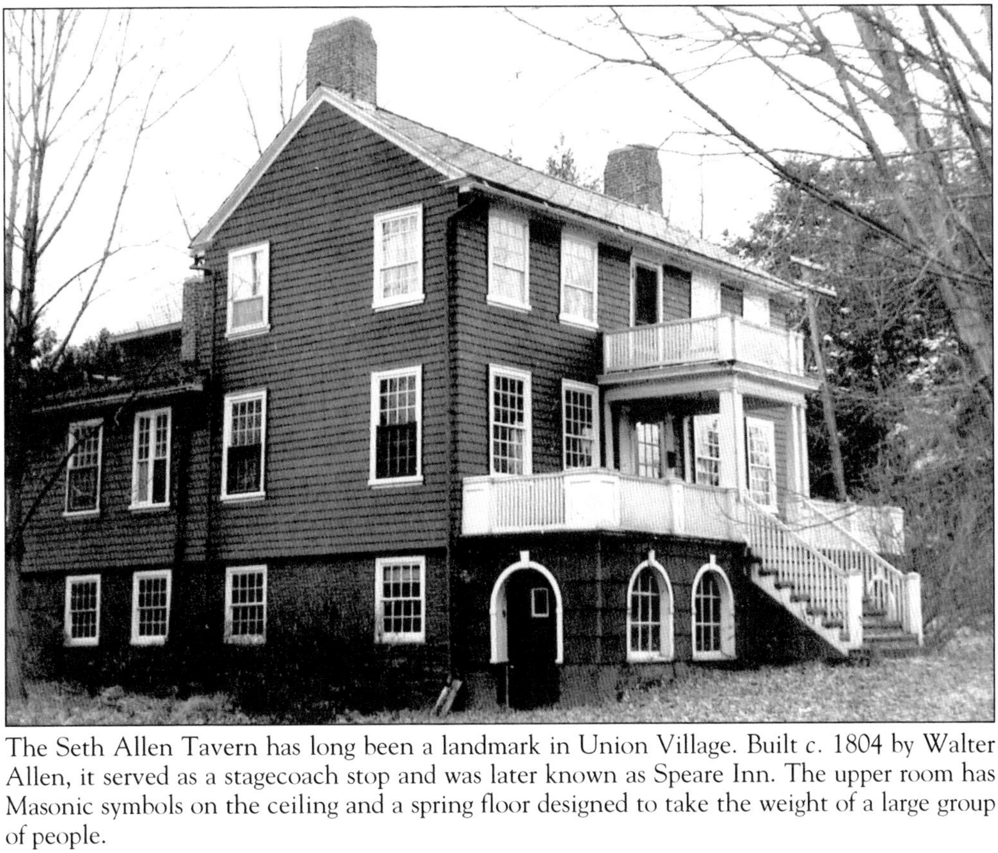

The Seth Allen Tavern has long been a landmark in Union Village. Built c. 1804 by Walter Allen, it served as a stagecoach stop and was later known as Speare Inn. The upper room has Masonic symbols on the ceiling and a spring floor designed to take the weight of a large group of people.

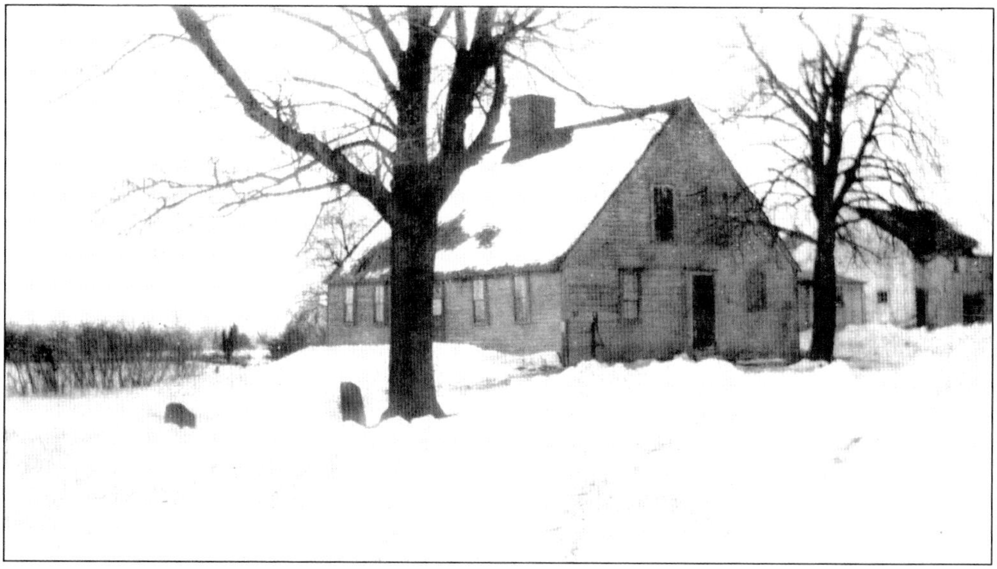

This house on Buxton Street was owned by Ellery Christiansen in 1923, when this photograph was taken. The house dates to 1690–1700 and was part of a farm originally comprising 130 acres, bought by Samuel Buxton from Israel Phillips in 1741. (GS.)

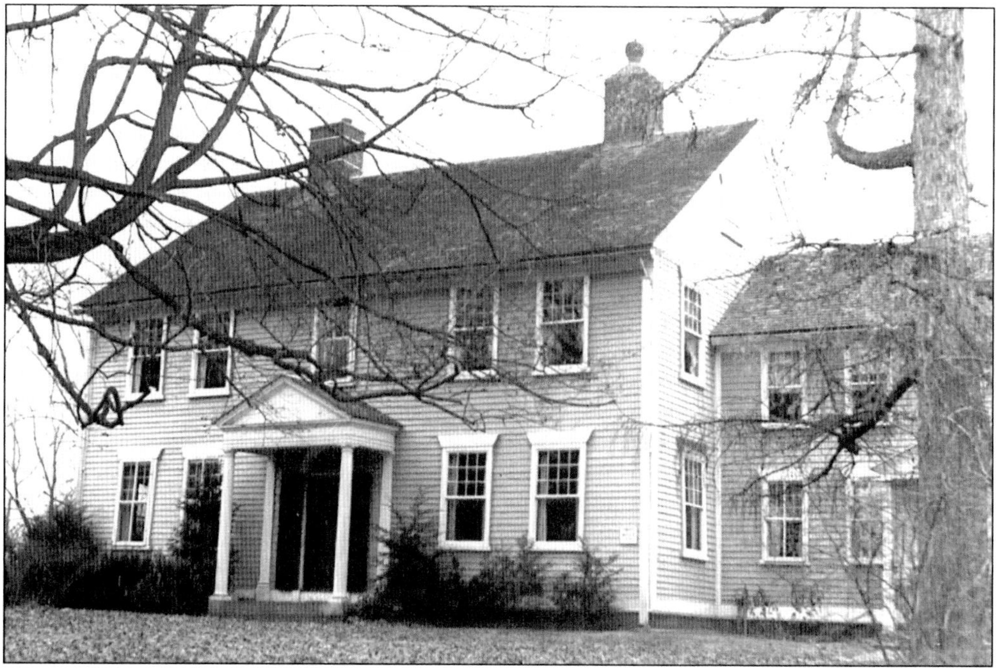

Walter Allen worked on a number of houses in Union Village, none boasting more intricate interior decoration than this one at the corner of Great Road and Pound Hill Road. Although the main house is dated c. 1802, the ell is often attributed to Hazadiah Comstock, whose dwelling occupied the site in the 18th century.

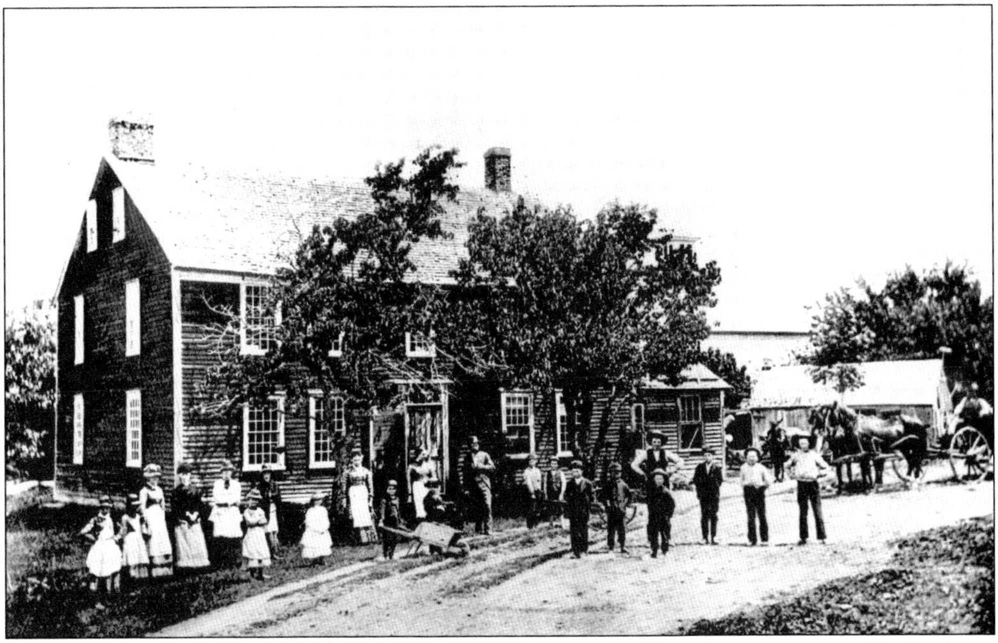

Rock Cliff Farm, located on Old Louisquisset Pike, is named for a large outcrop of bedrock on the hill behind the house. It was built in the mid-18th century or earlier on land that was once part of the Inman-Mowry grant. The land has one boundary, "whereon a Baptist meeting house formerly stood," according to an early deed. That early Six Principle Baptist structure had been built in 1706 and dismantled soon after. (MT.)

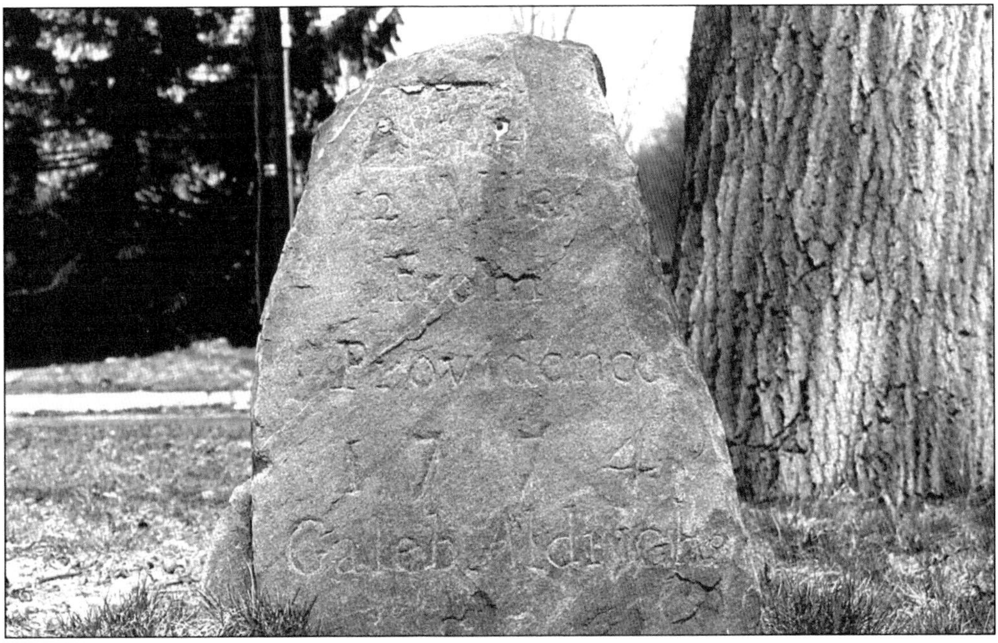

This milestone, erected and inscribed by Caleb Aldrich in 1774, was located along the Great Road from Mendon to Providence and indicates the distance to Providence as 12 miles. The stone rests today at the junction of Old Louisquisset Pike and Eddie Dowling Highway, not far from its original location.

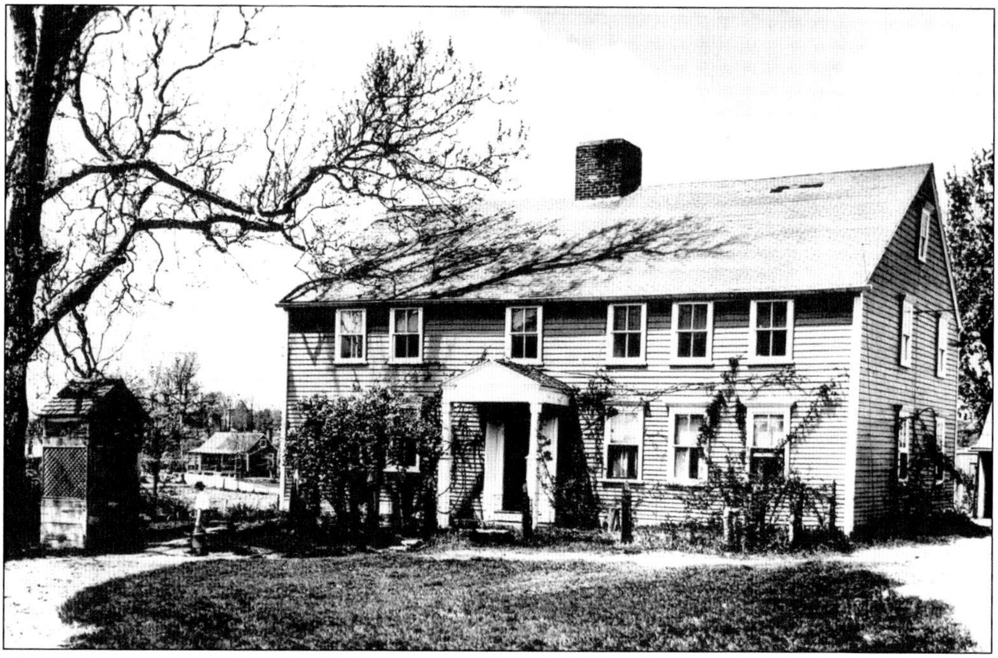

The 18th-century Hotchkiss-Thayer house, at the edge of Union Village, burned in a tragic fire in the early 1970s. Identified with the early years of the Quaker movement, the house was the center for many gatherings of Friends, some meetings even taking place under the sycamore tree to the left.

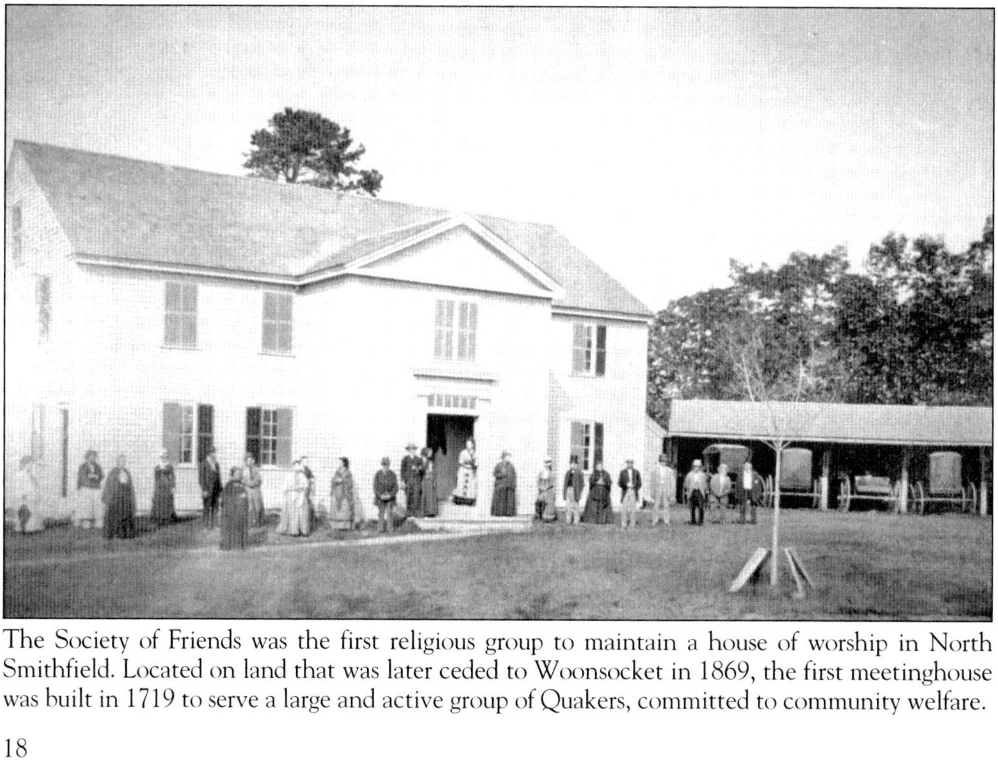

The Society of Friends was the first religious group to maintain a house of worship in North Smithfield. Located on land that was later ceded to Woonsocket in 1869, the first meetinghouse was built in 1719 to serve a large and active group of Quakers, committed to community welfare.

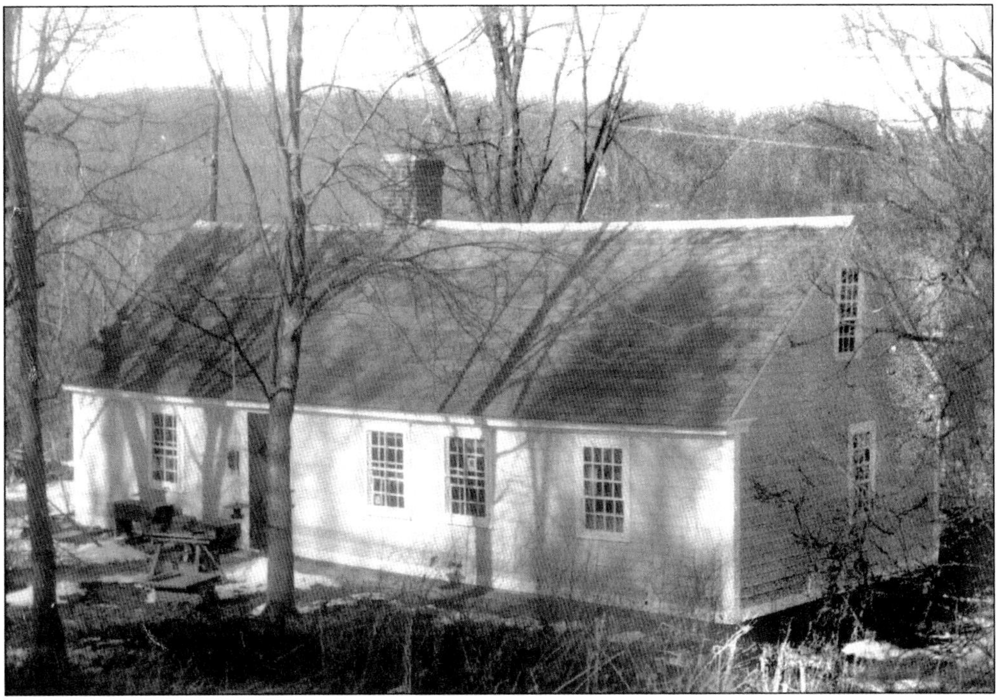

Built by James Brayton, a former slave, this house between Great Road and the railroad tracks at the edge of Union Village dated to the end of the Revolution. Using the money from his military service, Brayton constructed a small house; the southern end was added by his daughter Patience. The house remained in the Brayton family until 1961, after which it fell into disrepair and was burned.

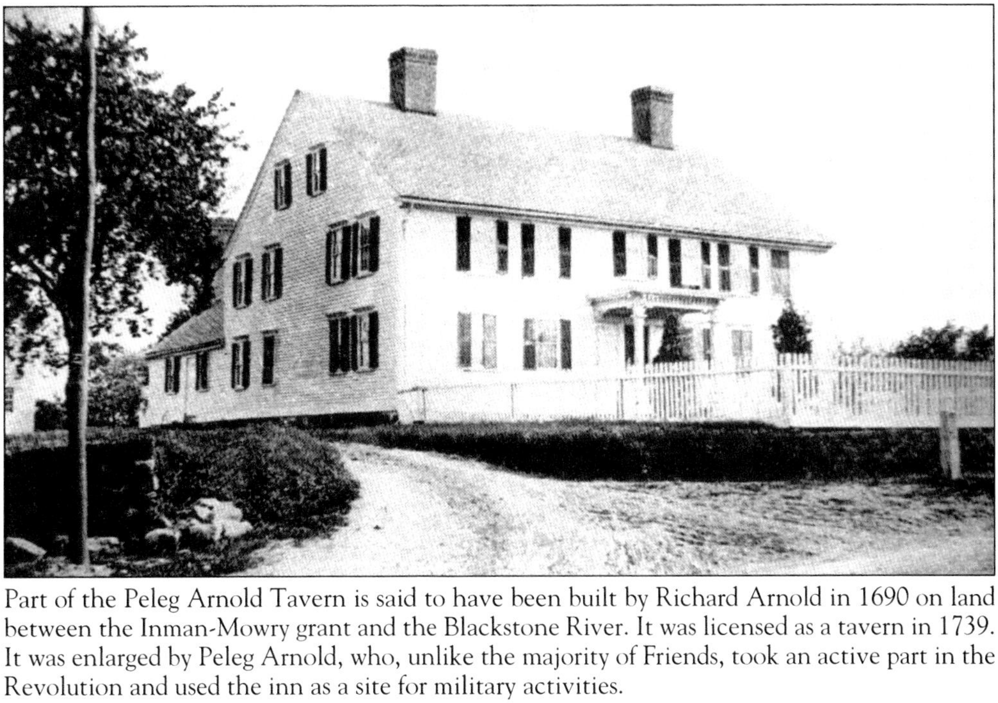

Part of the Peleg Arnold Tavern is said to have been built by Richard Arnold in 1690 on land between the Inman-Mowry grant and the Blackstone River. It was licensed as a tavern in 1739. It was enlarged by Peleg Arnold, who, unlike the majority of Friends, took an active part in the Revolution and used the inn as a site for military activities.

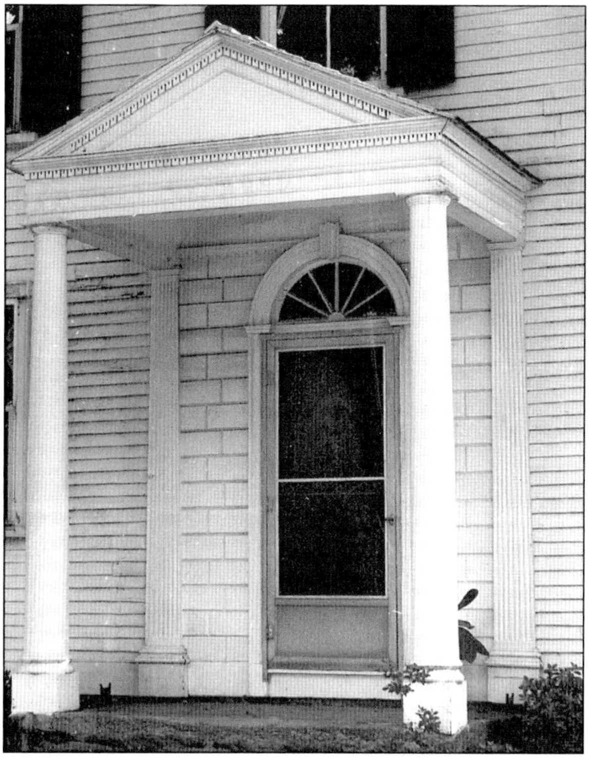

The pedimented porch, present on both the Walter Allen and Daniel Arnold houses, is shown here in detail. The arched fanlight above the door is set off by the rusticated wooden blocks on either side. Round columns on the front, and pilasters defining the edges of the rustication, create a unique portico that can be found on four Union Village houses.

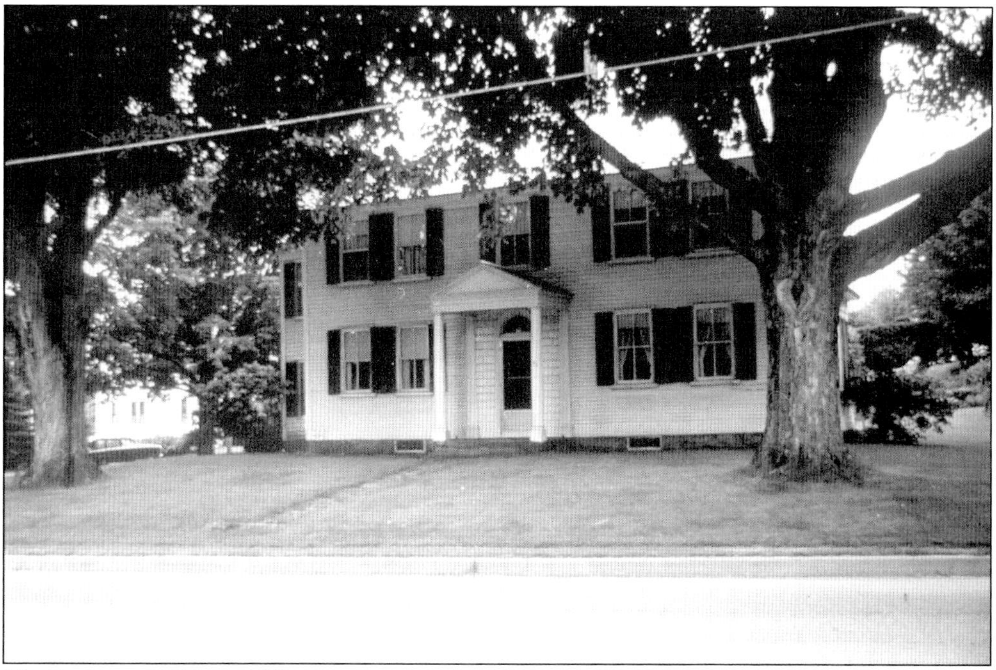

The Capt. Daniel Arnold house, in Union Village, is dated 1714. Arnold's daughter Elizabeth married blacksmith Daniel Ide, and the property remained in the Ide family for several generations. The house is distinguished by the later addition of a unique Union Village pedimented porch with rustication on either side of the front door.

Two

THE 19TH CENTURY 1801–1900

This was a century of change as the urban areas grew and prospered. This was a century of a certain stability in the rural parts of town. Mostly, it was a century of growth, in industry, in ideas, and in population.

The production of textiles left the cottage for the factory; education moved out of the home into established school buildings; travel and communication became easier; the Grange enhanced the lives of farm families.

Slatersville assumed the role of leader in this dynamic. A planned village, it placed work, housing, worship, and education in a close community context, fostered by a benevolent but strict proprietary management that set the rules. The Branch River worked harder and harder to power the expanding mills in Slatersville, Forestdale, and Branch Village. Union Village took on a gracious aspect, the substantial homes and well-known academies lending a dignity of purpose. With connection by trolley to Woonsocket, Slatersville, and points west, transportation widened the horizons of many residents.

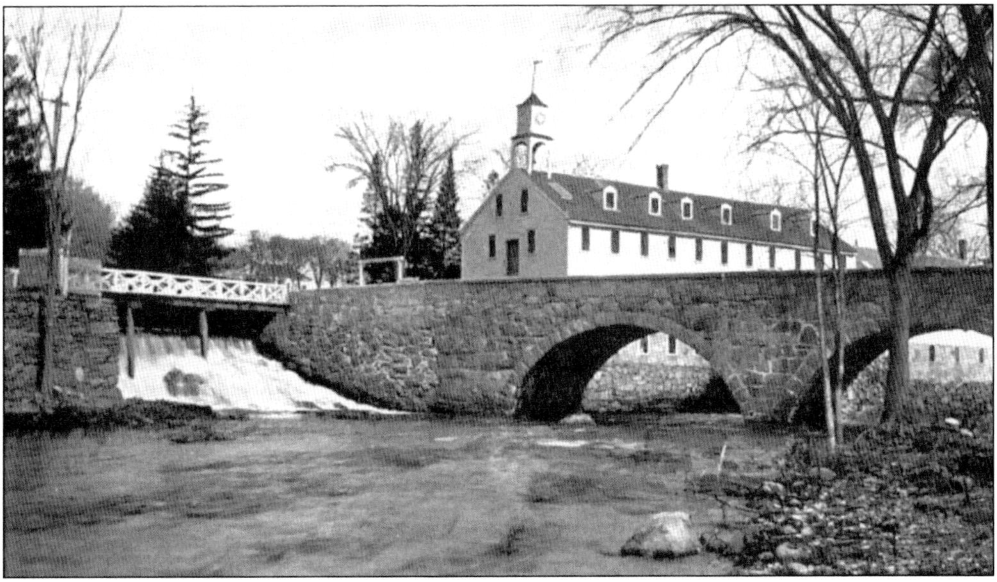

One of the early wooden Slatersville mill buildings is set off by the stone arch bridge carrying Providence Pike across the Branch River, the footbridge across the trench, and the waterfall from the trench that separated two of the large Western Mills buildings.

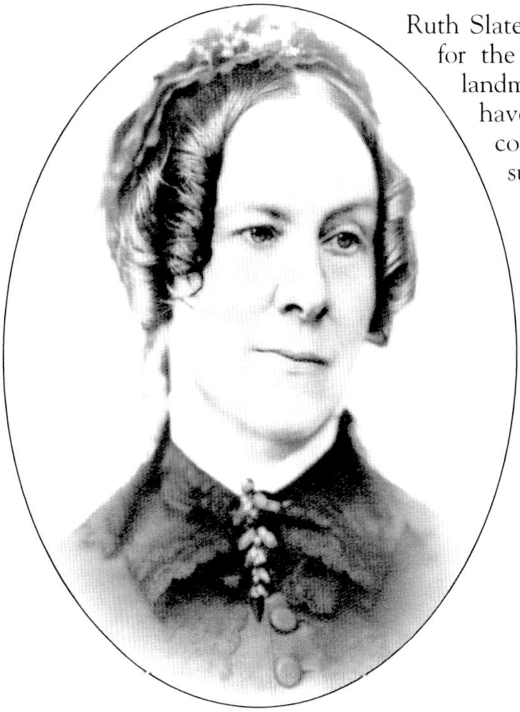

Ruth Slater, wife of John Slater, is largely responsible for the imposing "Village Church," a Slatersville landmark. Concerned that the village should have a sound moral foundation, she urged the construction of a church and, lest the youth succumb to moral lapse and ignorance, she organized a Sunday school. The values of the Slater family were carried through three generations of mill proprietorship. (SCC.)

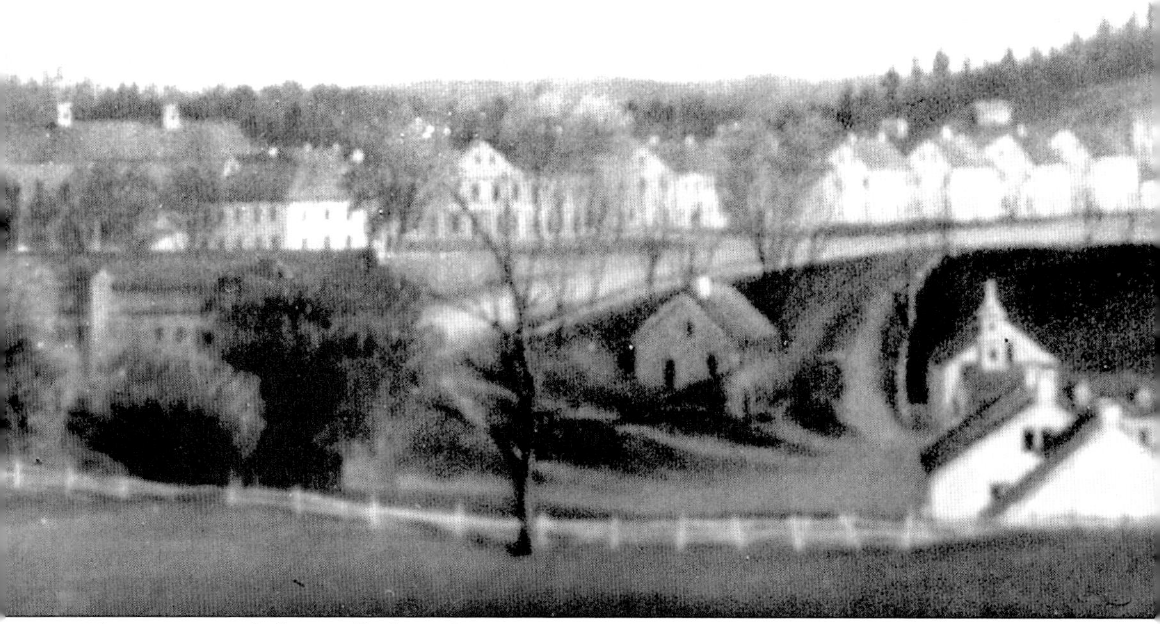

This painting of Slatersville from the perspective of today's Church Street hill illustrates the

John Slater, younger brother to Samuel, emigrated from Belper, England, to Pawtucket, where he was sent by his brother to find sites for new textile mills. John's choice of the Branch River falls was based in part on the success of earlier small saw- and gristmills nearby. John located the factory along the river and housing for the workers on the heights above, thereby constructing the first planned mill village in the country between 1806 and 1810. (SCC.)

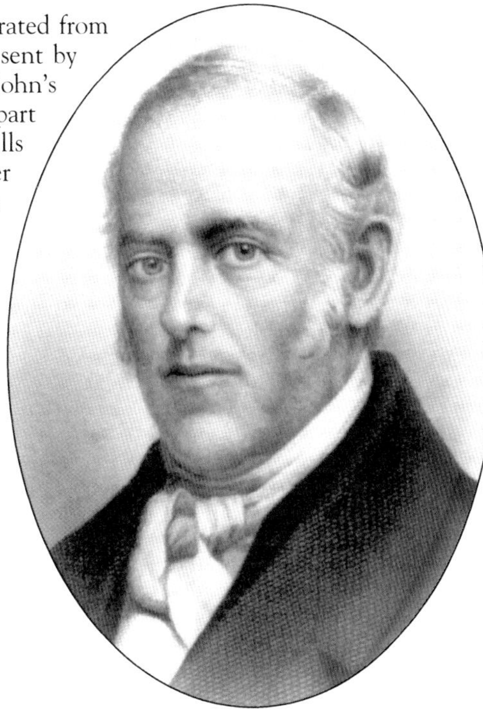

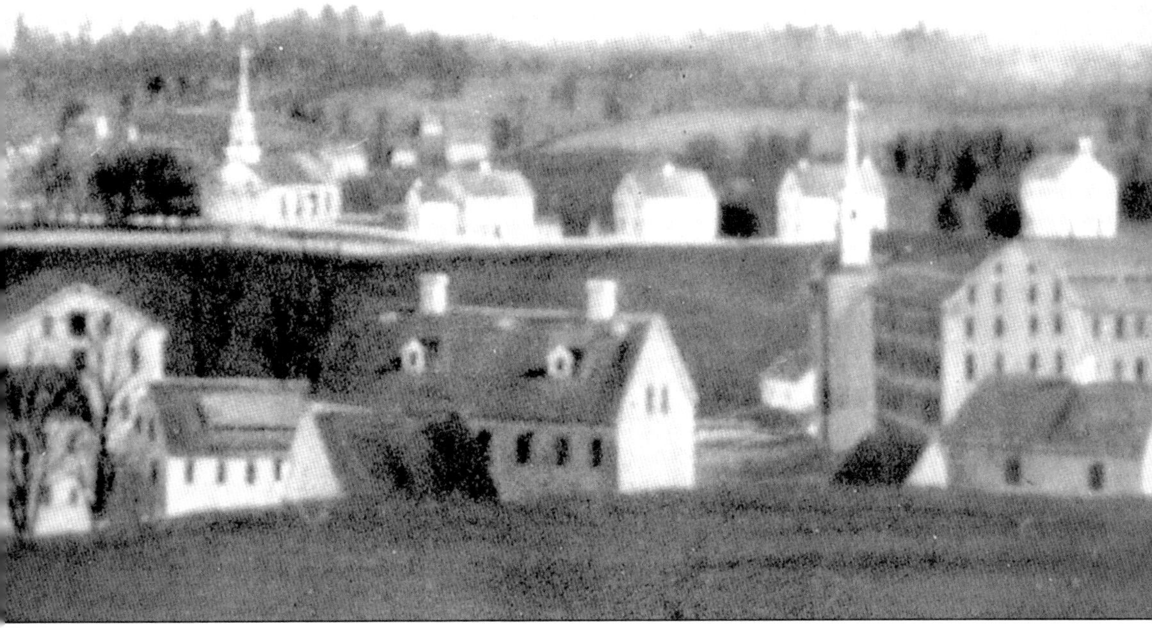

development of the village *c.* 1860. (SCC.)

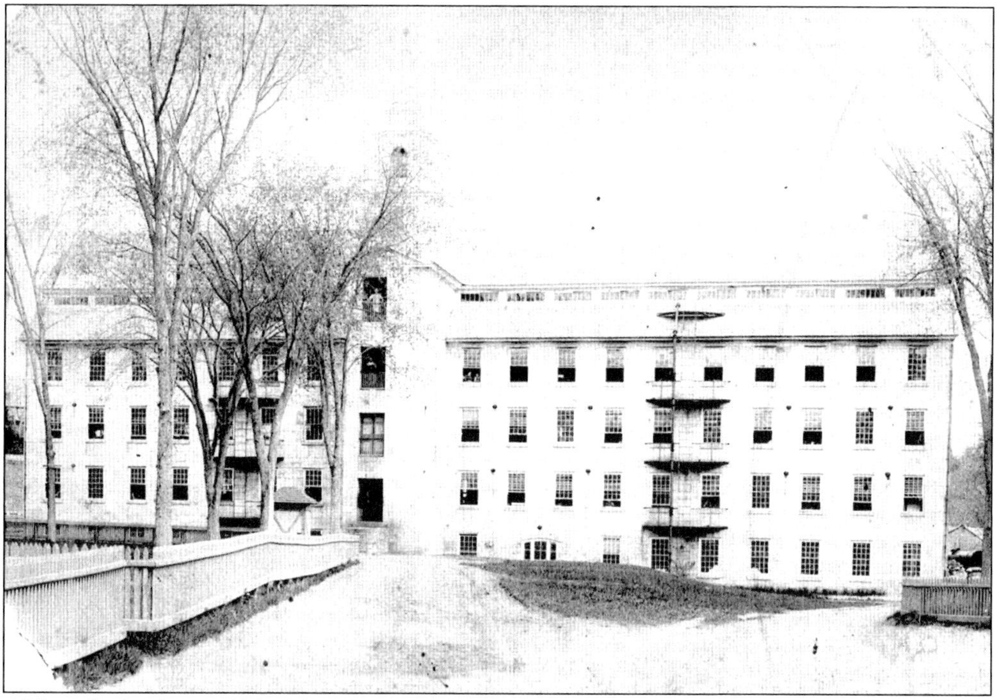

Although the first mill buildings were of wood, the gray stone 1826–1828 mill, with its bell tower, has become symbolic of Slatersville. Constructed after the earlier building was destroyed by fire, this mill became the anchor of the developing mill complex.

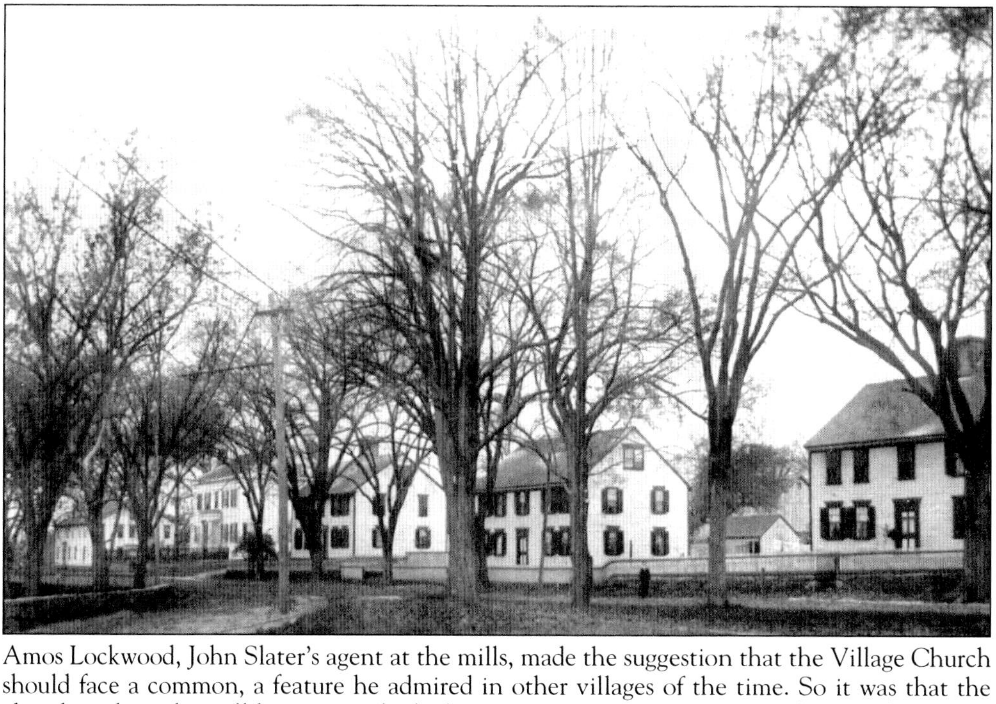

Amos Lockwood, John Slater's agent at the mills, made the suggestion that the Village Church should face a common, a feature he admired in other villages of the time. So it was that the church and nearby mill houses overlooked a grassy common, or green, set later with graceful elm trees.

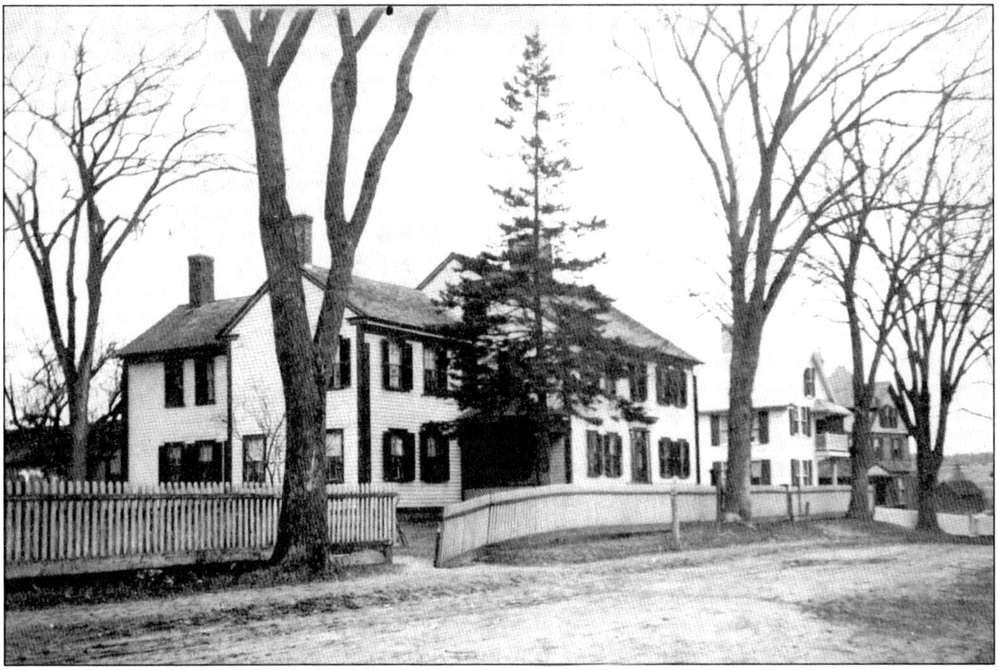

The parsonage of the church was the home of several notable pastors whose sermons dealt often with important issues of the day, such as temperance and slavery. The pastors also recruited well-educated teachers, such as William A. Mowry, for the Sunday school.

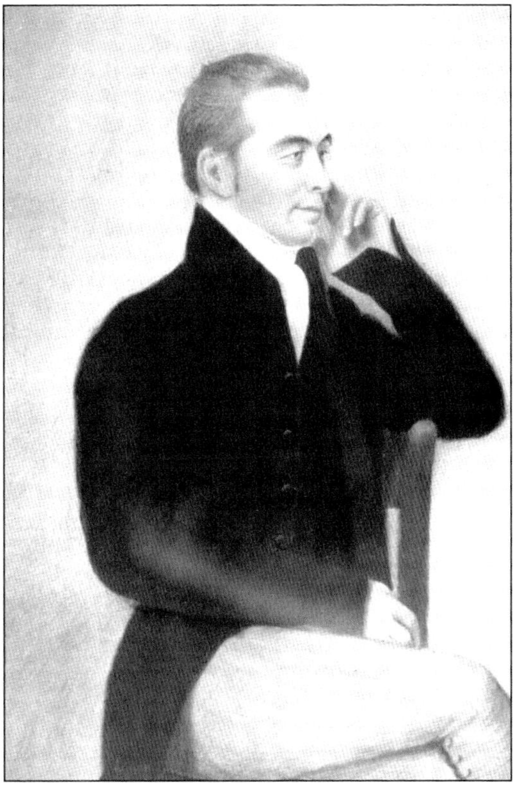

Prominent in the antislavery movement in Slatersville was Arnold Buffum, whose family had lived in the area for several generations. Buffum is listed as president of the New England Anti-Slavery Society in 1832, and William Lloyd Garrison as corresponding secretary. The church sponsored abolition lectures that were open to the public.

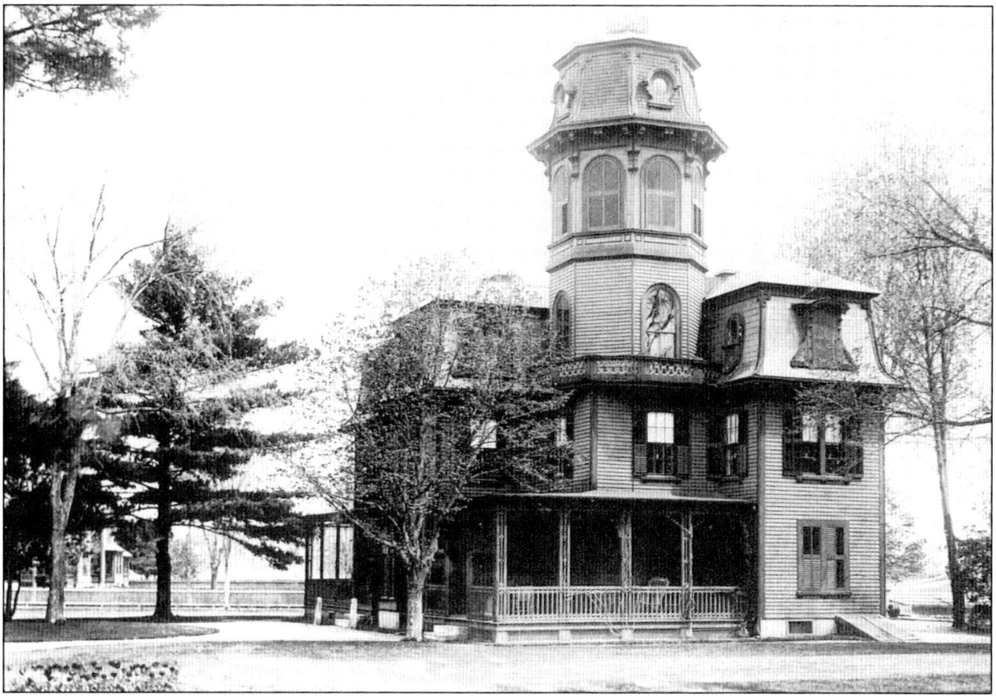

William Slater, manager of the Slatersville mills, built this mansion c. 1854. Designed by architect Thomas A. Tefft, the original house was embellished by the additions of a tower and a mansard roof c. 1868. It stood where Halliwell Drive is today. (RA.)

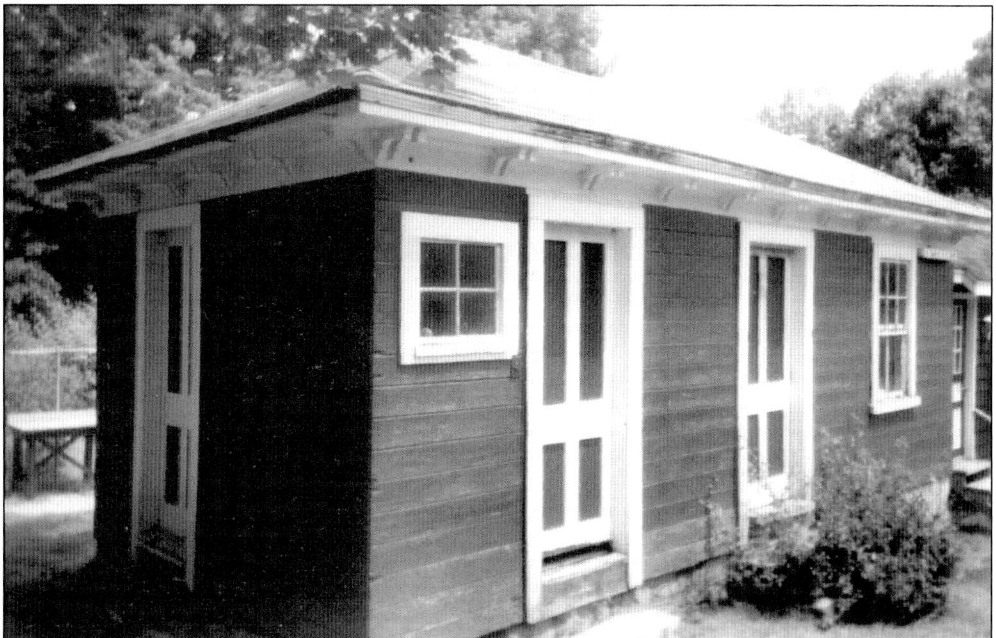

An auxiliary to the Slater mansion was this modest utilitarian servants' building and two-hole outhouse, with the ornamental bracketing on the eaves, similar to that of the mansion itself. (WSt.)

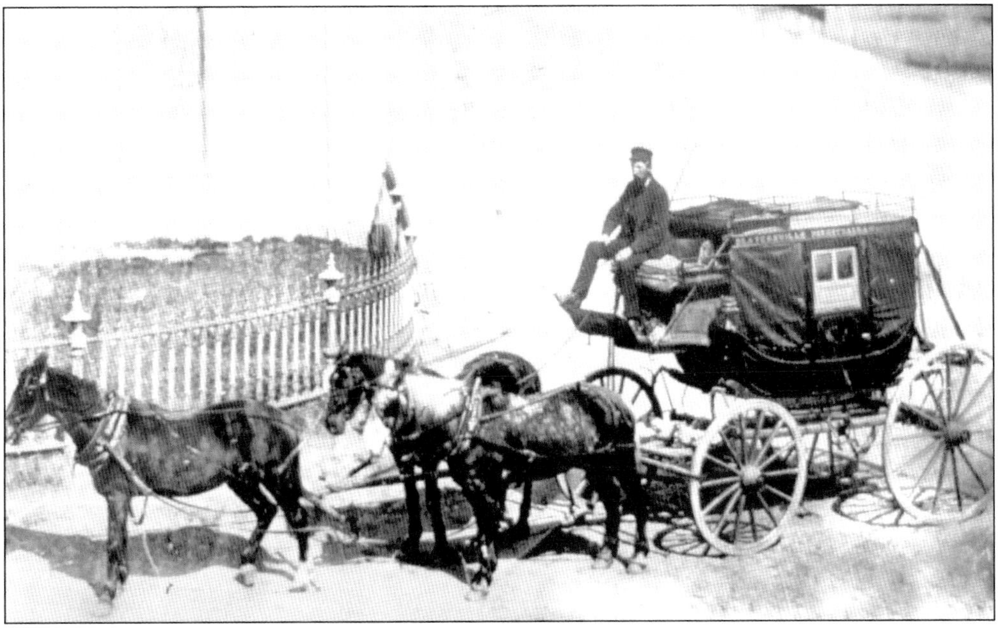

In the mid-19th century, the stagecoach was still a main conveyance for land travel. The Slatersville-Forestdale-Woonsocket stage made stops along Great Road in Union Village, as well as in Forestdale and in Slatersville at the inn where the town hall now stands. Other stages connected the area to Providence and Worcester.

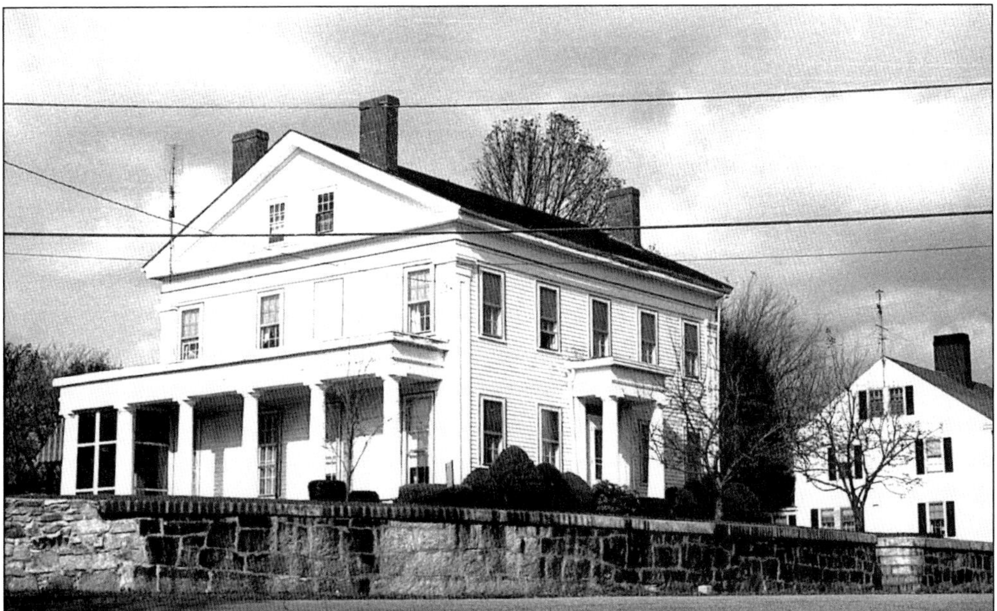

Dr. Elisha Bartlett was the husband of Elizabeth Slater, daughter of John and Ruth Slater. Bartlett built this house *c.* 1850 on the site of John Slater's house, which was removed to its present location on School Street to allow Bartlett to build there.

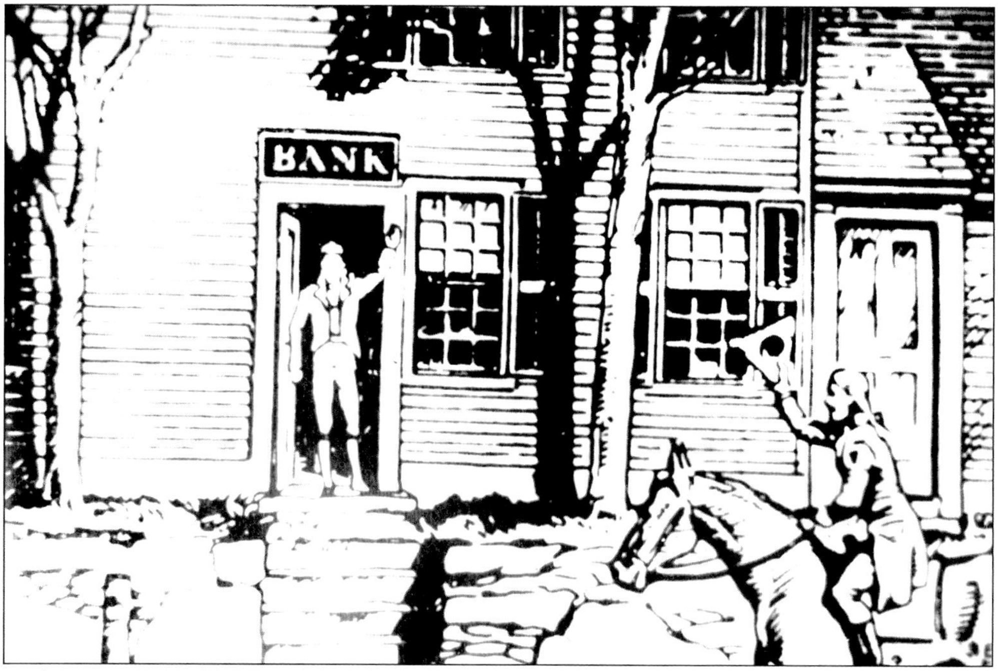

Built *c*. 1803, the Smithfield Union Bank building shown in this sketch still exists today on Pound Hill Road, but it is altered so that it is unrecognizable. Originally located at the corner of Great Road, where it functioned as a bank and general store, it was moved a few hundred feet westward when bank operations were transferred to Woonsocket in 1851.

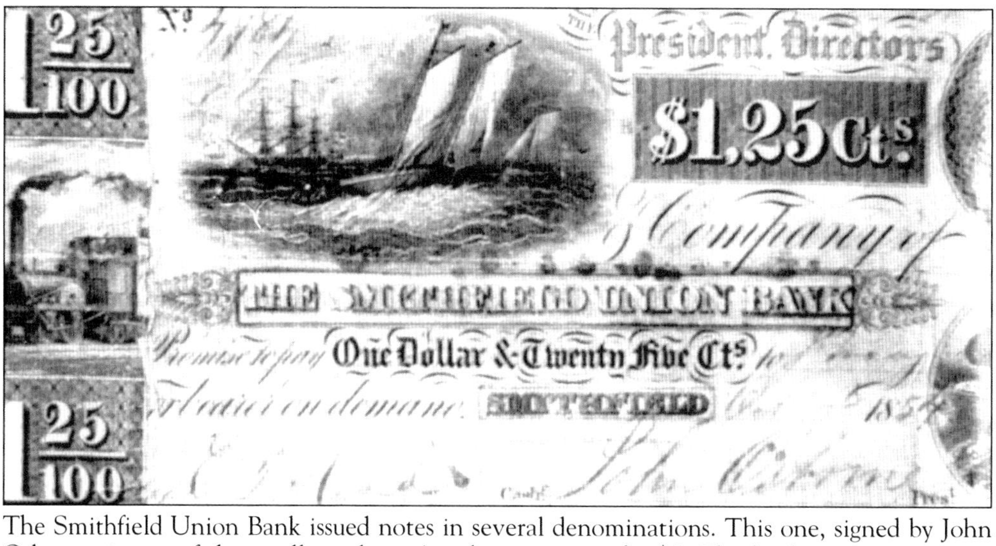

The Smithfield Union Bank issued notes in several denominations. This one, signed by John Osborne, is one of the smaller values. Another note was for $3. The bank gave its name to Union Village.

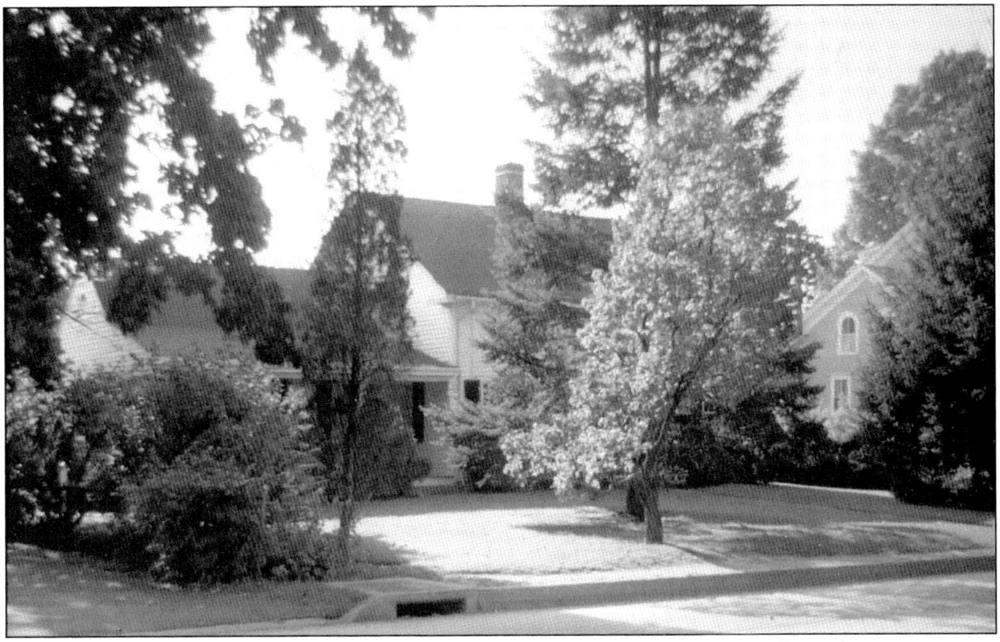

The Almy-Marble house, built *c.* 1805, is attributed to Christopher Almy, first postmaster of Woonsocket (Union Village), with additions to the early simple structure made by his daughter Phoebe Almy Marble. Sarah Marble, Almy's granddaughter, traveled by stagecoach to Woonsocket and then by train to Providence to teach at the Rhode Island Normal School.

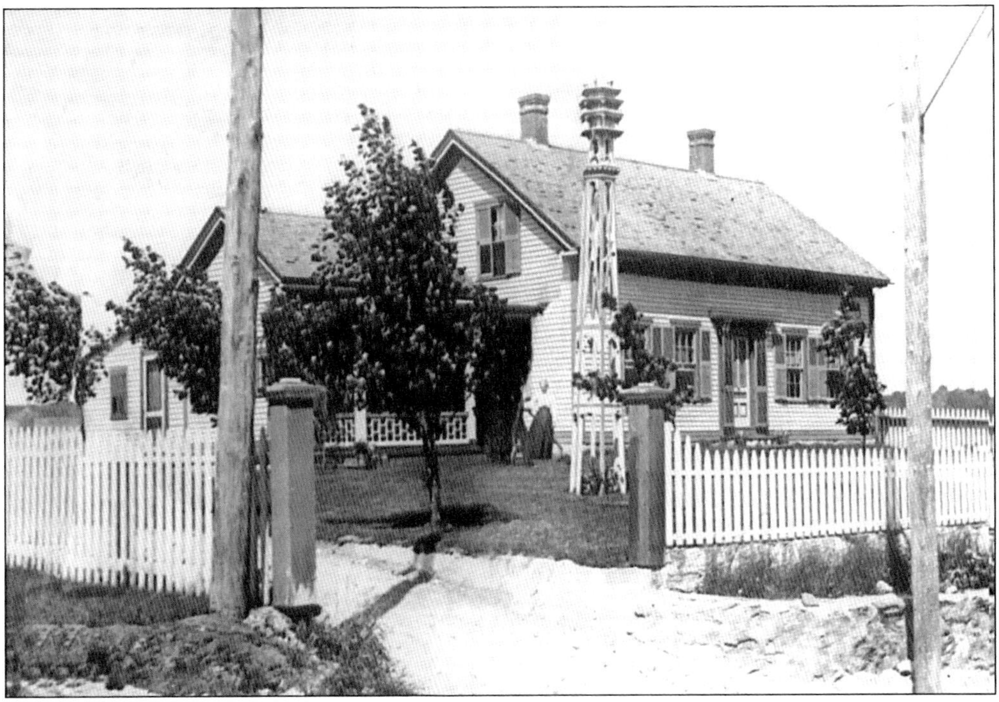

This *c.* 1834–1840 house in Slatersville was once owned by Stephen Slater and later sold to others, including Hemingway Hamlin and Robert Cole. In this early-20th-century photograph, the front yard features what appears to be a very elaborate birdhouse.

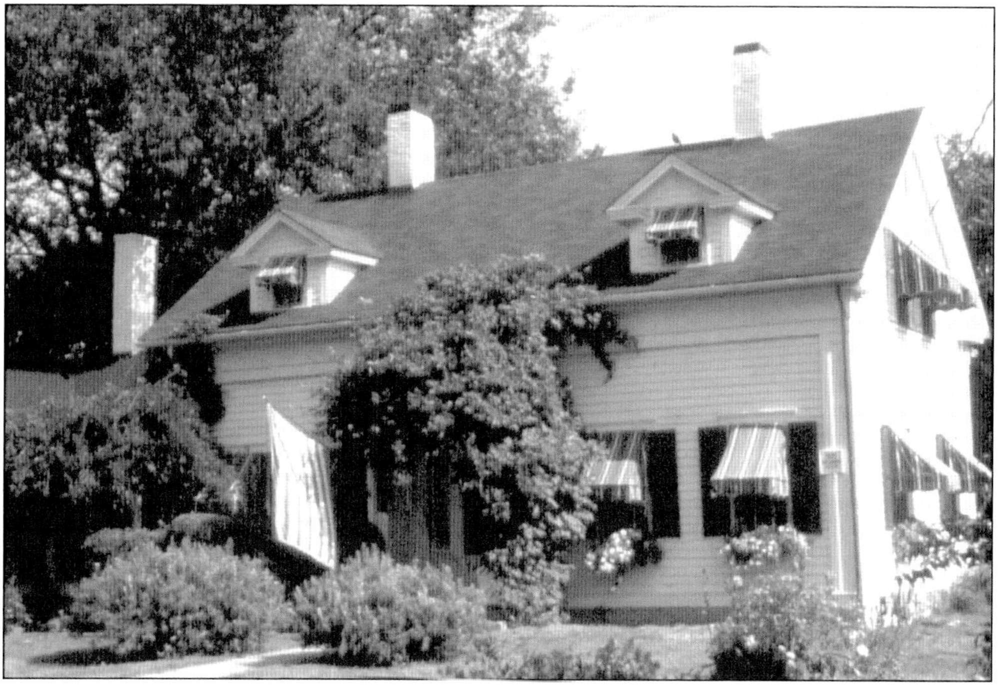

Hannah Southwick built the Captain Landers house *c.* 1835 on part of the farm of Joseph Arnold. She succeeded James Bushee at the Smithfield Academy, operating the "Young Ladies Seminary" until the building burned. Captain Landers succeeded Southwick as resident and is noted for the cannon he kept on the front lawn to mark his participation in the Dorr War.

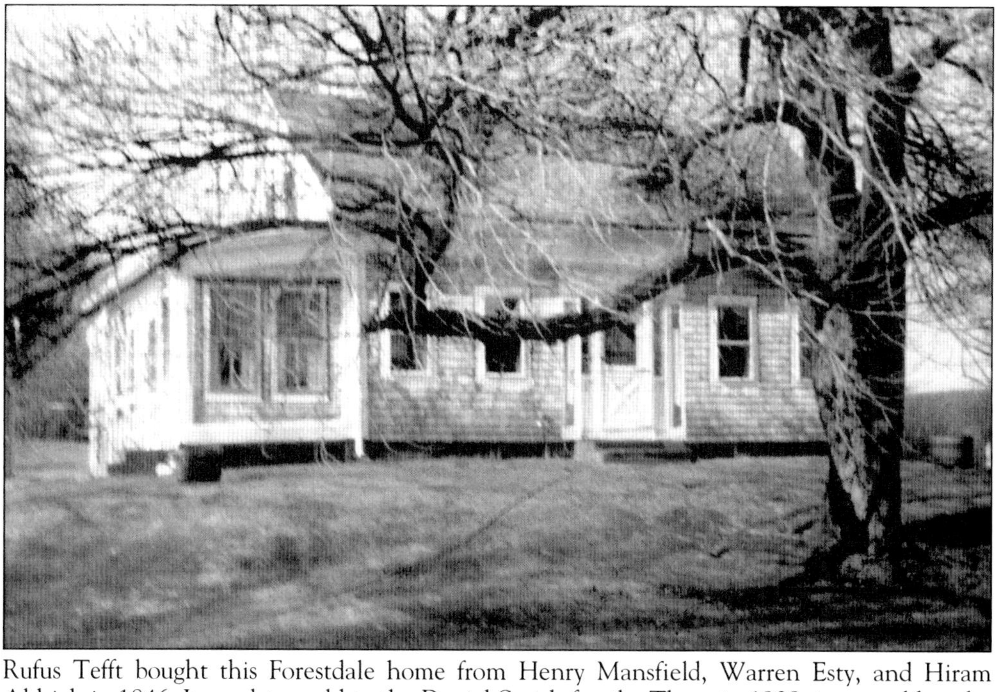

Rufus Tefft bought this Forestdale home from Henry Mansfield, Warren Esty, and Hiram Aldrich in 1846. It was later sold to the Daniel Smith family. Then, in 1908, it was sold to the Harpin family, whose descendants held it until the late 20th century. (LV.)

James Bushee, a prominent name in the history of education in North Smithfield, and contemporary of Henry Barnard, began his schooling at an academy in Union Village in the early 1800s. After teaching in Massachusetts, he returned to Union Village to become teacher and principal of the Smithfield Academy. Later, he established his own academy in the Aldrich Inn, where the science facilities were said to rival those of Brown University and where his methods were those of most successful teachers today.

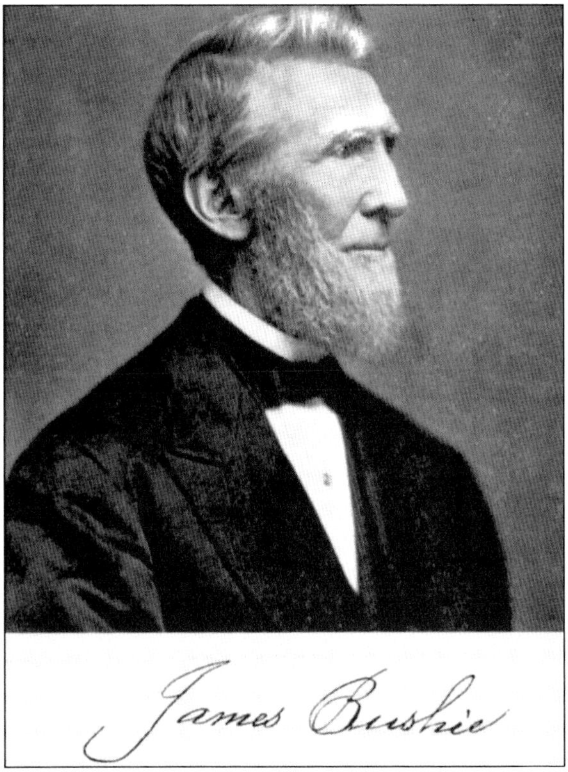

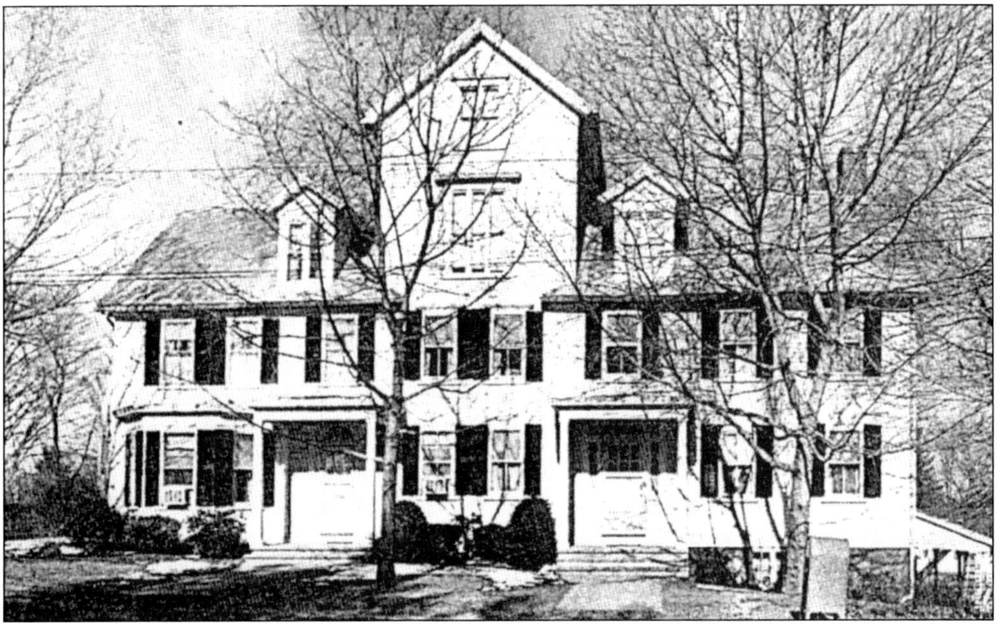

The George Aldrich Inn, on Great Road, is distinguished by its association with James Bushee and his academy. Built in 1804 by Marcus Arnold, it was sold in 1809 to George Aldrich and then enlarged. It functioned as an inn from 1821 to 1834. In 1832, Aldrich's daughter married James Bushee. They settled in the Aldrich home and, in 1843, opened the Smithfield Union High School for Males and Females in their home.

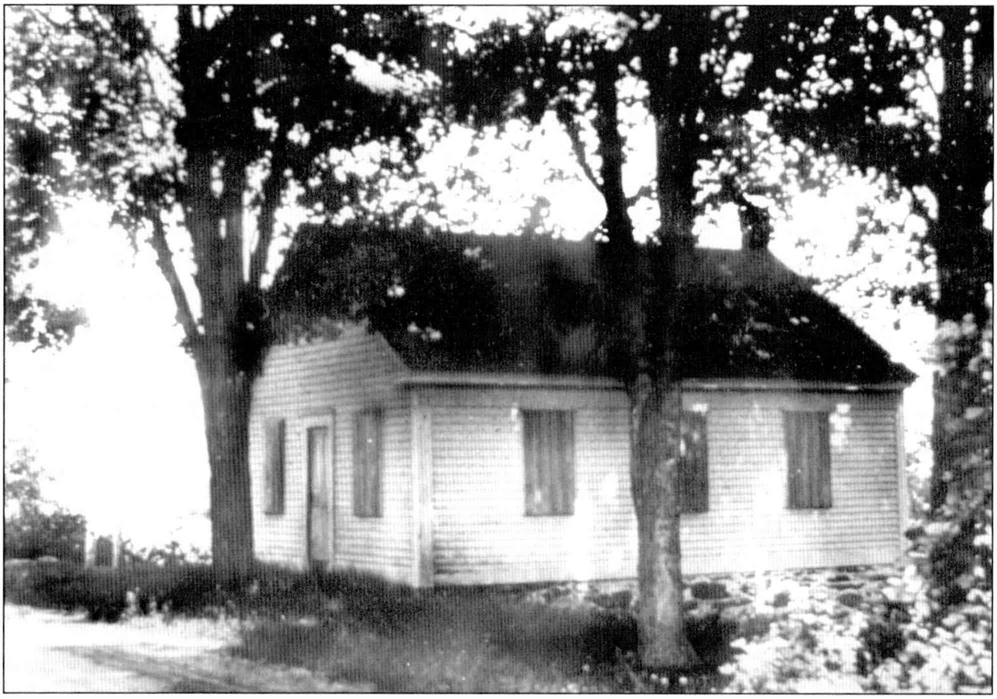

By the mid-19th century, North Smithfield had been divided into 11 school districts, each one responsible for setting the school term and hiring a teacher. The earliest schoolhouse (*c.* 1803), serving the Remington district, was on Pound Hill Road near Douglas Pike. The Mowry School (above) was located on Kendall Mowry's land on Greenville Road near Douglas Pike. It is said that at one time, every child in the school was surnamed Mowry except for a Smith, and his first name was Mowry. The Mansfield School was located near the corner on North Main and Mechanic Streets in Slatersville. Today, it is a private home.

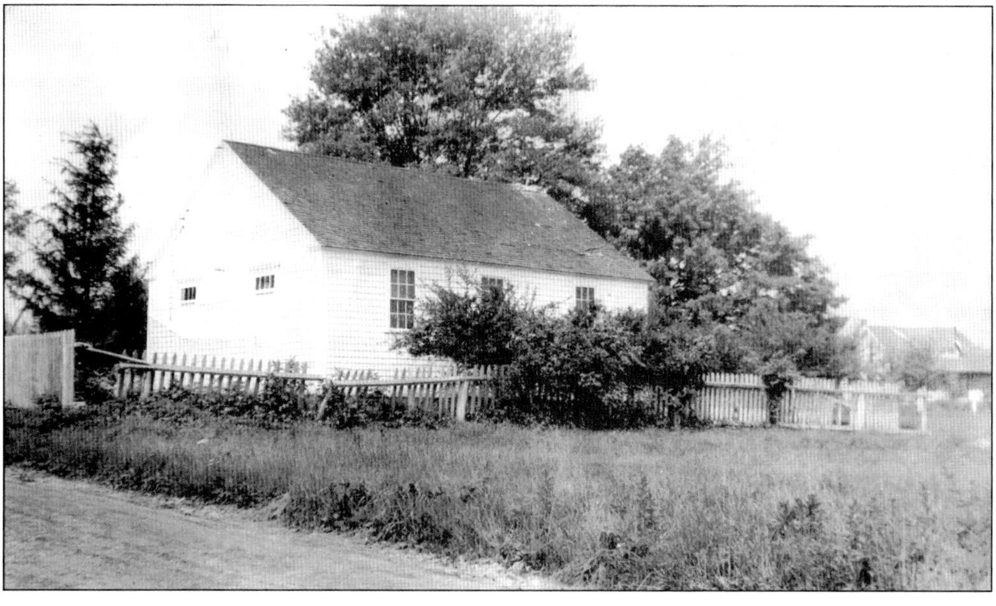

It is logical that the earliest large school building was the Slatersville School built in 1886. It replaced a much smaller schoolhouse just behind this new school, where a playground is today.

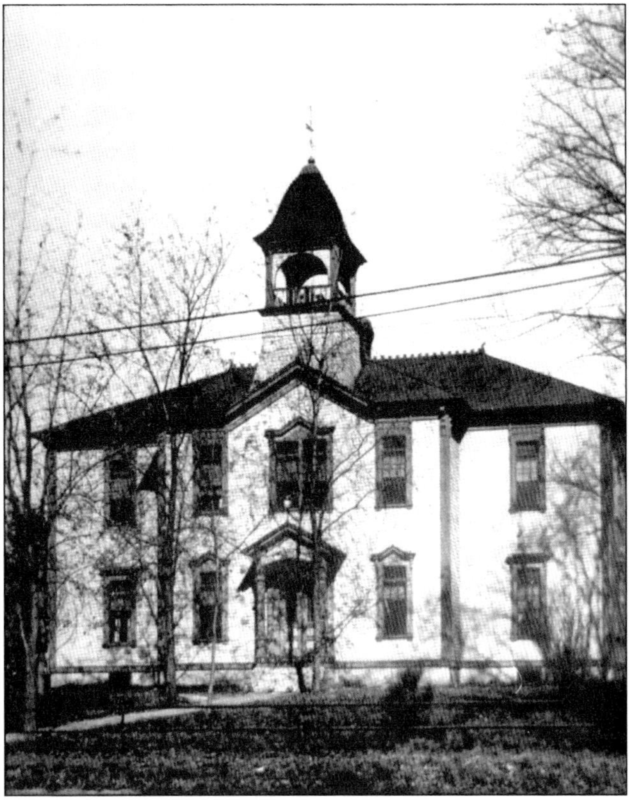

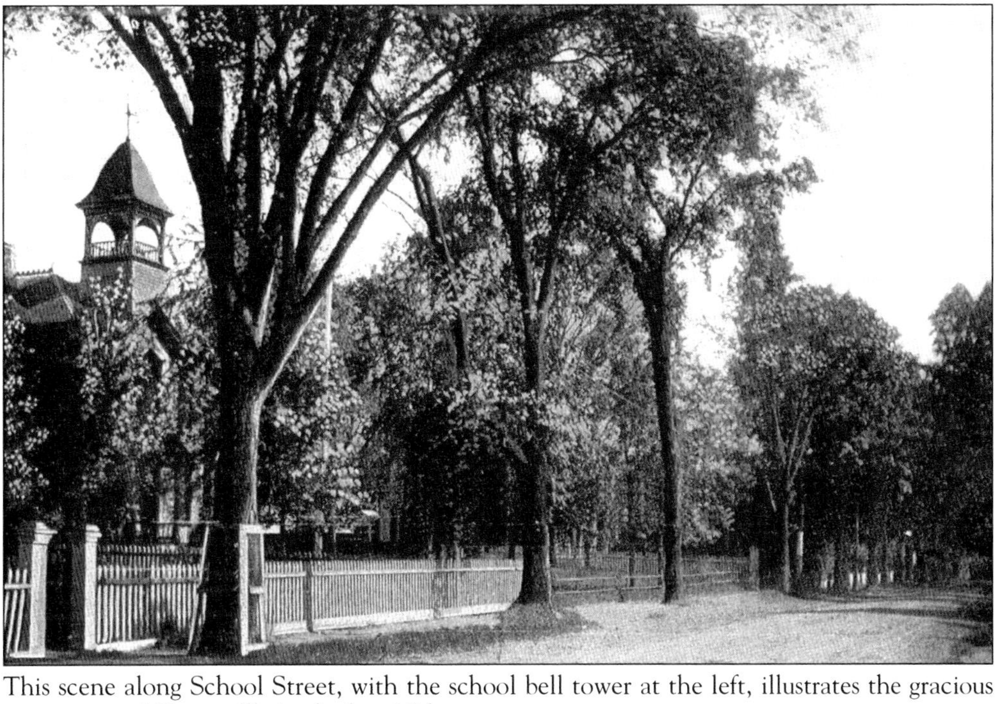

This scene along School Street, with the school bell tower at the left, illustrates the gracious appearance of Slatersville in the late 19th century.

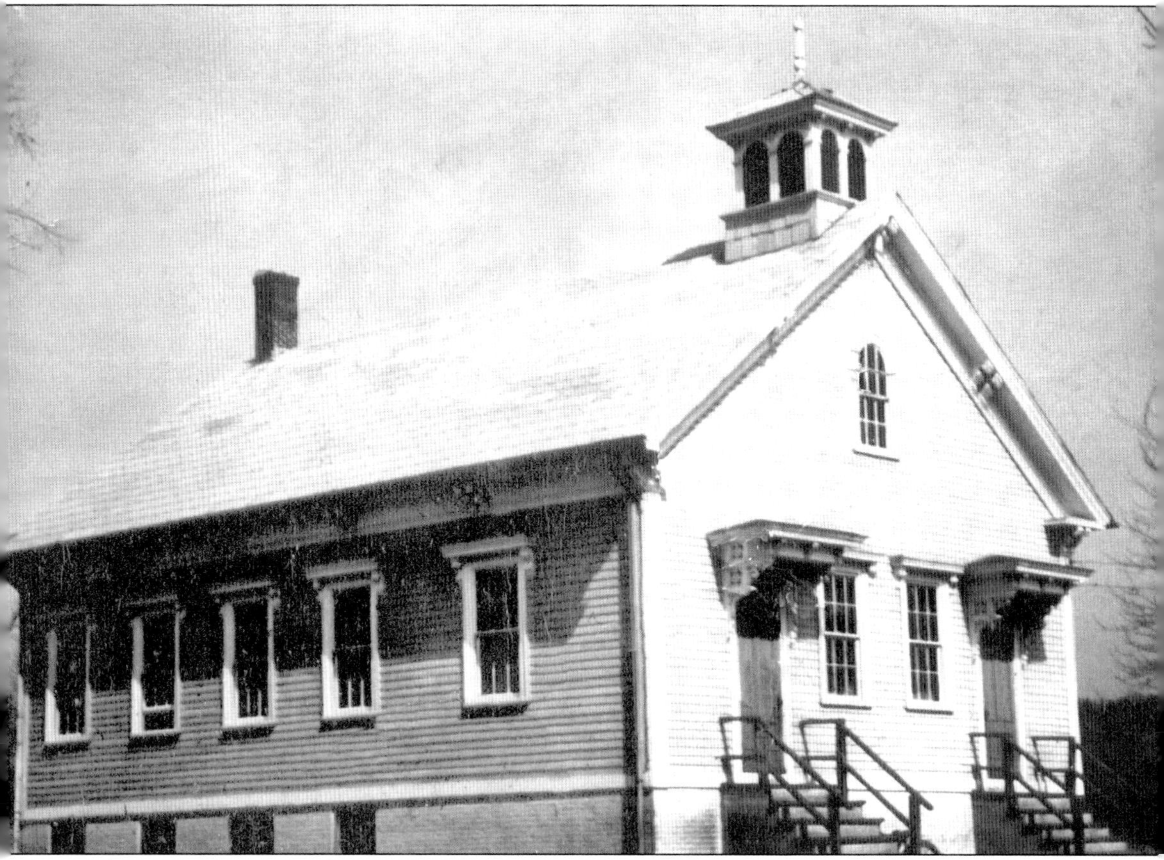

The Forestdale School was built in 1877 on land deeded by the Forestdale Manufacturing Company. It replaced the earlier Branch School of District No. 3, located at the corner of Maple Avenue and Great Road. It served as a one-room school for many years. In 1958, the Eleanor Howard Kindergarten was moved here from Kendall-Dean School; it was returned there in 1975. The North Smithfield Heritage Association then leased the building for its headquarters. The group has restored and maintained the structure, using the premises for its collections and presentations, thus continuing the building's original educational purpose.

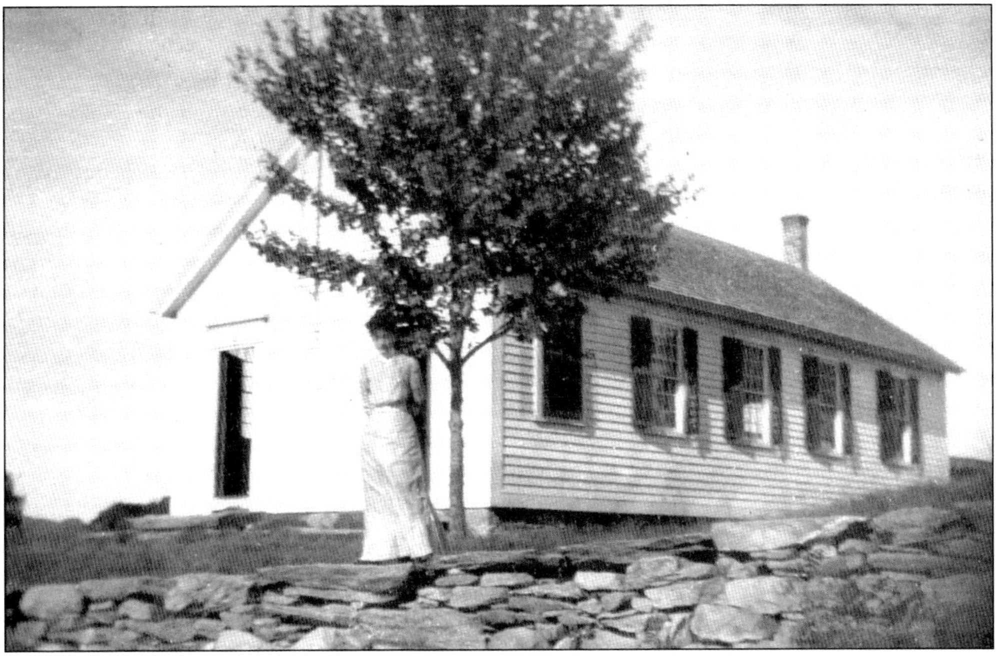

The Union Village School was set on a rise along Woonsocket Hill Road beyond the junction with Great Road. Somewhat larger than the rural schools, it served the students in and around Union Village. Later, it was replaced by a two-story four-room brick school, which burned in the early 1970s.

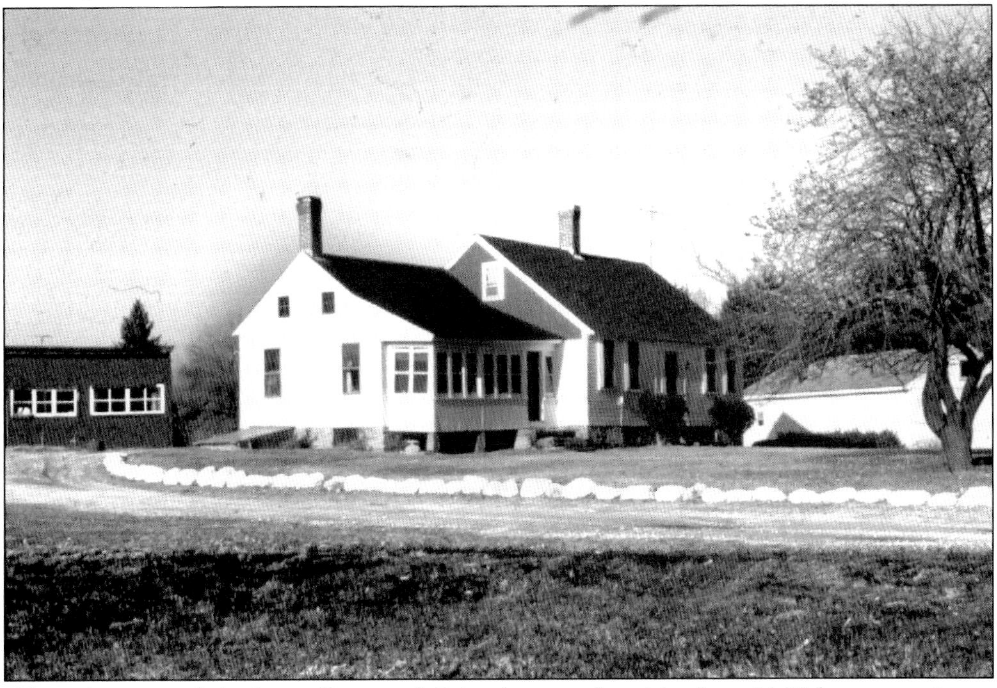

When the original Andrews (Primrose) School was replaced in the mid-19th century, it was moved over the snow and ice from its location on Grange Road to become the ell on the Goodwin house at Primrose Four Corners. The glassed-in porch was a later addition. (WAN.)

Town of North Smithfield.

APPORTIONMENT

Of School Money to each District for Teachers' Wages, 1888.

District No. 1.—Mansfield,	- - -	$300.00
" " 2.—Slatersville,	- - -	1,500.00
" " 3.—Branch,	- - -	400.00
" " 4.—Union,	- - -	330.00
" " 5.—Blackstone,	- - -	700.00
" " 6.—Remington,	- - -	280.00
" " 7.—Staples,	- - -	300.00
" " 8.—Aldrich,	- - - -	330.00
" " 9.—Sayles Hill,	- - -	290.00
" " 10.—Mowry,	- - - -	200.00
" " 11.—Andrews,	- - -	350.00
Total,	- - - - -	$4,980.00

Bills for incidentals not to exceed five dollars for each district and department will be allowed.

The organization of the Committee for 1888 is as follows: JOHN H. BAILEY, JR., Chairman; JAMES I. HOTCHKISS, Clerk; GEORGE R. SMITH, M. D., was elected by the committee to be Superintendent.

Trustees will send all school returns and bills for fuel and incidentals to the clerk who will issue all money orders.

Post office address of each member of the committee, Woonsocket, R. I.

This notice details the apportionment of money to each school district for teachers' wages.

Toward 1840, a constitutional crisis grew in Rhode Island. Under the existing charter, only certain male property owners could vote. A growing population, many of them immigrants, were deprived of voting rights. Thomas Wilson Dorr led the movement to extend suffrage, supported by Dr. Metcalf Marsh of Slatersville, organizer of the Slatersville Suffrage Association. A controversial election in 1842 named Dorr as governor, but the militia was called out, Dorrites' homes were entered, and the election was invalidated. (NSHA.)

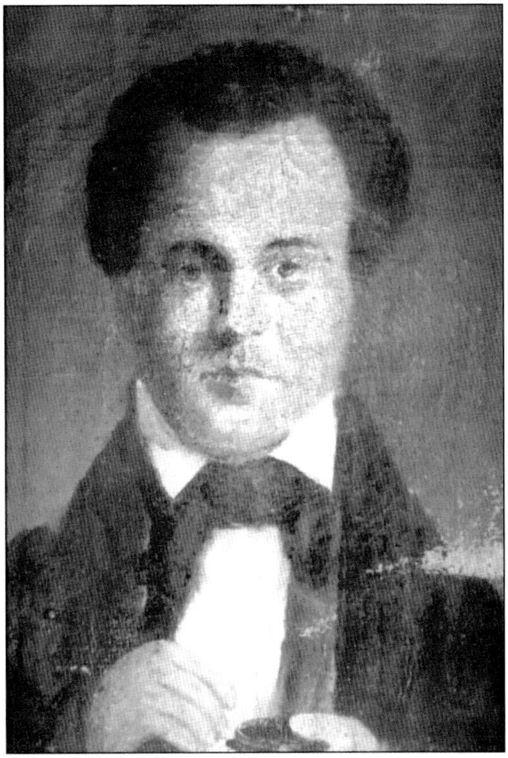

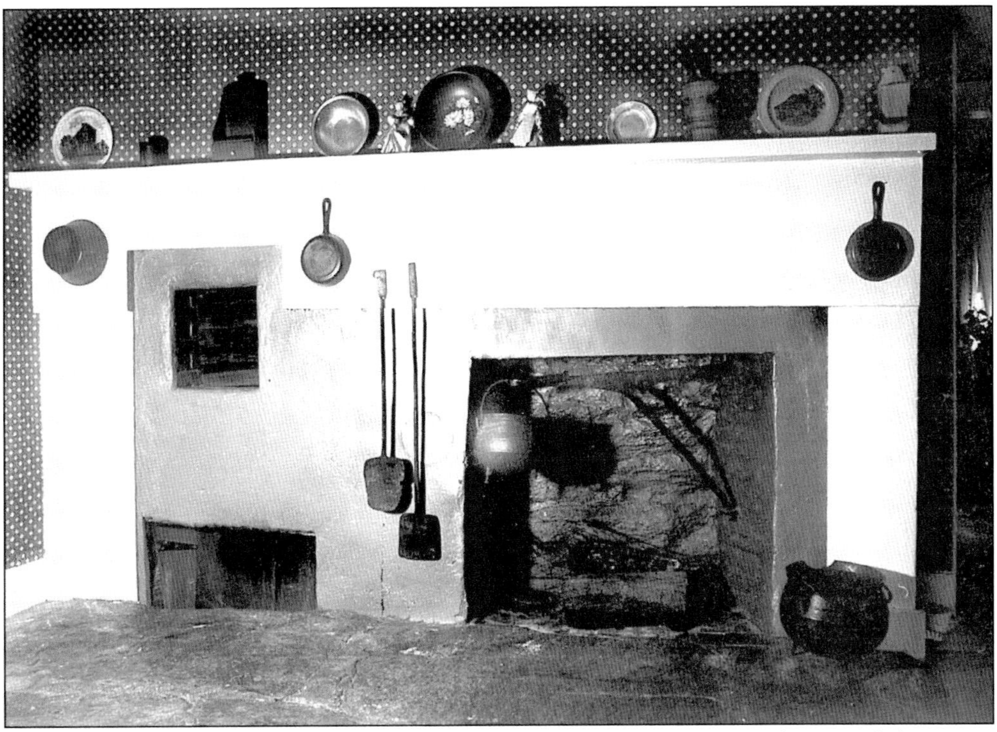

Around this fireplace in his home on Mechanic Street, Dr. Metcalf Marsh counseled patients as well as politicians.

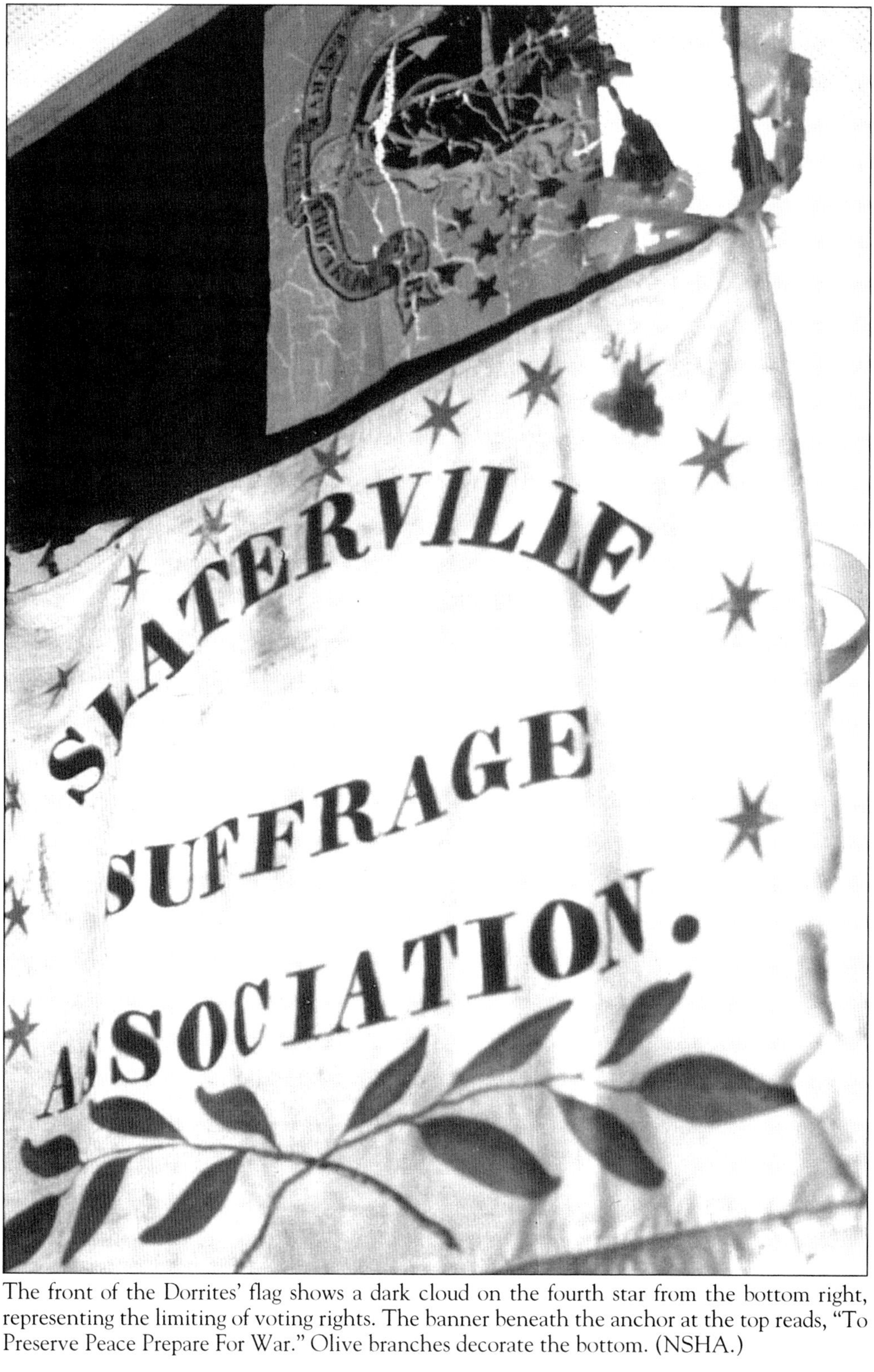

The front of the Dorrites' flag shows a dark cloud on the fourth star from the bottom right, representing the limiting of voting rights. The banner beneath the anchor at the top reads, "To Preserve Peace Prepare For War." Olive branches decorate the bottom. (NSHA.)

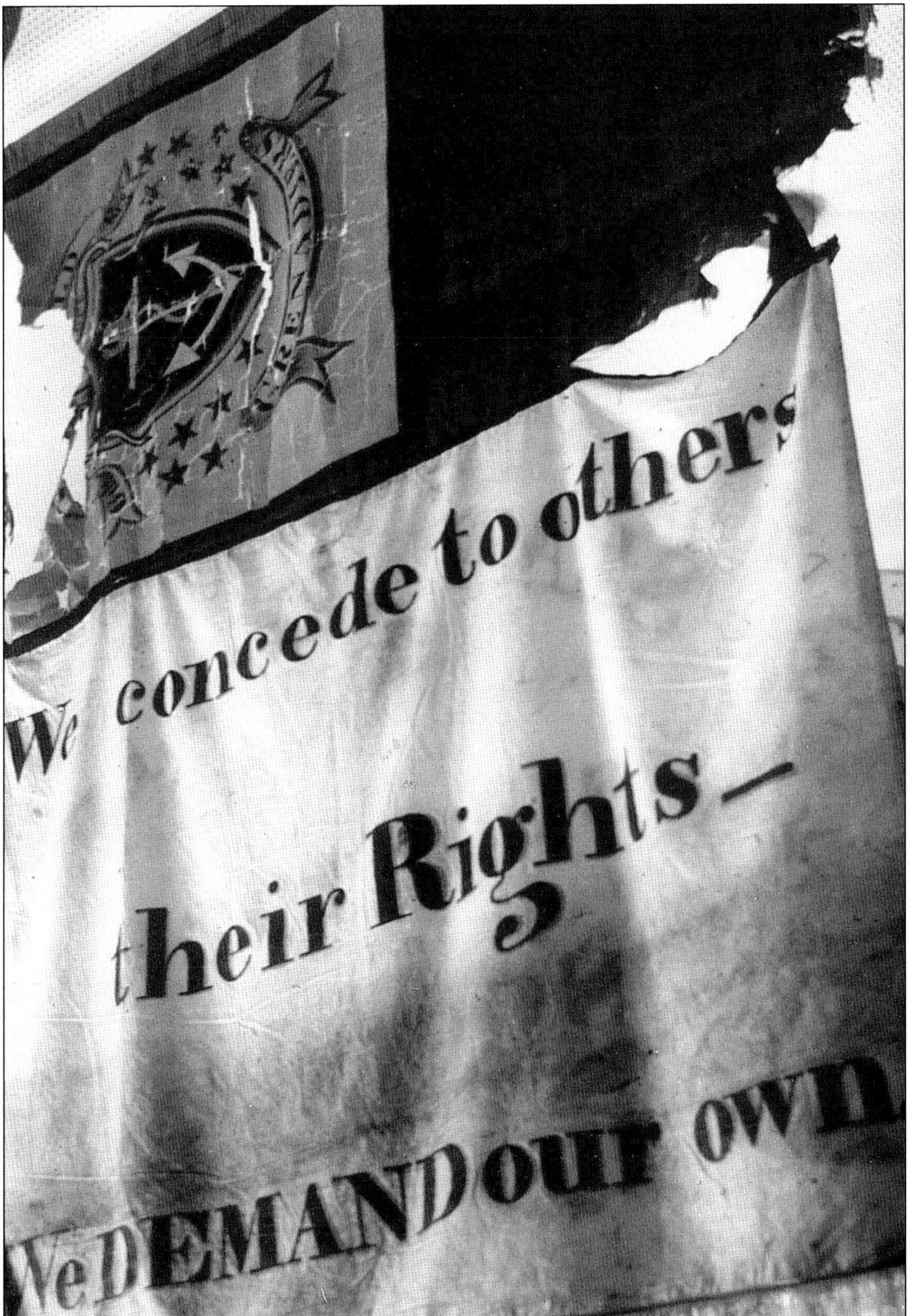

The other side of the flag reflects the Dorrites' attitude toward the extension of the franchise, rather than any restrictions. Banners around the anchor emblem read, "Smithfield" and "Grenadiers," suggesting militancy. (NSHA.)

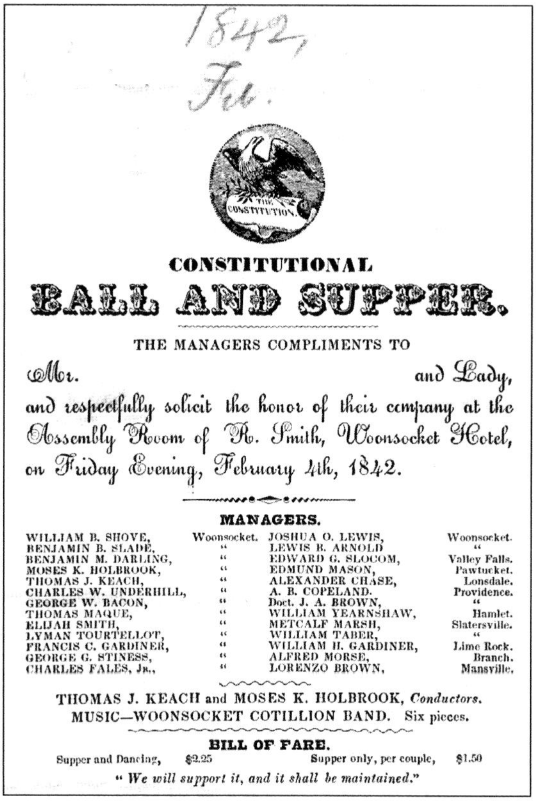

1842,
Feb.

THE CONSTITUTION.

CONSTITUTIONAL

BALL AND SUPPER.

THE MANAGERS COMPLIMENTS TO

Mr. and Lady,

and respectfully solicit the honor of their company at the Assembly Room of R. Smith, Woonsocket Hotel, on Friday Evening, February 4th, 1842.

MANAGERS.

WILLIAM B. SHOVE,	Woonsocket.	JOSHUA O. LEWIS,	Woonsocket.
BENJAMIN B. SLADE,	"	LEWIS B. ARNOLD	"
BENJAMIN M. DARLING,	"	EDWARD G. SLOCOM,	Valley Falls.
MOSES K. HOLBROOK,	"	EDMUND MASON,	Pawtucket.
THOMAS J. KEACH,	"	ALEXANDER CHASE,	Lonsdale.
CHARLES W. UNDERHILL,	"	A. B. COPELAND.	Providence.
GEORGE W. BACON,	"	Doct. J. A. BROWN,	"
THOMAS MAQUE,	"	WILLIAM YEARNSHAW,	Hamlet.
ELIJAH SMITH,	"	METCALF MARSH,	Slatersville.
LYMAN TOURTELLOT,	"	WILLIAM TABER,	"
FRANCIS C. GARDINER,	"	WILLIAM H. GARDINER,	Lime Rock.
GEORGE G. STINESS,	"	ALFRED MORSE,	Branch.
CHARLES FALES, Jr.,	"	LORENZO BROWN,	Mansville.

THOMAS J. KEACH and MOSES K. HOLBROOK, *Conductors.*
MUSIC—WOONSOCKET COTILLION BAND. Six pieces.

BILL OF FARE.

Supper and Dancing, $2.25 Supper only, per couple, $1.50

" We will support it, and it shall be maintained."

The list of managers on this invitation to a constitutional ball and supper shows the extent of support for Dorr's cause among many prominent men of the region. (NSHA.)

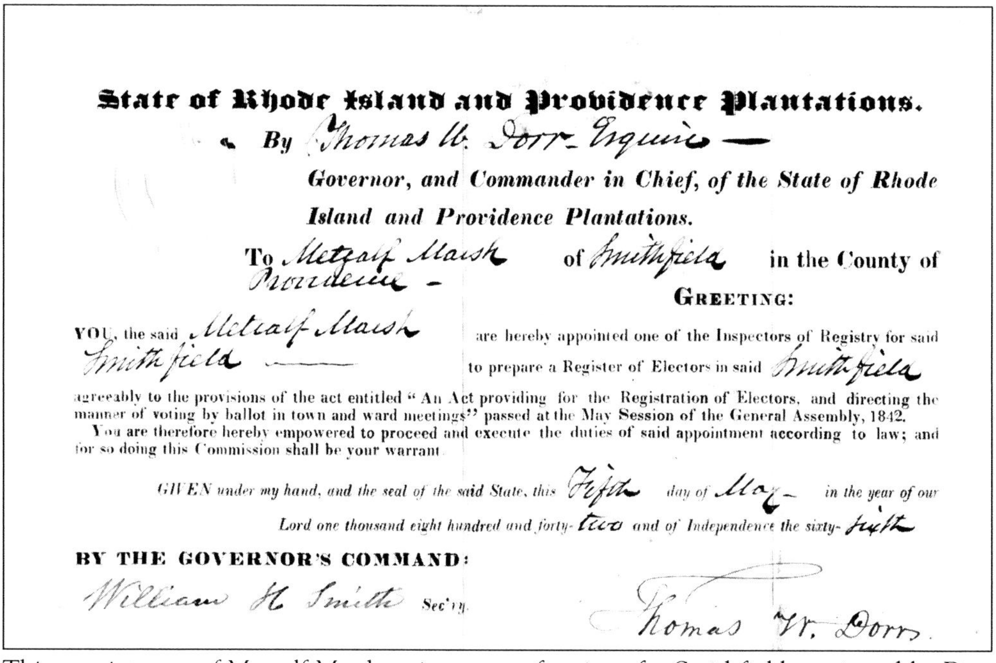

State of Rhode Island and Providence Plantations.

By Thomas W. Dorr Esquire —

Governor, and Commander in Chief, of the State of Rhode Island and Providence Plantations.

To Metcalf Marsh of Smithfield in the County of Providence -

GREETING:

YOU, the said Metcalf Marsh are hereby appointed one of the Inspectors of Registry for said Smithfield ——— to prepare a Register of Electors in said Smithfield agreeably to the provisions of the act entitled " An Act providing for the Registration of Electors, and directing the manner of voting by ballot in town and ward meetings" passed at the May Session of the General Assembly, 1842.

You are therefore hereby empowered to proceed and execute the duties of said appointment according to law; and for so doing this Commission shall be your warrant.

GIVEN under my hand, and the seal of the said State, this Fifth *day of* May *in the year of our Lord one thousand eight hundred and forty-* two *and of Independence the sixty-* sixth

BY THE GOVERNOR'S COMMAND:

William H. Smith Sec'ry.

Thomas W. Dorr.

This appointment of Metcalf Marsh as inspector of registry for Smithfield was issued by Dorr himself as "Governor, and Commander in Chief" of the state on May 15, 1842. The defeat of his armed supporters came later that year. (NSHA.)

CIRCULAR.

Dear Sir:—In order to produce concert of action throughout the State, and secure the adoption of our CONSTITUTION by a triumphant majority, a general plan of operations has been fixed upon by the Executive Committee of the R. I. Suffrage Association, and arrangements made to have Addresses delivered by gentlemen engaged in this great work of Reform, in all the Towns, at the times and places named in the annexed schedule.

The Committee look to you to use your utmost exertions in the cause, to make arrangements to secure a full attendance of the citizens of your town, and if there is not a complete organization already, to have your Town fully organized by choosing a Vigilance Committee for the Town, and a Sub-committee in every district, to canvass the town, and register in a book for the purpose, the name of every male citizen, that on the days set forth, the vote of every citizen who does not distinctly refuse, shall be secured in favor of the Constitution.

For the Executive Committee.

Metcalf Marsh Esq.
Slatersville

Saml Low
Cor. Secy.

Pawtucket,	Monday 6th,	At Centreville, Warwick.
Lonsdale,	Tuesday 7th,	" Washington Village, Coventry.
Cumberland Hill,	Wednesday 8th,	" Meeting House, W. Greenwich.
Centreville,	Thursday 9th,	" State House, E. Greenwich.
Greenville,	Friday 10th.	" Wickford, North Kingstown.
Burrillville.	Saturday 11th,	" Hill School House, Exeter.
Dyersville,	Monday 13th,	" Brands Iron Works, Richmond.
Simmonsville,	Tuesday 14th,	Hopkinton.
Cranston,	Wednesday 15th,	" Pawcatuck, Westerly.
Pawtuxet,	Thursday 16th,	Charlestown.
Woonsocket Falls,	Friday 17th,	" Wakefield, South Kingston.
Slatersville,	Saturday 18th,	" Jamestown.
Glocester,	Monday 20th,	" Newport.
Foster,	Tuesday 21st,	" Portsmouth.
Scituate,	Wednesday 22d,	" Little Compton.
Lime Rock,	Thursday 23d,	" Tiverton.
(Meetings simultaneously,	Friday 24th, throughout the State)	Bristol.
Burrillville,	Saturday 25th;	Warren.

The Ex Comee will forward Bills calling the meeting in your town to your address.

S Low
Cor Secy

This circular was issued by the Executive Committee of the Rhode Island Suffrage Association in an effort to gain support for reform and a new constitution to replace the Royal Charter. (NSHA.)

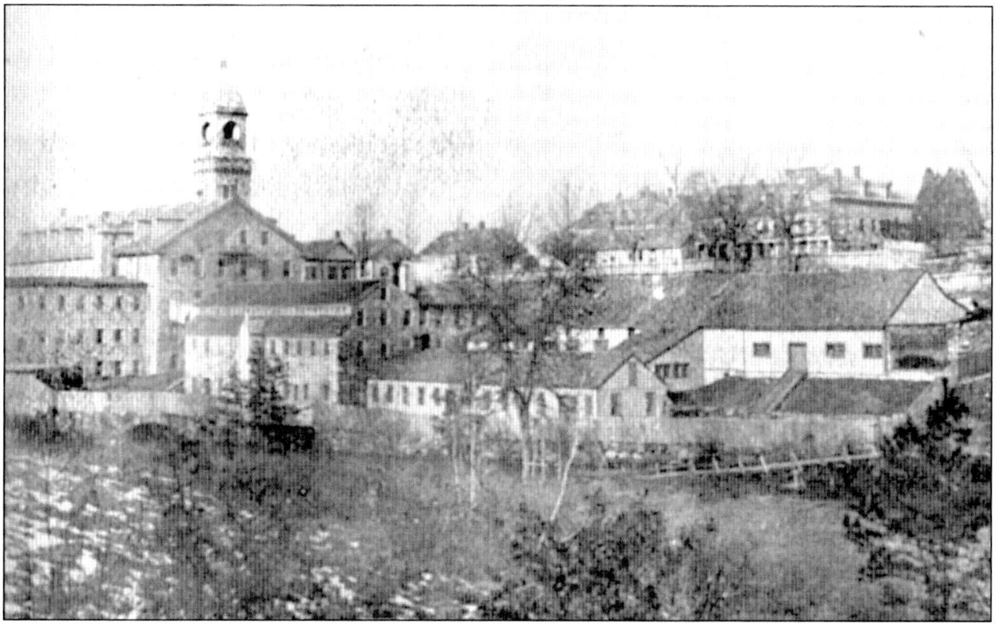

A view of Forestdale in 1901 shows the entire mill complex developed from the 1860s on. The commercial block is at the upper right, and the old scythe works along the river is at the lower right. (Hall, 1901.)

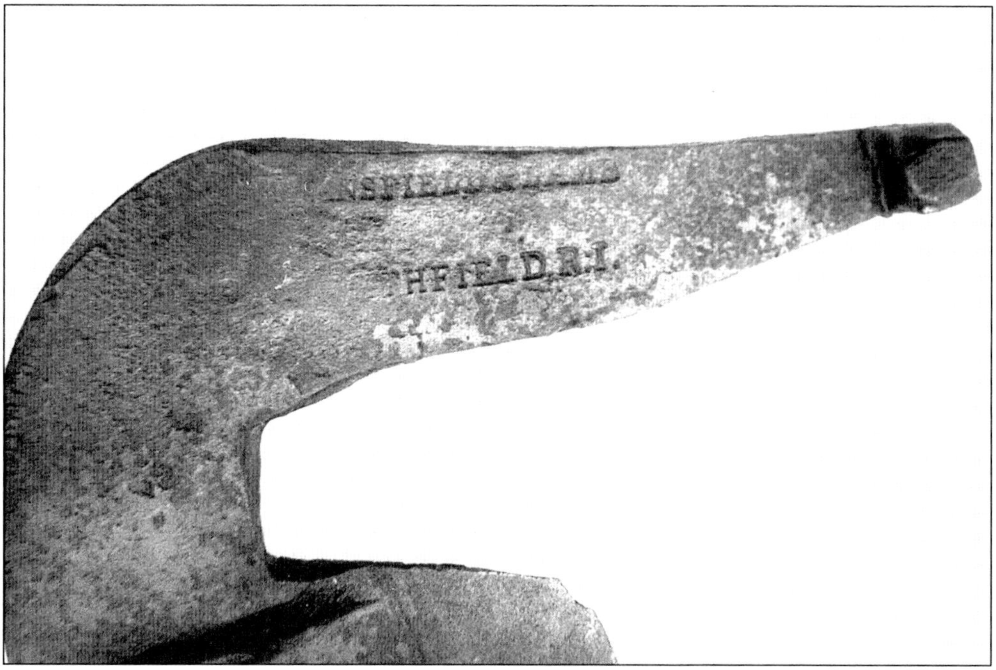

Mansfield and Lamb did not forget the farmers, even as they produced their finely crafted sabers. This plow blade, owned by the North Smithfield Heritage Association, is an example of the many that the Forestdale works produced for use by the region's farmers. (NSHA.)

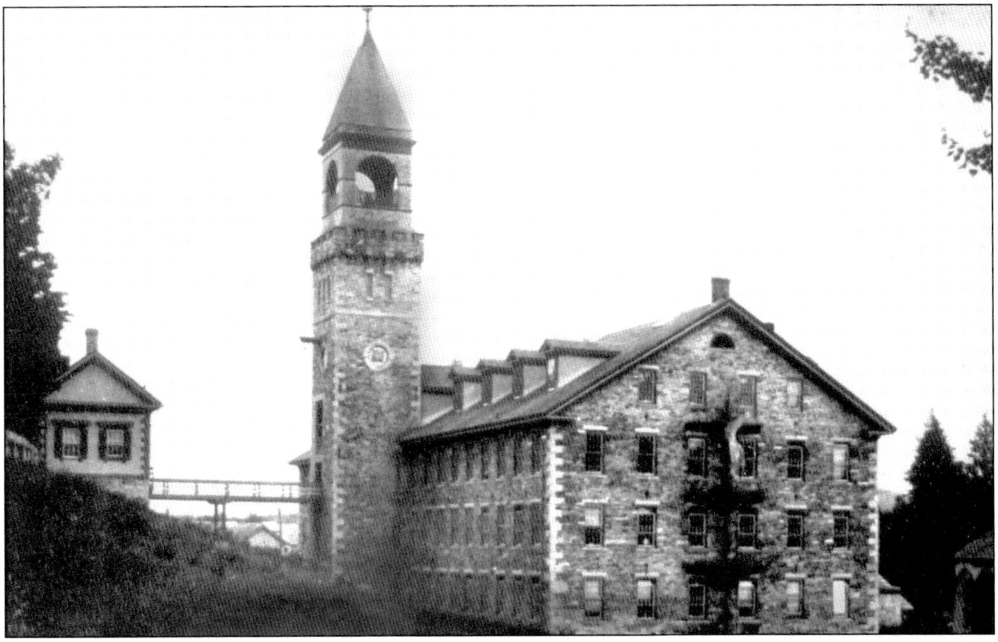

The imposing stone cotton mill was the landmark of Forestdale until it burned in the late 1970s. The bell tower was visible above the trees from a great distance. A wooden footbridge connected the mill with the frame office building, distinguished by its rusticated quoins similar to the stone quoins of the mill itself.

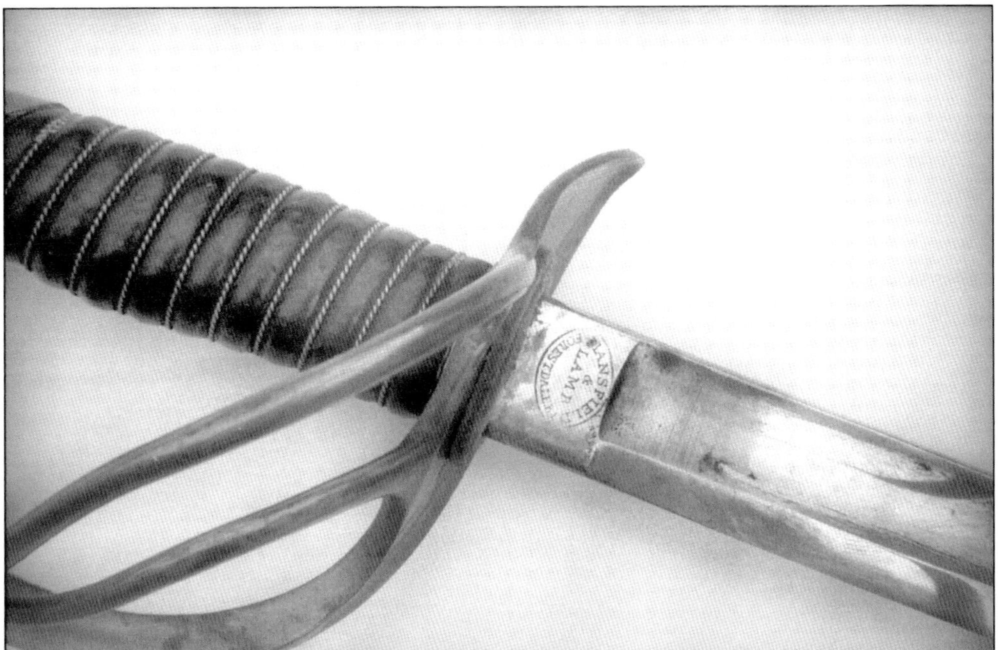

Early scythe factories at Forestdale had evolved into a prosperous business by the 1850s under the ownership on Mansfield and Lamb. Early in the Civil War, Mansfield and Lamb received a contract to make sabers for the Union army. The sabers were so highly regarded that a second contract was issued. (NSHA.)

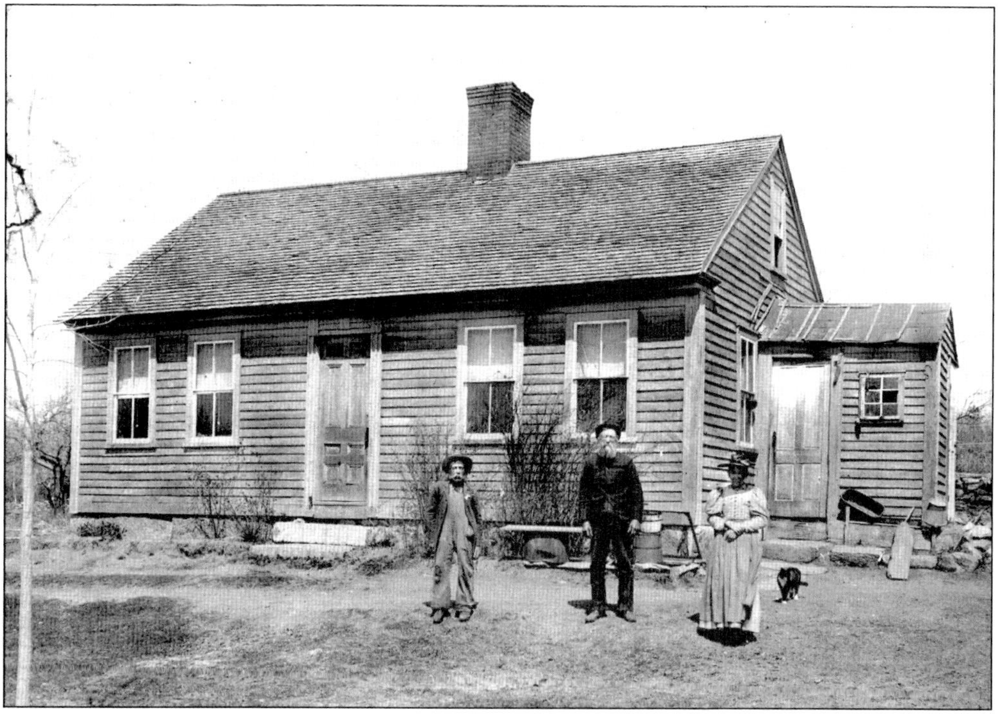

The Ichabod Allen house on Old Smithfield Road is a story-and-a-half farmhouse with an off-center chimney. Dated *c.* 1851, this house has remained in the Allen family continuously to the present. (RP.)

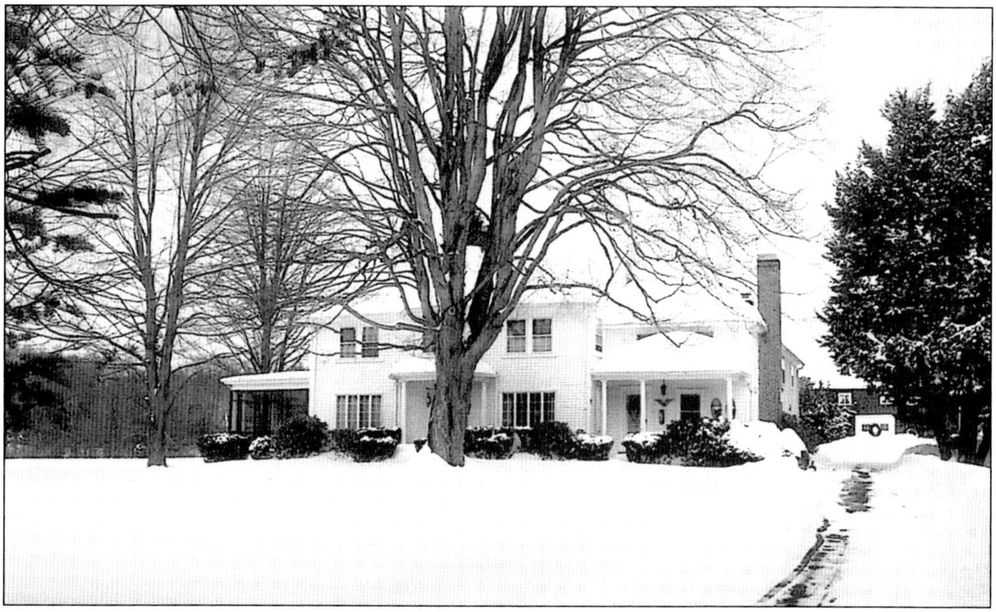

The David Wilkinson house is a two-and-a-half-story center-chimney structure dating to *c.* 1829. Wilkinson was associated with Samuel Slater in the cotton-manufacturing business. Several generations of Wilkinsons occupied the house, which shows evidence of embellishment over time. (IS.)

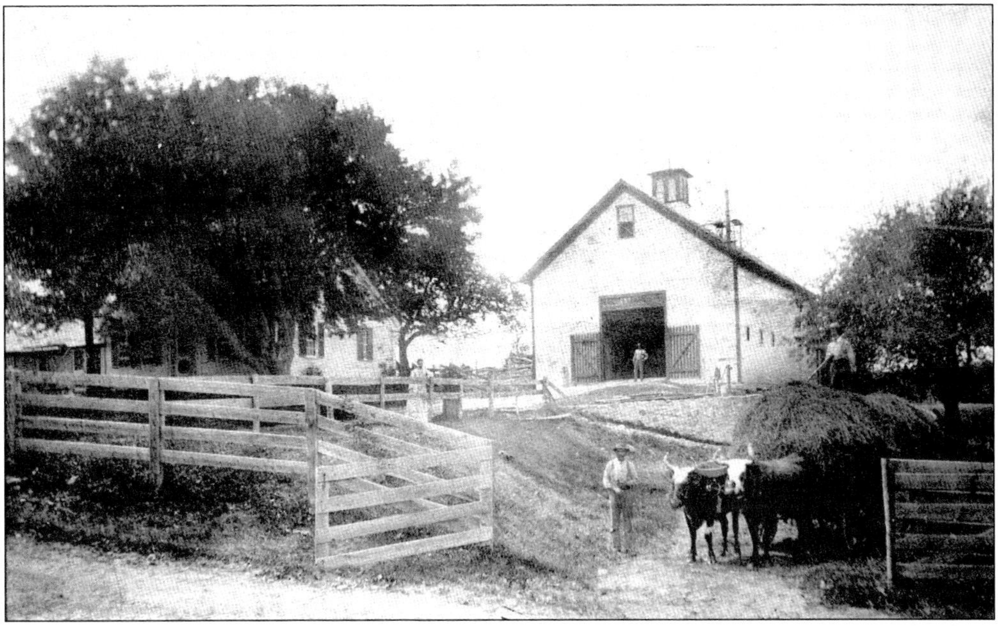

At the Lewis Chilson farm on Buxton Street, a yoke of oxen hauls a load of hay in this late-19th-century photograph. The substantial barn dwarfs the modest farmhouse. The farm was later owned by the Fredette family. (GS.)

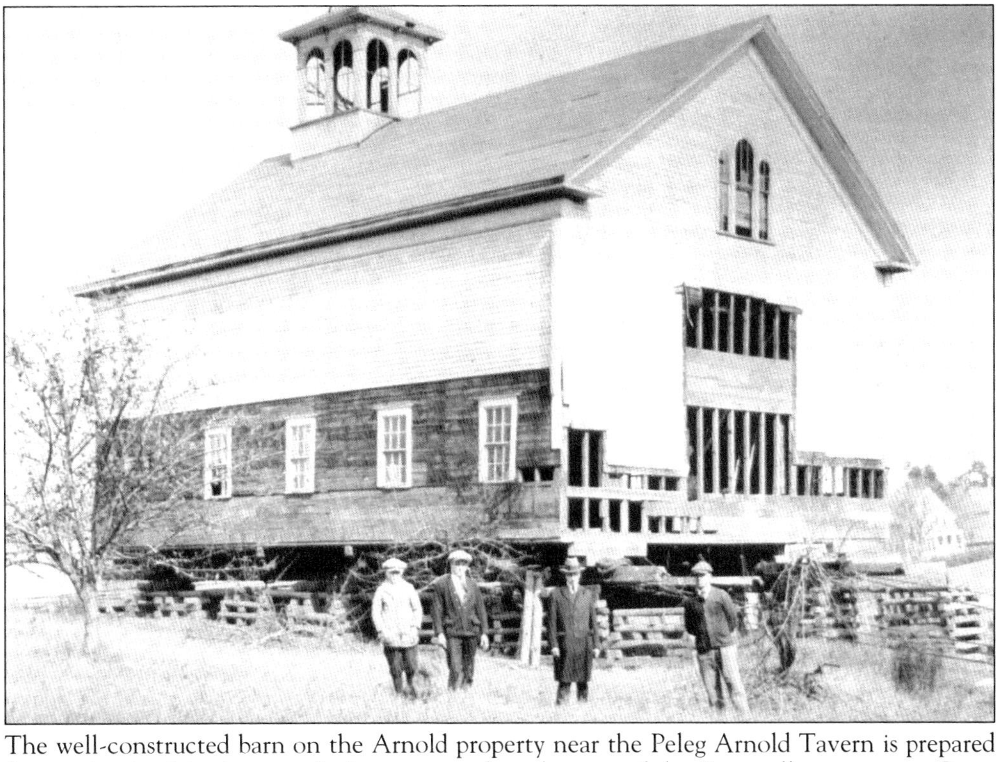

The well-constructed barn on the Arnold property near the Peleg Arnold Tavern is prepared for moving in this photograph. It was moved to the rear of the Brownell property on Great Road. Note the nicely designed cupola.

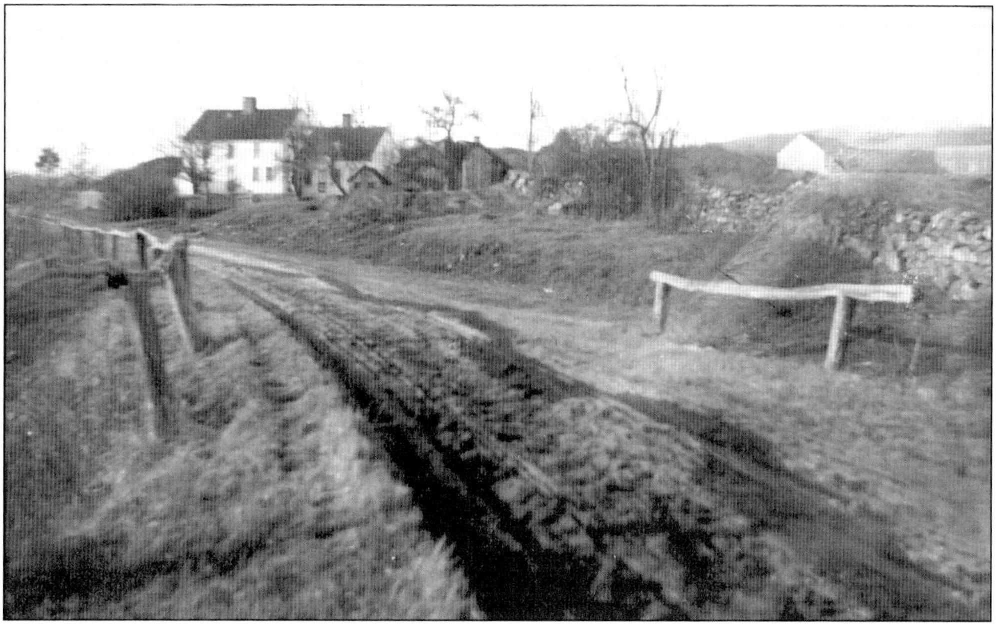

Some of the problems of the early dirt roads are well illustrated by this photograph of Providence Pike on the bend by the "King" David Mowry house. Ruts and an unstable roadbed are evident. (DPM.)

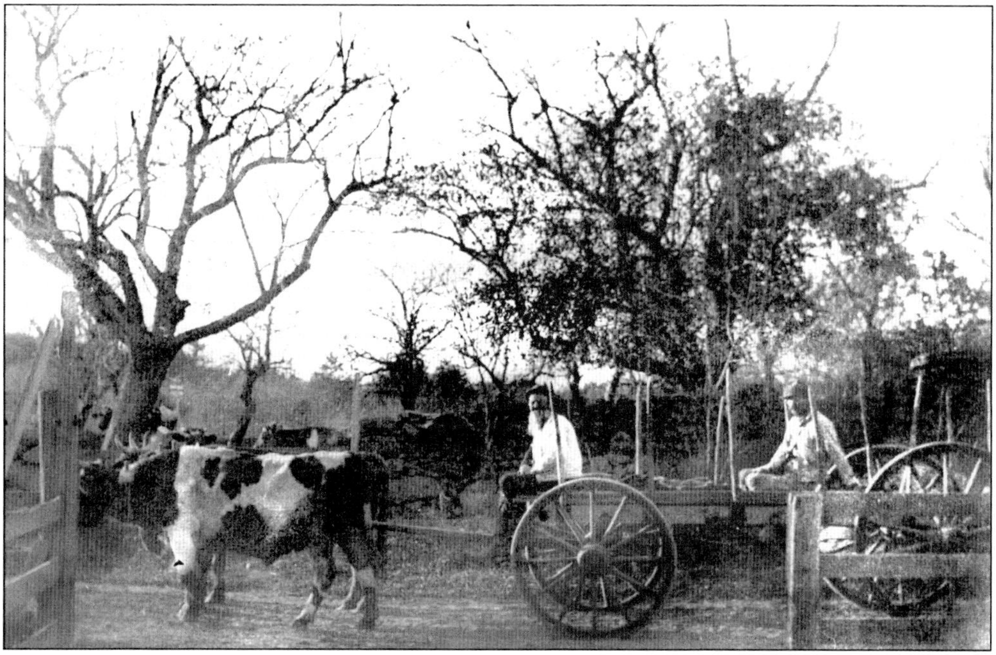

Along with the stagecoaches, oxcarts were common on town roads as the trained teams slowly hauled heavy loads of furniture, hay, wood, and stone between the farms. Making the trip to market in Woonsocket would take most of the day.

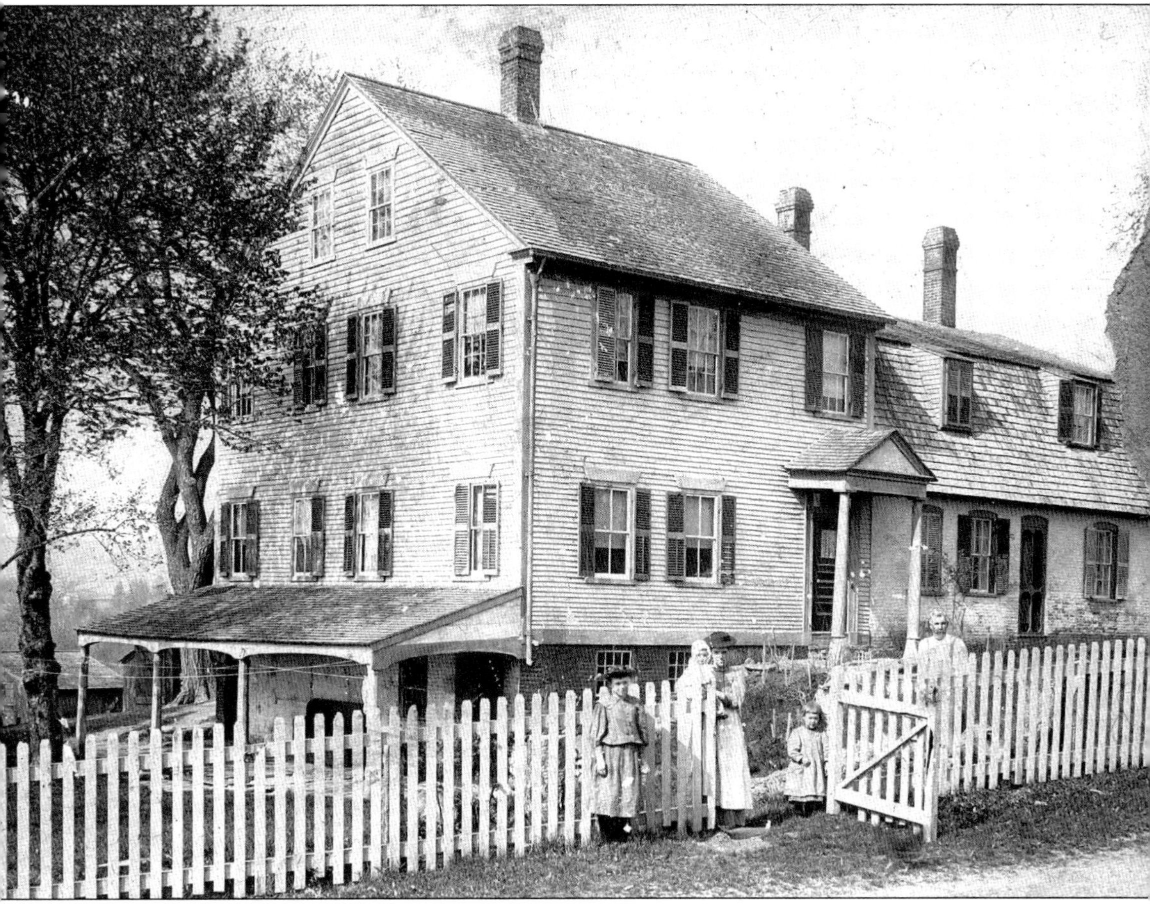

Pictured in 1889, the Moses Aldrich house, on Great Road, was constructed in two parts; the brick ell with the gambrel roof and dormer windows is dated 1774, and the wooden part is later. The family members at the gate are Harts and Aldriches. The house was torn down in the 1960s to make room for a Shell gas station. (Tabor.)

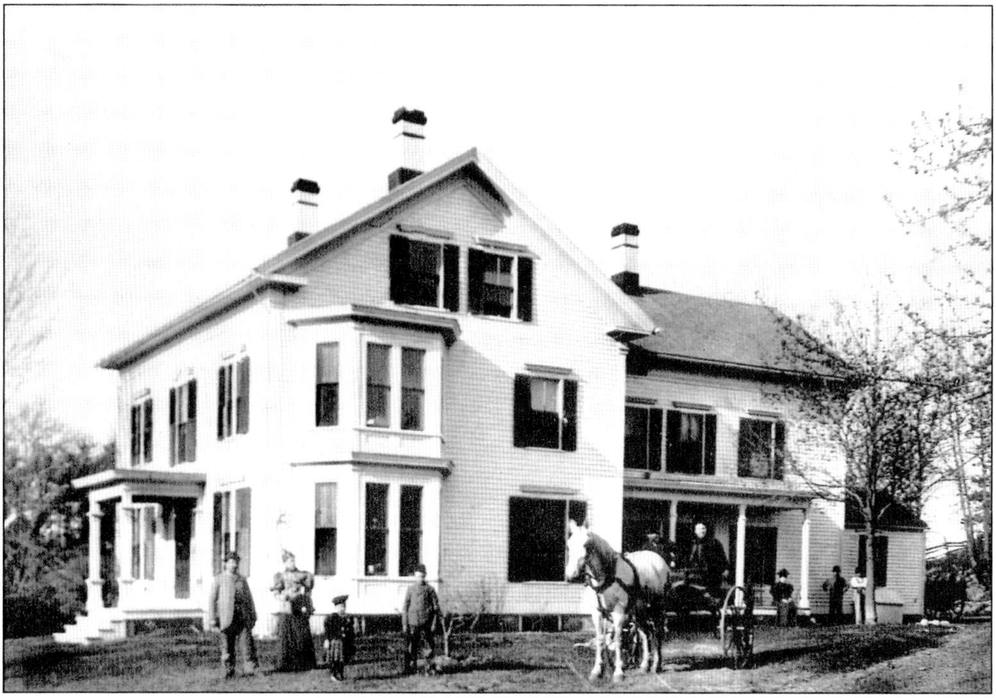

Rock Cliff Farm took on new life in 1876, when Hiram and Julia Paine Thayer decided to tear down the old Colonial house and build the "modern" one (above) with bay windows and a large ell. Inside were some of the newest conveniences of the day. One family member noted that behind the house was a barn "so large that a huge load of hay could be driven in one end and out the other." The old barn was used for storage of wood and cartons of glass milk bottles for their growing dairy business. The adjacent windmill pumped plenty of water. The pleasant aspect of the new farm is evident (below), the line of Great Road (Old Louisquisset Pike) running between the stone walls that mark the oldest roads in town. (MT.)

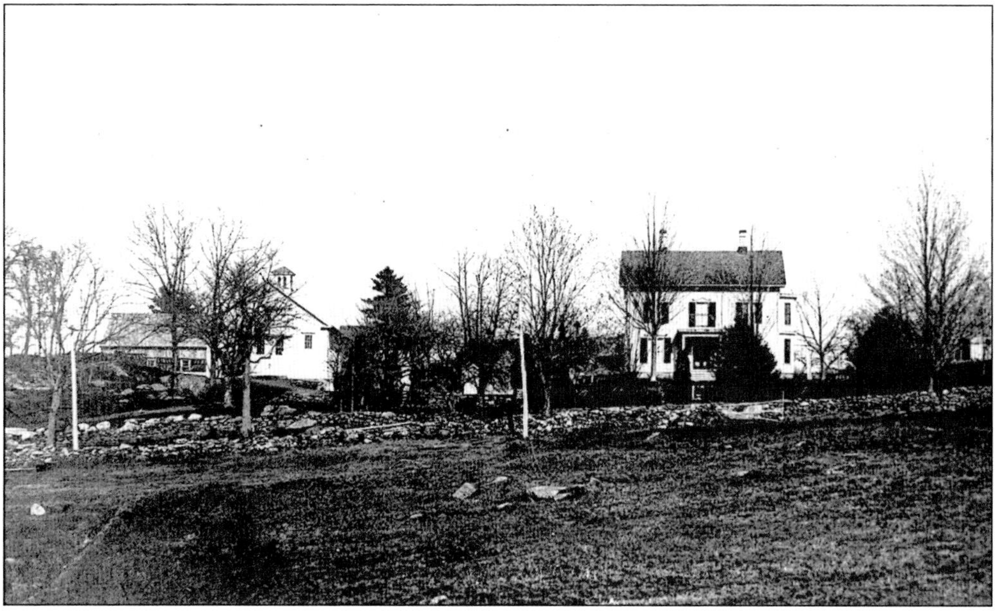

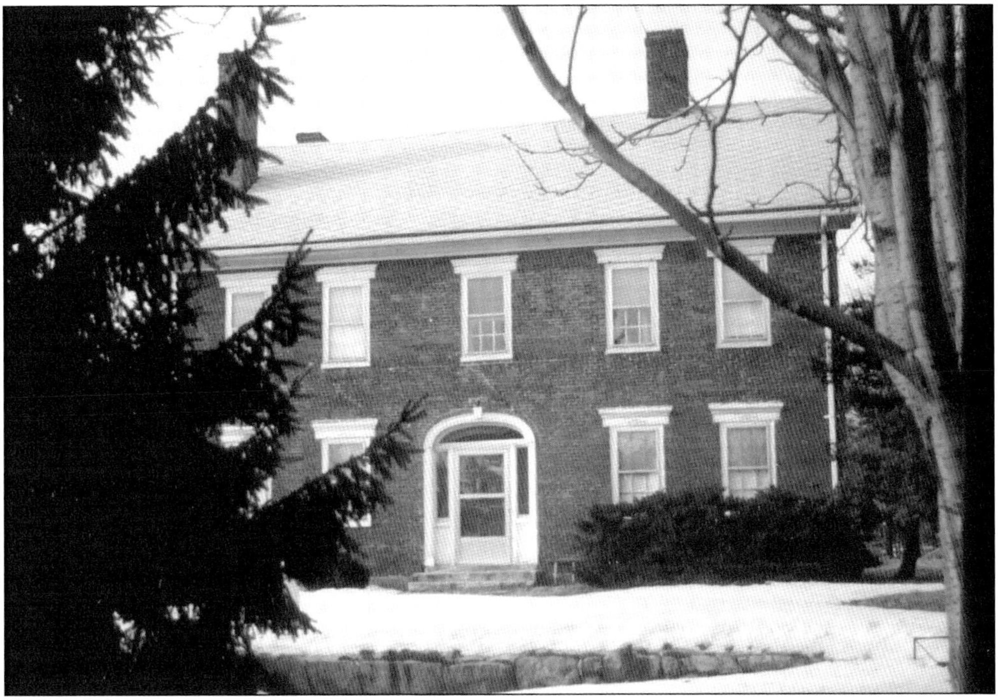

The Brick Tavern, on Great Road opposite Green Street, is said to have been a stop on the stage route connecting Providence and Worcester. One of the few brick buildings in town, it is dated *c*. 1825 and operated as an inn after the proprietor of the inn on the town hall site in Slatersville moved his business to this location.

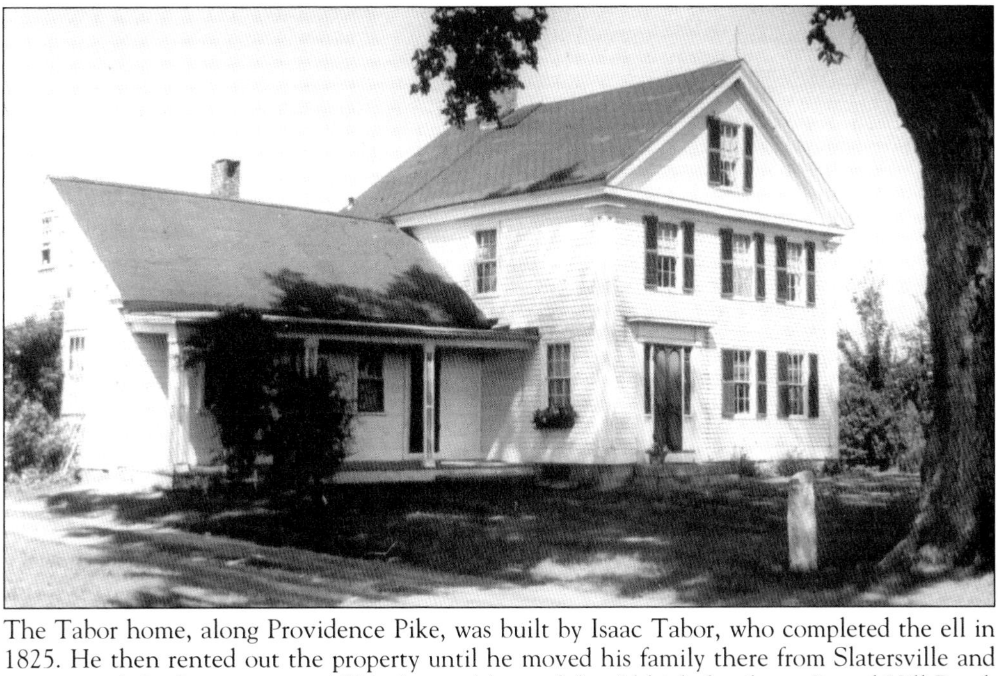

The Tabor home, along Providence Pike, was built by Isaac Tabor, who completed the ell in 1825. He then rented out the property until he moved his family there from Slatersville and constructed the larger part in 1836. As neighbors of the Aldrich family on Pound Hill Road, several Tabors were interred in the Aldrich burying ground. (Tabor.)

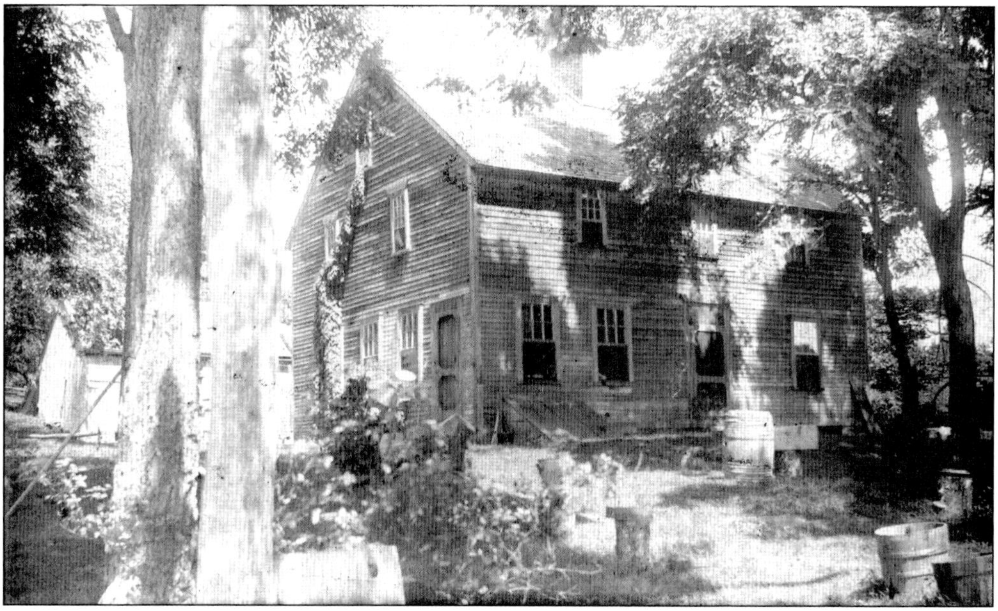

This 18th-century Mowry homestead on Woonsocket Hill Road was the scene of many family gatherings, when the view across the Sandy Plains and Smith's Pond could be enjoyed. In the photograph below are, from left to right, Alvah, Martha, Florence, and Forrest Mowry with daughter Ruth Hopkins Mowry. (Hurd.)

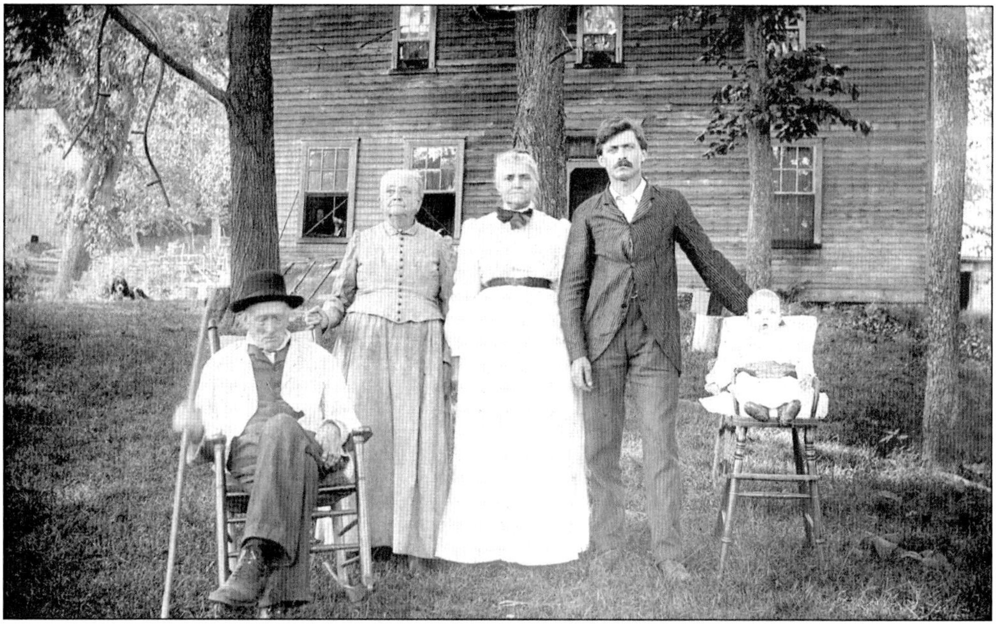

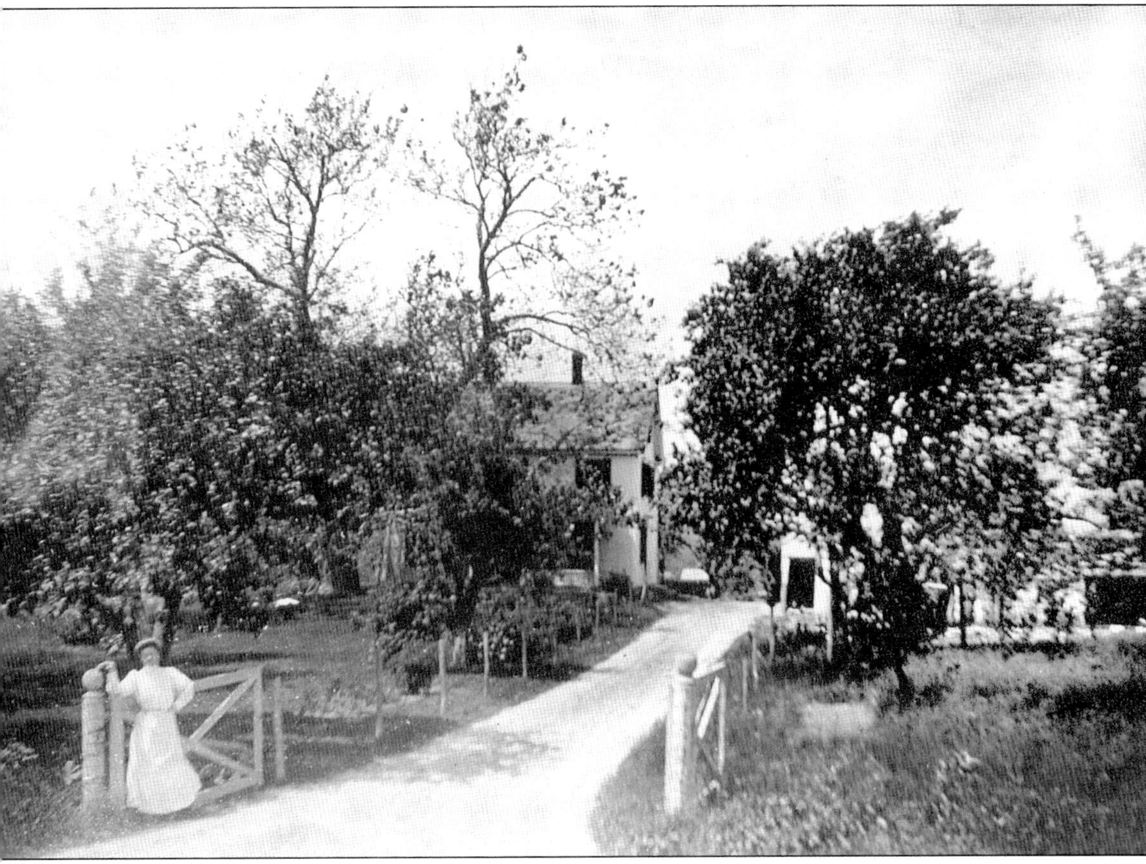

The Henry Green farm, on Pound Hill Road, was the scene of many family gatherings and friendly picnics and was a most attractive setting. The farm is now O'Donnell's Homestead Gardens, and the extensive grounds are open to all. (DG.)

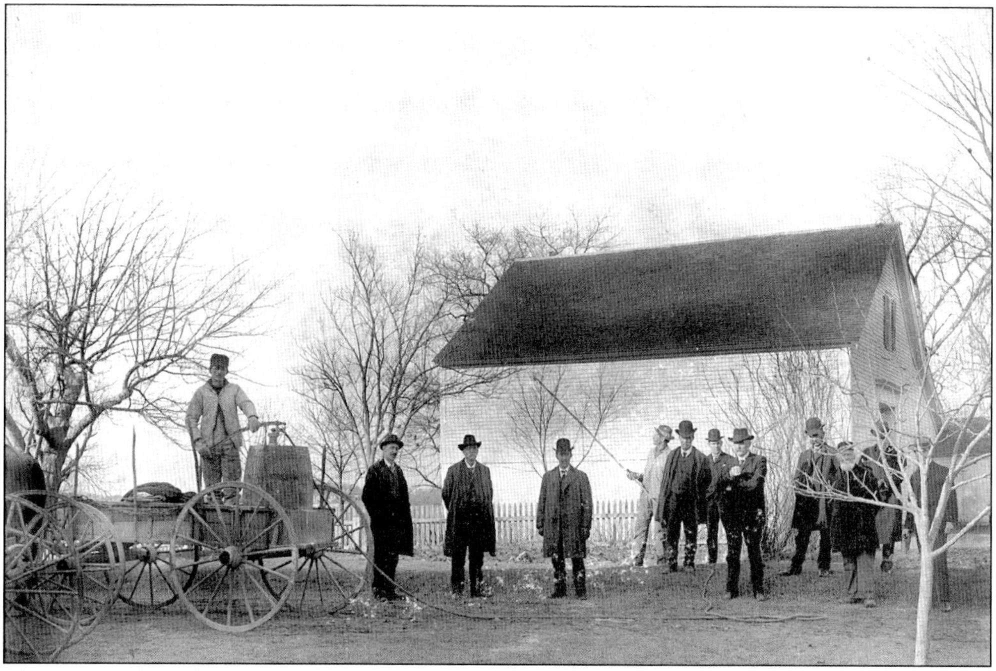

This scene of a gathering on a Mowry farm appears to have been a solemn occasion, judging by the formal attire. (Hurd.)

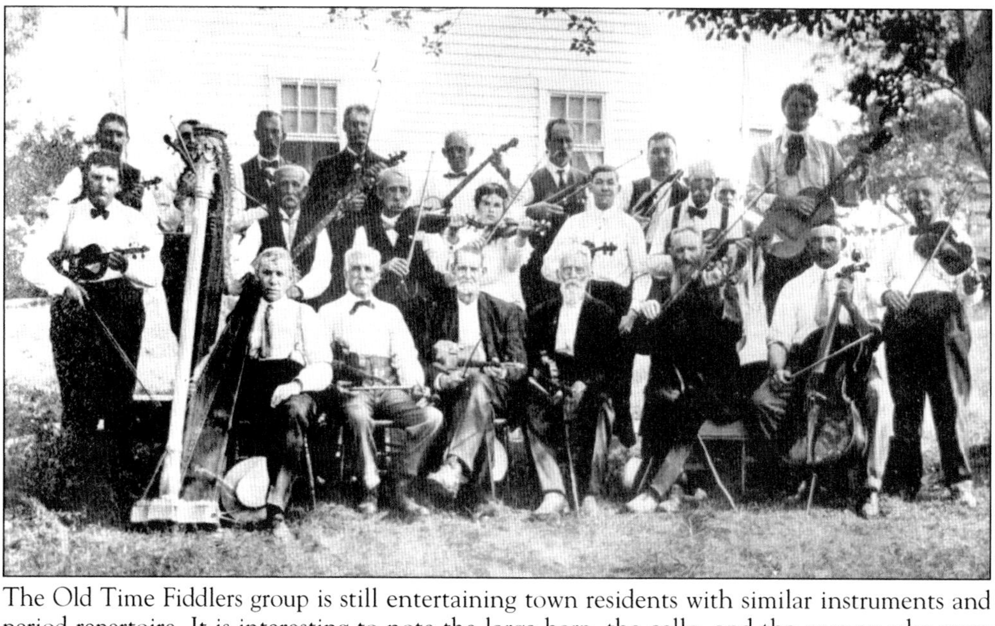

The Old Time Fiddlers group is still entertaining town residents with similar instruments and period repertoire. It is interesting to note the large harp, the cello, and the women who were part of this turn-of-the-century ensemble.

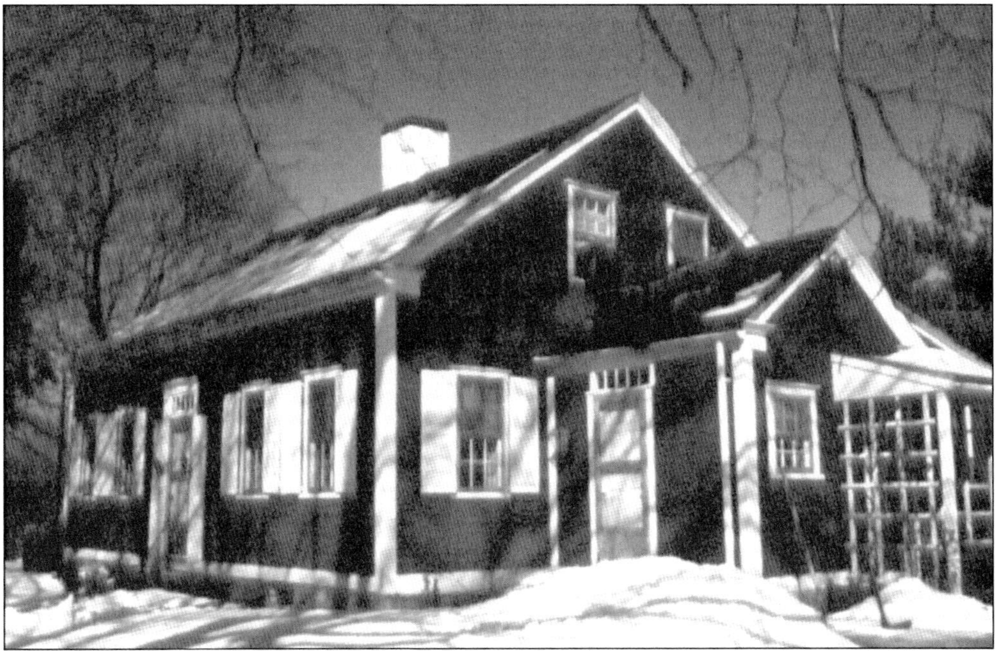

Dating to *c.* 1815, the Stephen Smith farm, on the corner of Douglas Pike and Mattity Road, included a substantial L-shaped barn, which was painted barn red with white trim to match the house. The house, which was the home for many years of Allan and Virginia Shepherd (charter members of the North Smithfield Heritage Association), was restored to beauty and comfort and boasted a model kitchen of the 1950s.

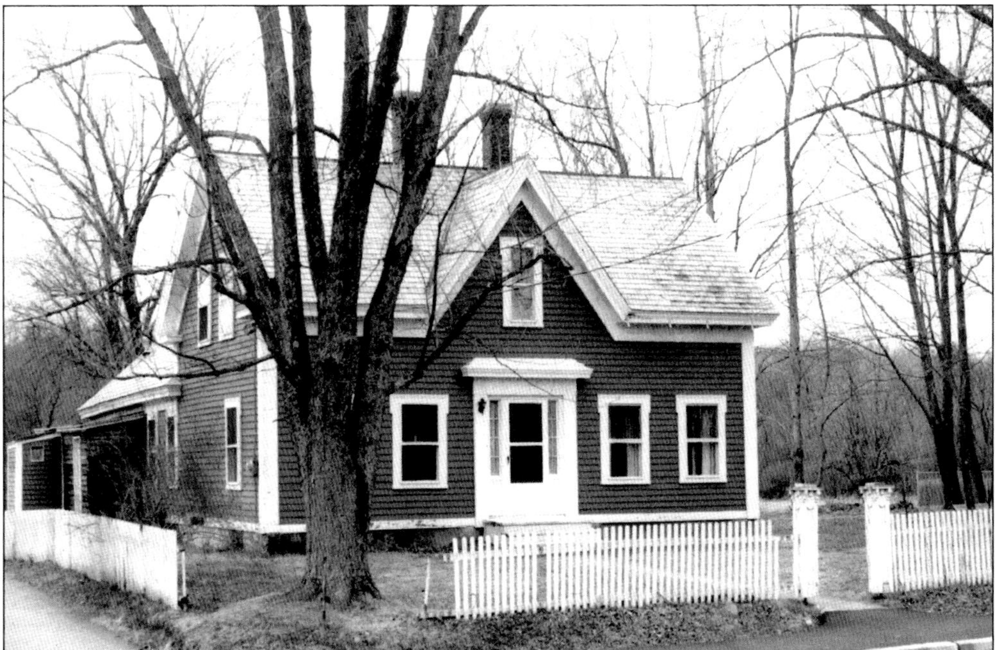

One of the mill houses along North Main Street in Slatersville, this two-story structure with front gable and Federal-style doorway reflects the architectural styles of several periods.

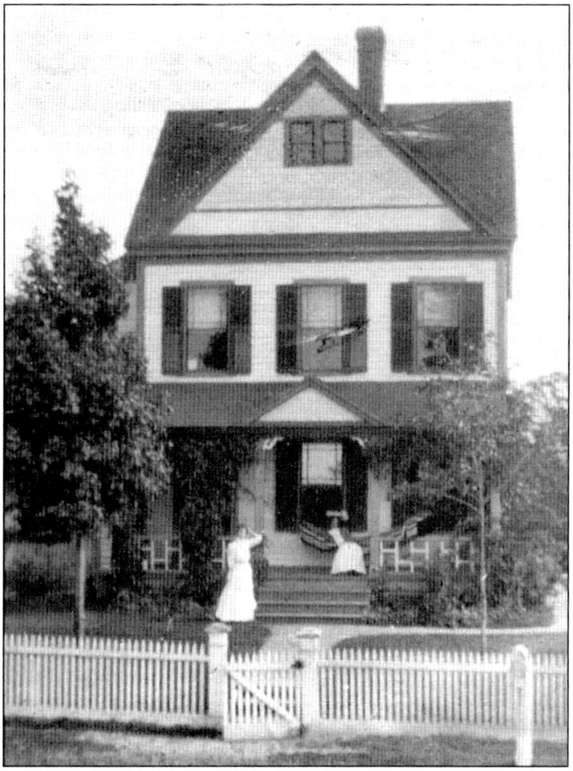

The Thomas Aldrich house, on Pound Hill Road, displays many features of late-19th-century architecture, including the front gable, the expansive front porch with open-work balusters, and stained glass around the front door.

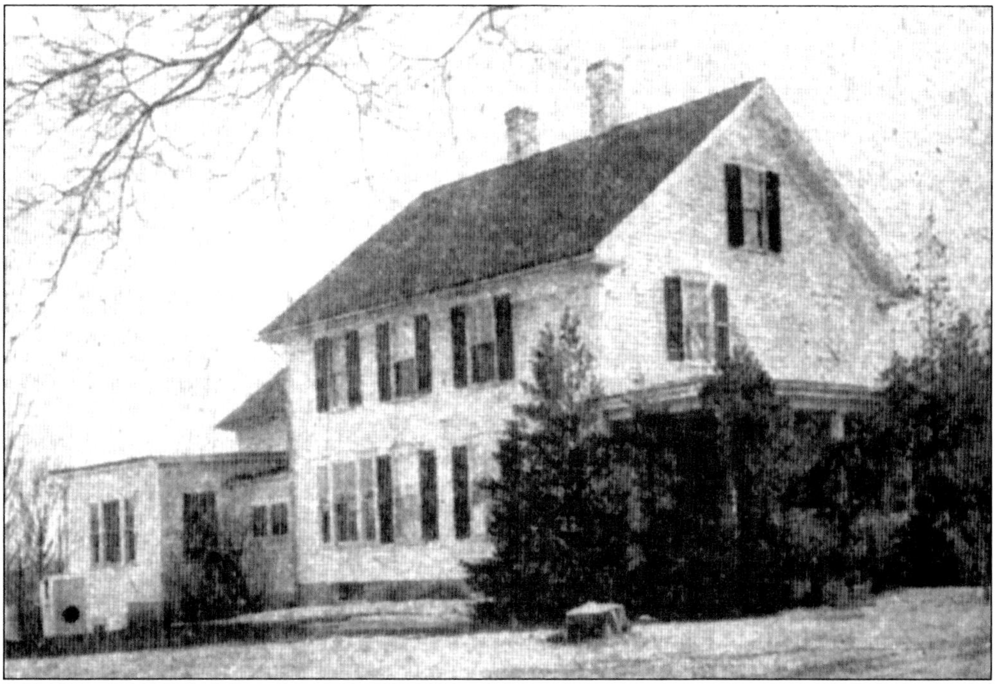

This house on Great Road is one of two, built just alike next to each other by Sylvester Aldrich. His mother occupied one, and his sister and her husband, John Metcalf (then minister for the Friends), lived in the other. It shows late-19th-century features.

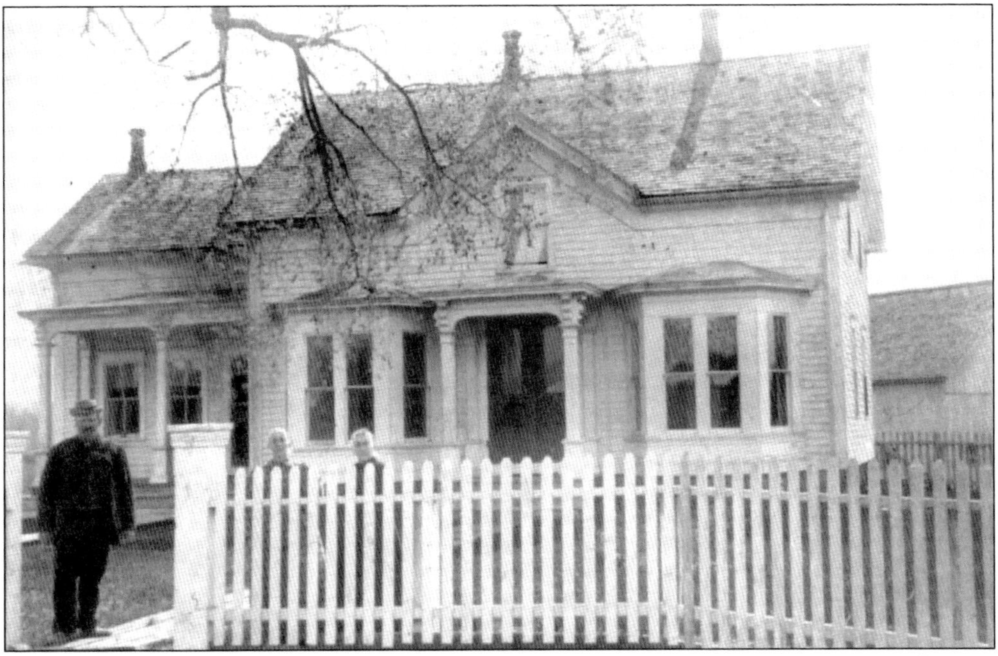

This Mowry house, located on Greenville Road near the Primrose railroad crossing, features a front gable and bay windows on both sides of the door. The house was owned by Marion Humes, a Mowry descendant, into the 1970s.

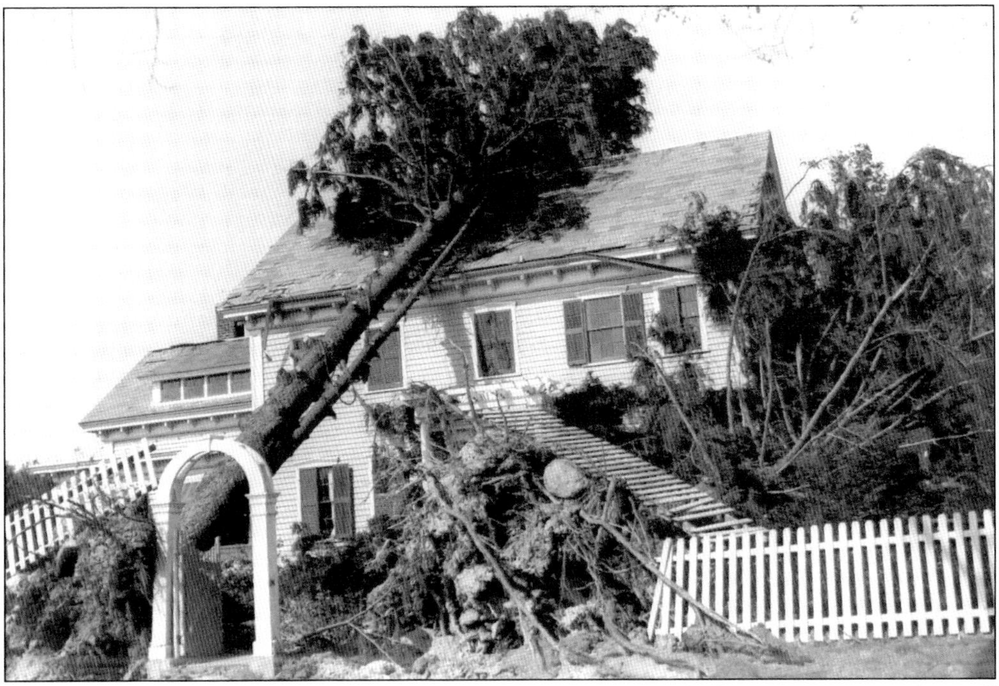

The sturdiness of the early houses was demonstrated by the Wright home on Woonsocket Hill Road, shown here amidst the aftermath of the 1938 hurricane, which hit New England hard. Despite the tree on the roof, the structure maintained its integrity, losing only some roof slates, part of the front gutter, and keeping its windows intact through closing the shutters.

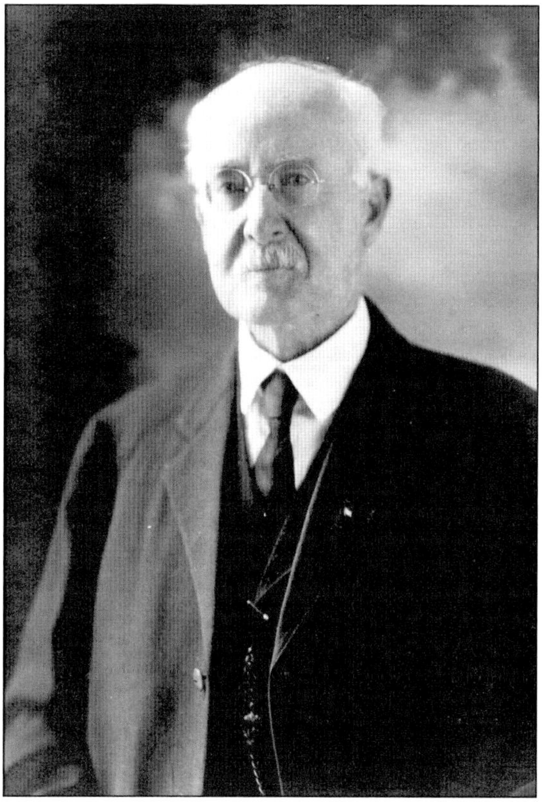

Joshua Wardle was the first resident of North Smithfield to become a state senator. He was widely respected.

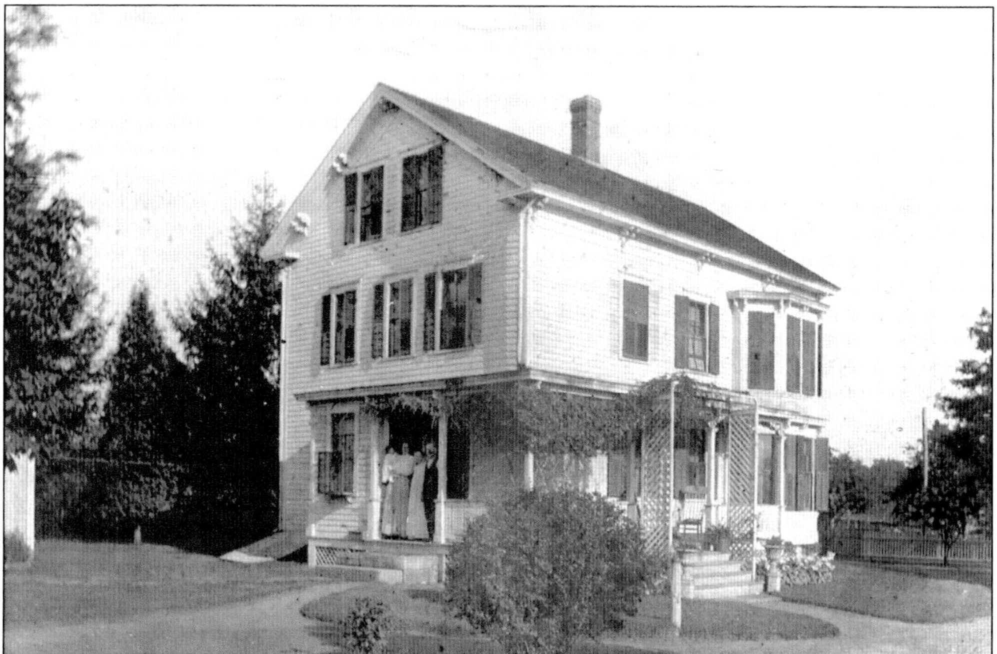

The Wardle residence, on Buxton Street, was known as "Bleak House" for reasons unknown. The porch and shrubs soften the lines of this 19th-century dwelling.

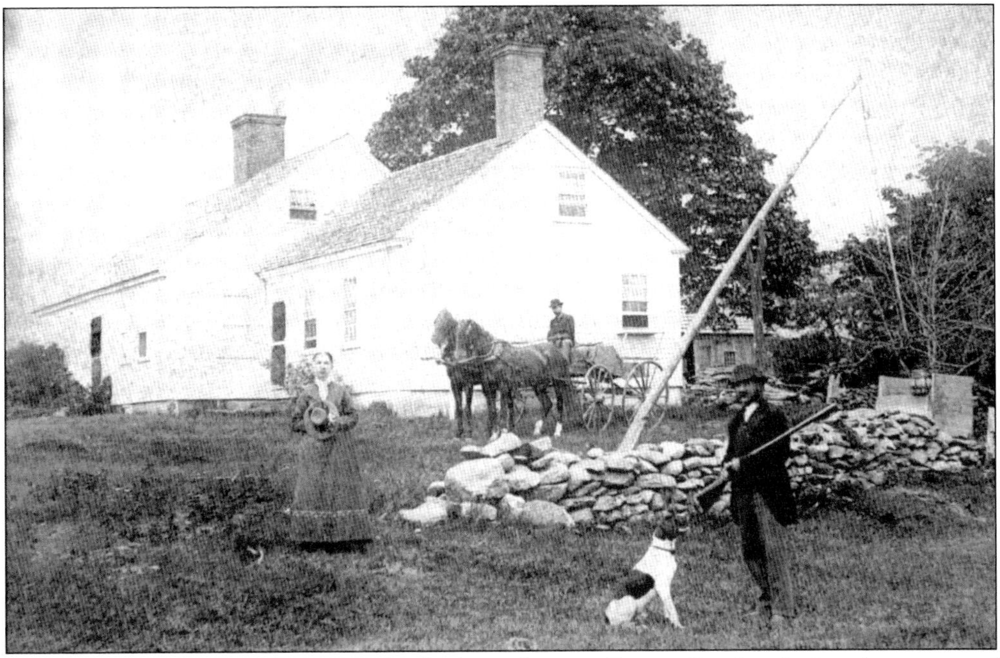

This 1880s scene at the Thayer-Jencks-Andrews farm on Grange Road embodies the essence of the Rhode Island farmer. Owen and Ardella Thayer, with their dog, are standing by a stone wall near the well sweep. The basement of the 1780 house was used as a neighborhood butcher shop when the Andrews family occupied the premises. (North.)

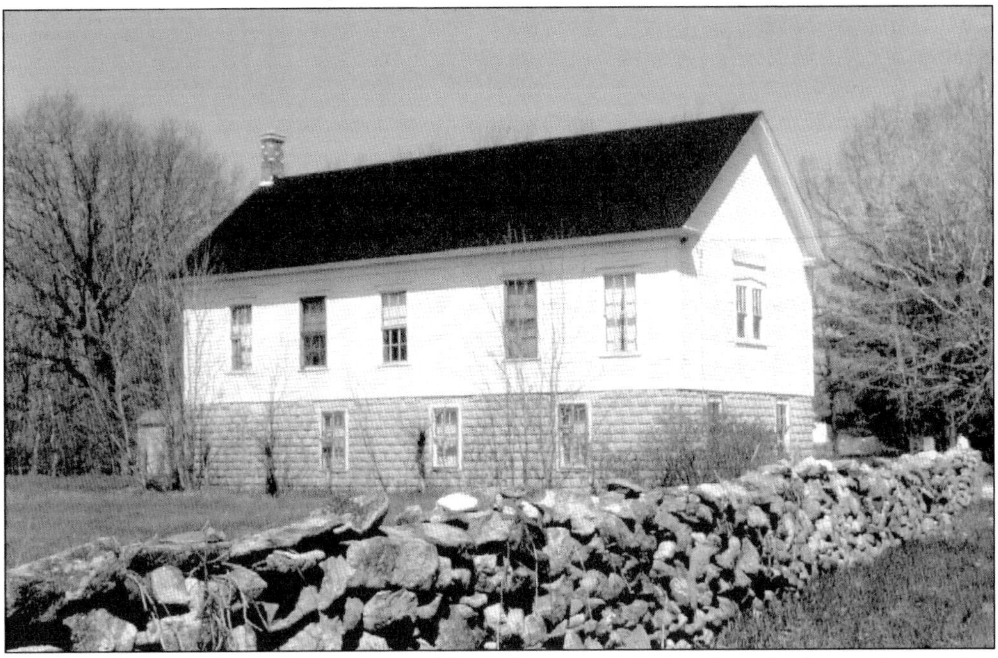

Across Grange Road is Primrose Grange No. 9, Patrons of Husbandry, which was chartered in 1887. The Grange building was purchased in 1911, moved to the location opposite Rocky Hill Road, and later raised on a foundation of concrete blocks. Just to the right of the Grange was the lot for the second Andrews School, moved to the former Andrews farm after the school was closed.

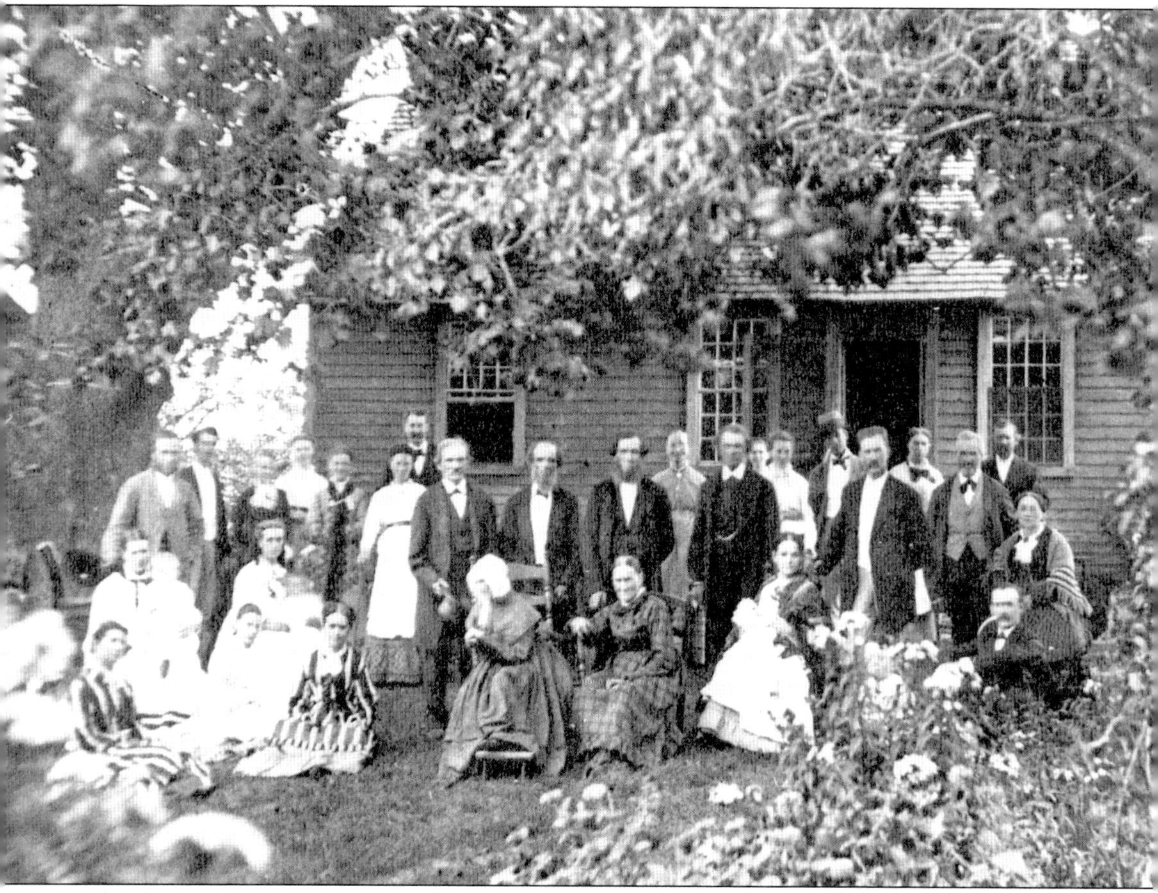

This large group from the Slatersville Congregational Church is gathered for a picnic at the Henry Green farm on Pound Hill Road toward the end of the 19th century. (DG.)

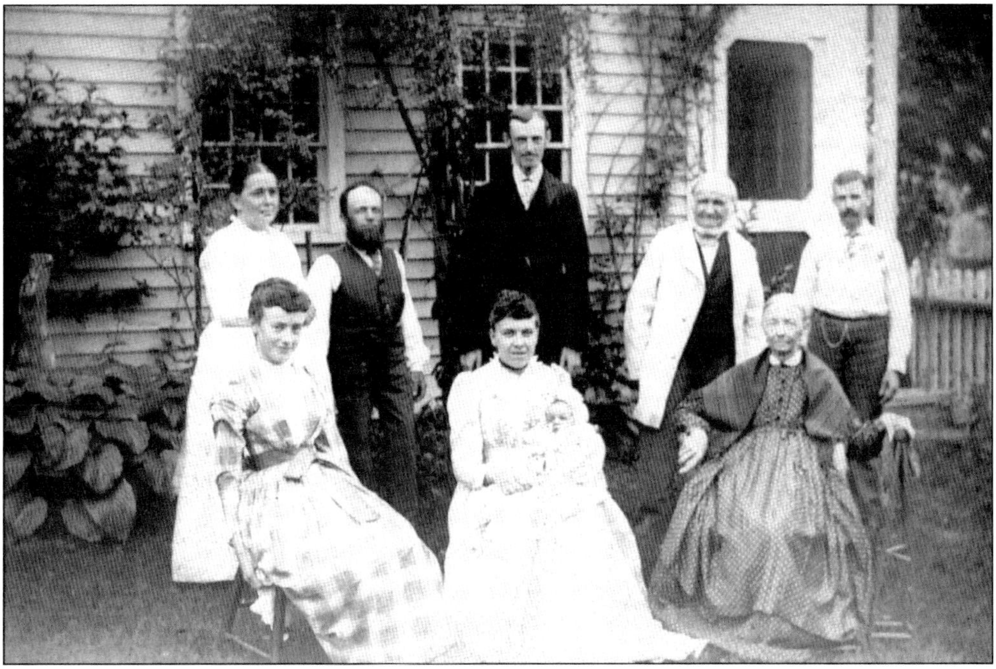

Members of the Todd family of Greenville Road pose in 1890 outside the farmhouse. The infant Col. Robert Todd is shown in his mother's arms. His father stands behind them. Colonel Todd and his wife, Louise Cole Todd, opened their homestead farm to many artists in the mid-1900s.

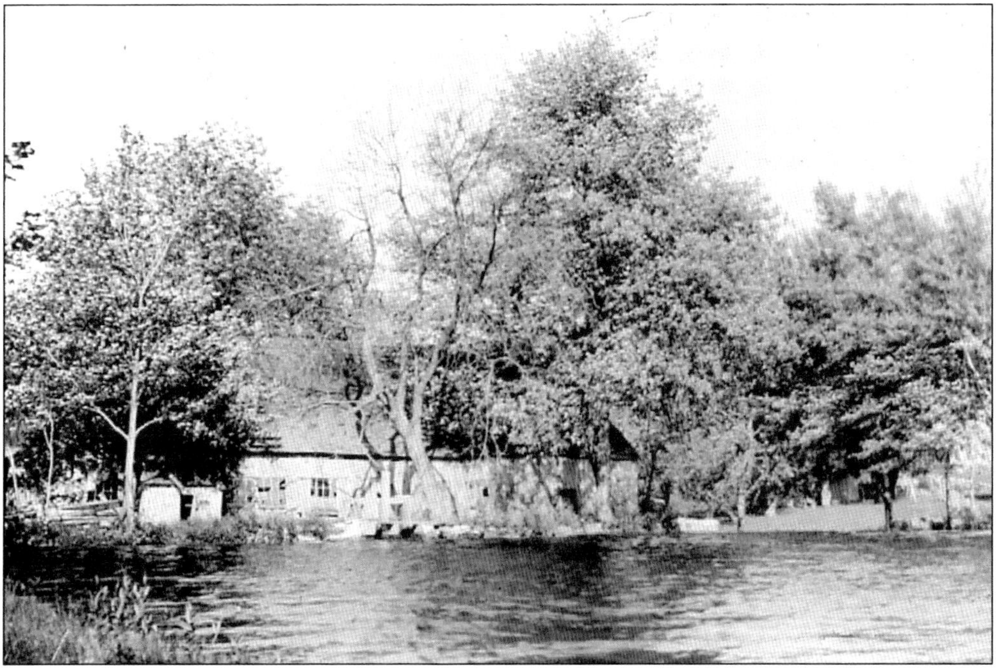

The sawmill at the outlet of Todd's Pond provided wood for the stove heating the Andrews school in the 1850s, as well as boards and shingles for local buildings. The farm also had its own icehouse.

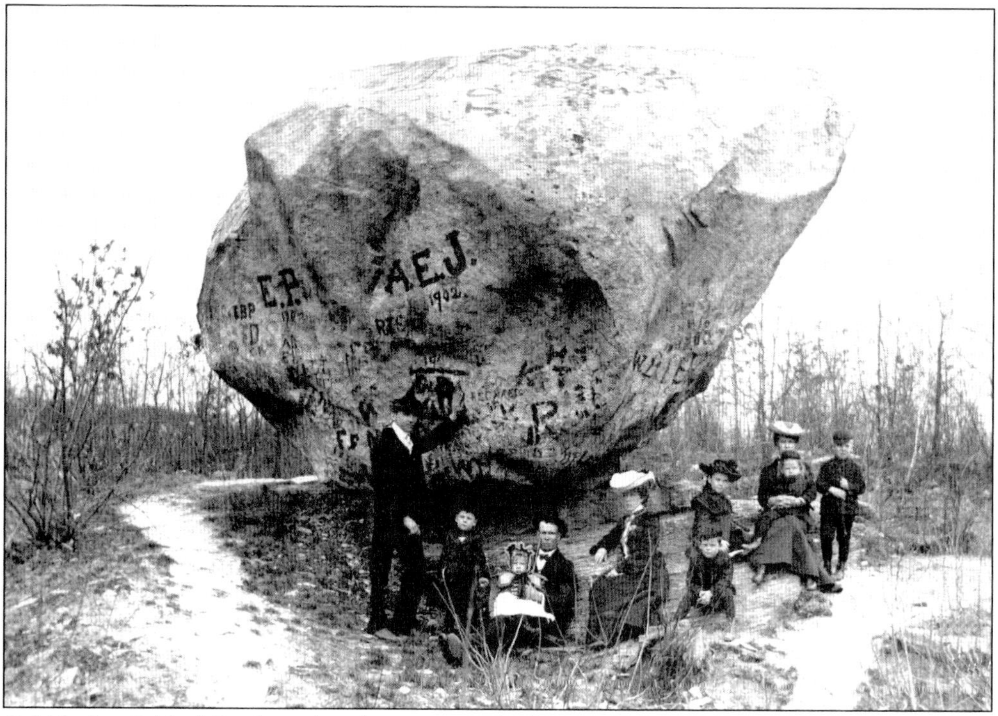

Cobble (or Coblin) Rock, a glacial erratic perched on a wooded hill near today's St. Antoine complex, was a popular picnic destination. Shown here in late-19th-century finery are members of the Hummel and Ainslie families. (TM.)

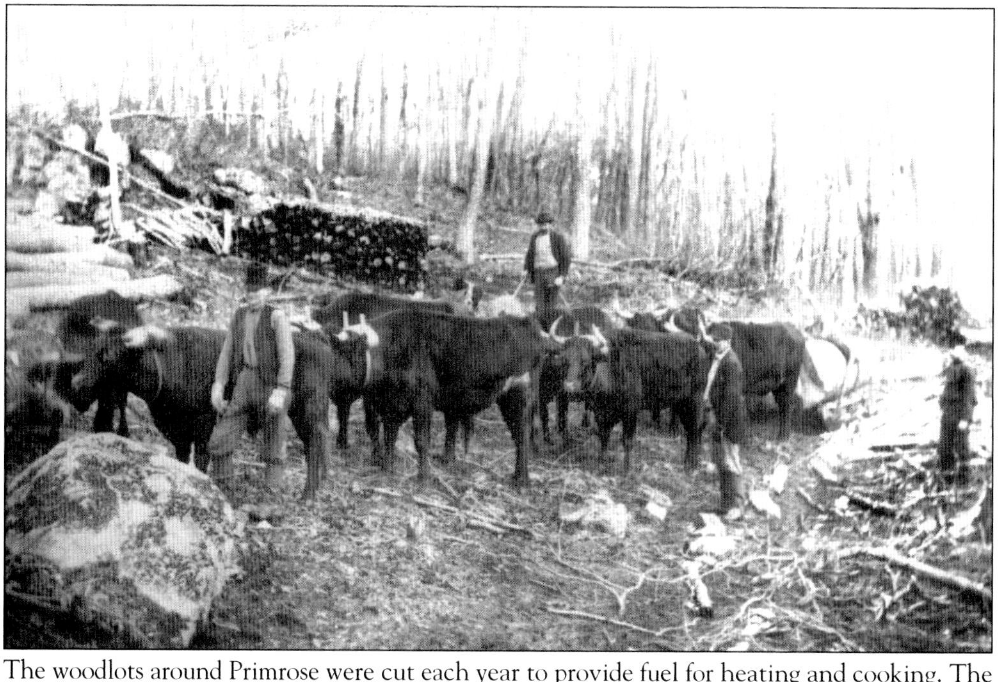

The woodlots around Primrose were cut each year to provide fuel for heating and cooking. The loads were carried on carts pulled by oxen, to be sold in Slatersville, Woonsocket, and to those families without woodlots of their own.

St. John's Roman Catholic Church in Slatersville was built in 1872 on Liberty (or Independence) Hill, part of a large tract of land bordering the lower reservoir given by William Slater. The original steeple shown here was 90 feet high. The rectory next door was built in 1895 in the Second Empire mansard-roof style.

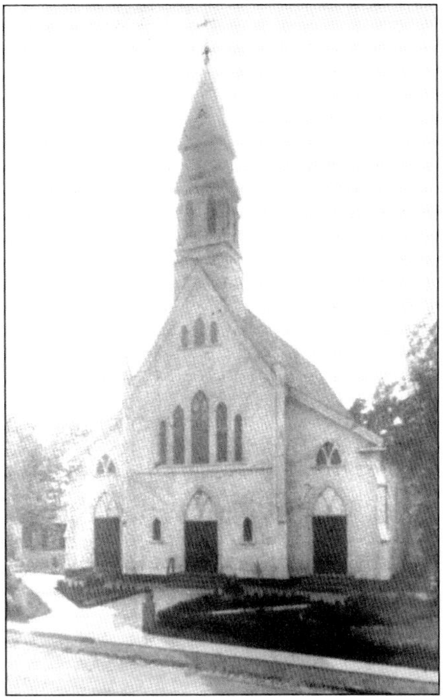

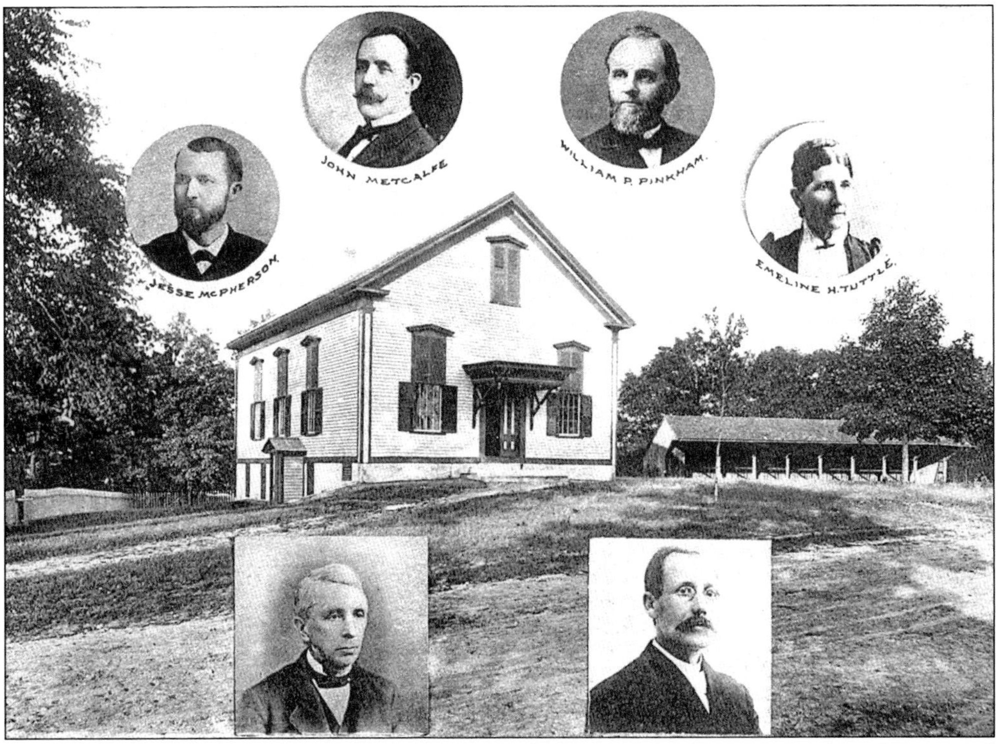

The rebuilt Friends meetinghouse was completed in 1881 on the same land as the original building. The carriage shed is still evident at the right. A cemetery in the Quaker tradition with uninscribed stones lies to the left and behind the meetinghouse. The first six ministers to serve in the new building are shown.

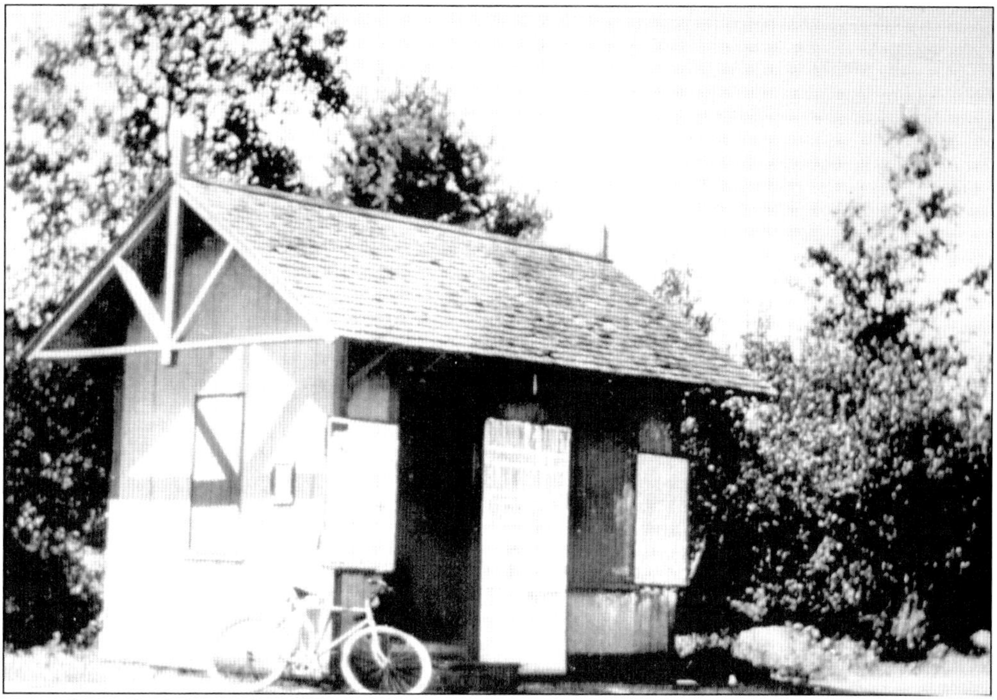

Near the end of the 19th century, railroads provided a sure conveyance and linked many parts of northern Rhode Island. One line, completed in 1873, followed the Wanasquatucket River and went through Primrose to Pascoag. The Primrose Station was located near the Greenville Road crossing.

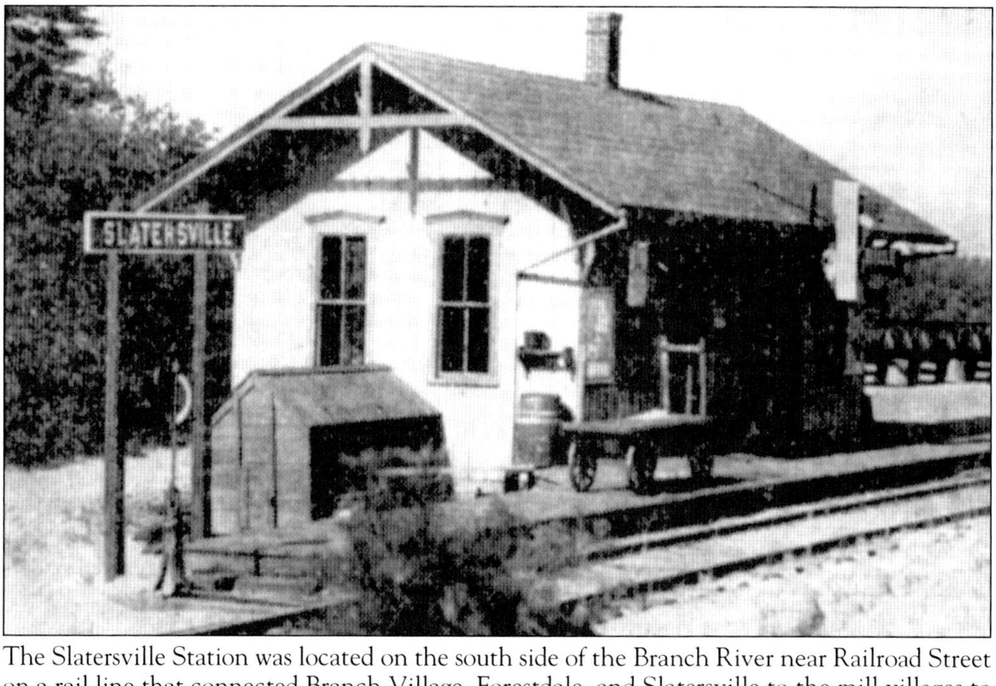

The Slatersville Station was located on the south side of the Branch River near Railroad Street on a rail line that connected Branch Village, Forestdale, and Slatersville to the mill villages to the west. (WHS-SSD.)

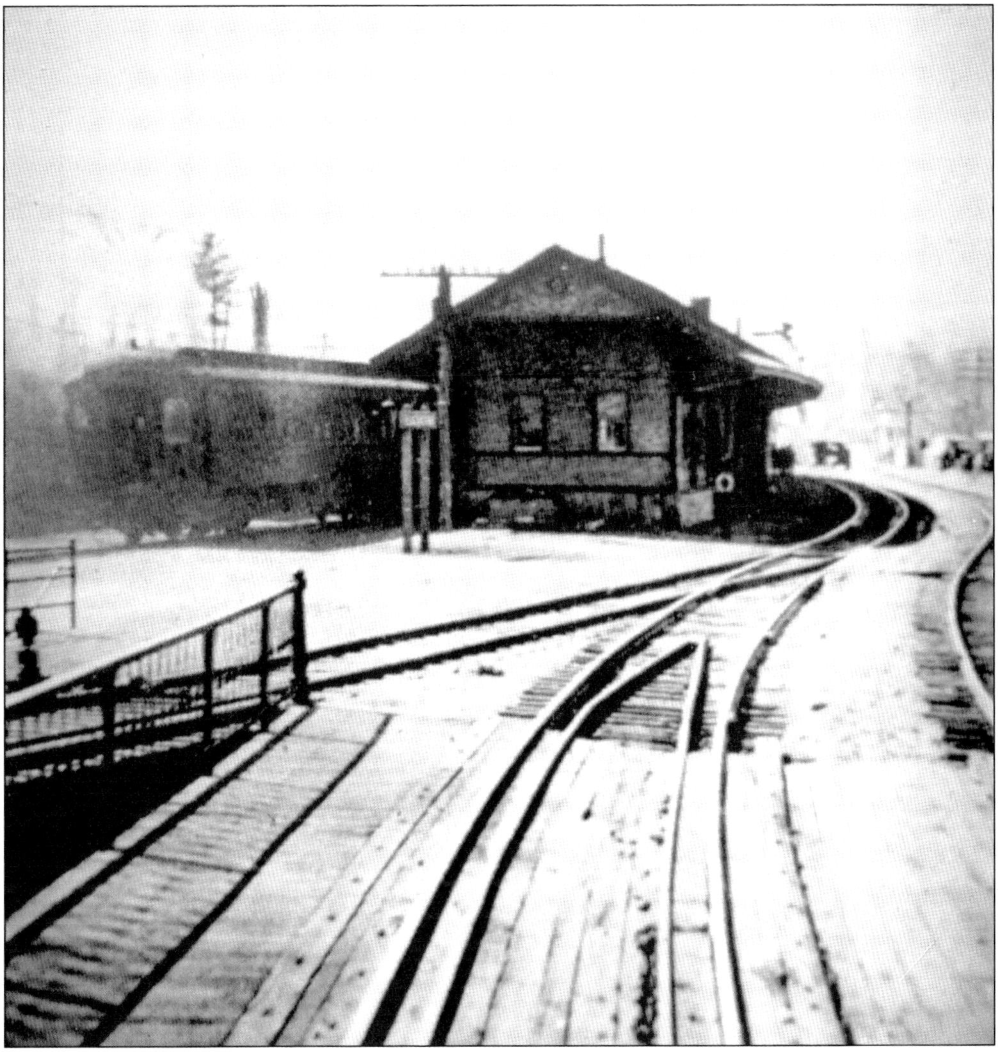

The Providence and Worcester Railroad, completed in 1847, ran through Woonsocket to Waterford. The Waterford Station, actually in Massachusetts, was large, had a switching operation, and led to greater growth of both places. (WHS-SSD.)

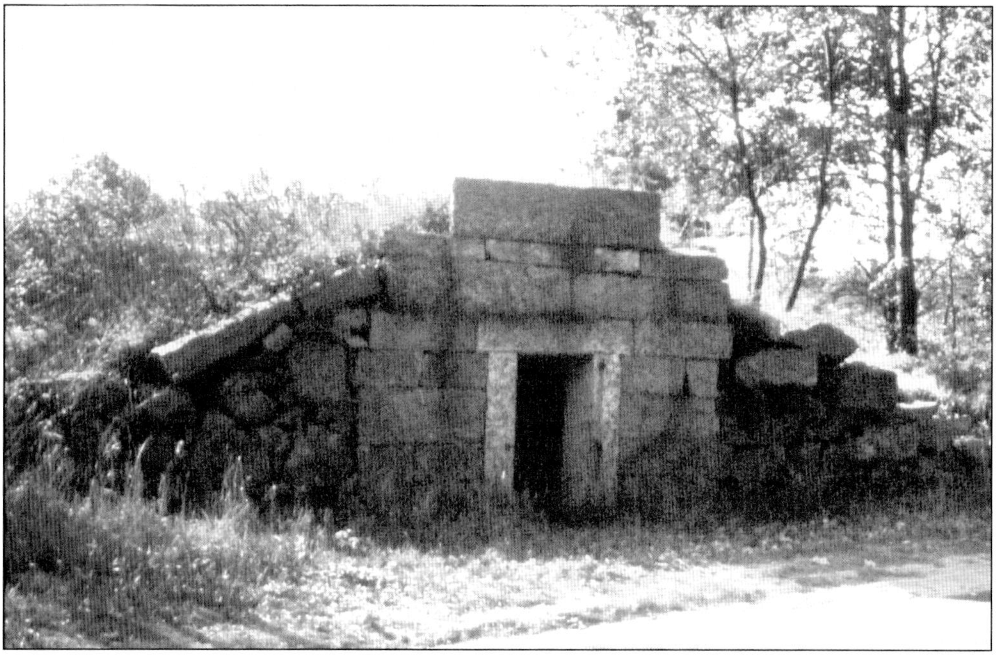

A landmark along the road to Millville was this tomb, which gave its name to Tomb Road. Used as a repository for remains when the ground was too frozen for digging, the structure was destroyed in the late 1970s.

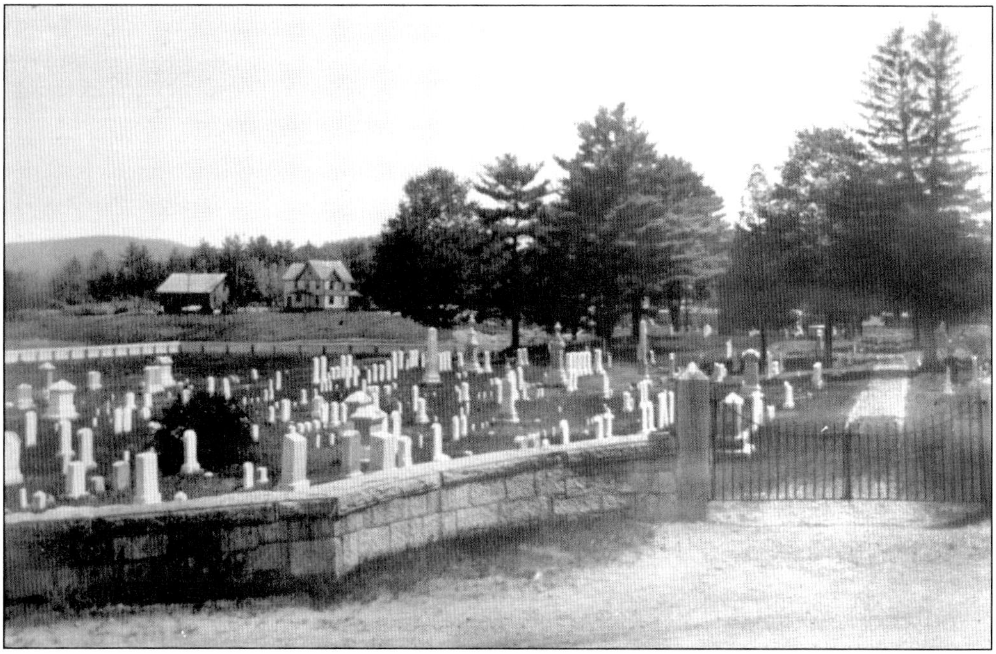

Slatersville Cemetery contains the marked stones of many of the village's early residents. The Slater family has its own fenced plot. The cemetery is still used today.

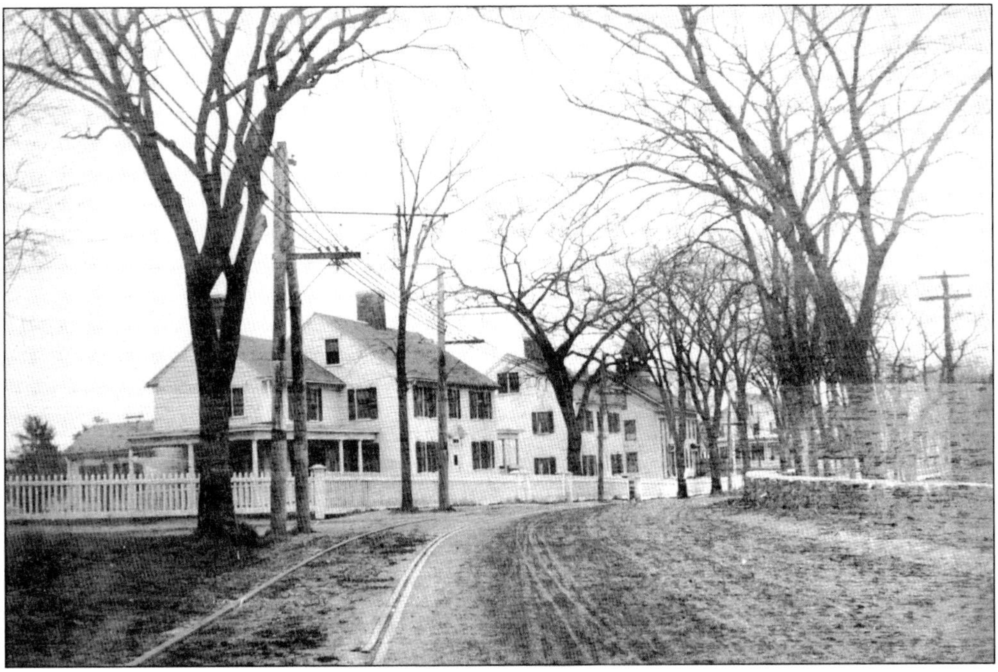

The electric railway reached Slatersville in the late 19th century, and trolley tracks became a feature of main roads. Here, the tracks follow the side of School Street. John Slater's home is on the left.

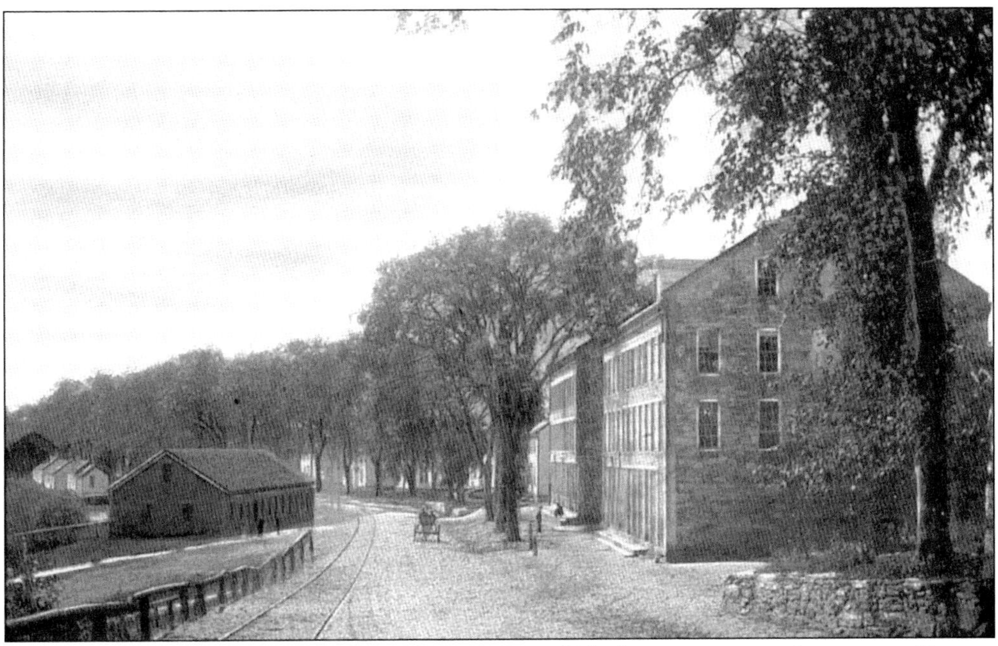

The trolley tracks extended past the 1850s commercial block to continue to Pascoag via Herring Pond (Spring Lake). A horse-drawn carriage illustrates another mode of transport.

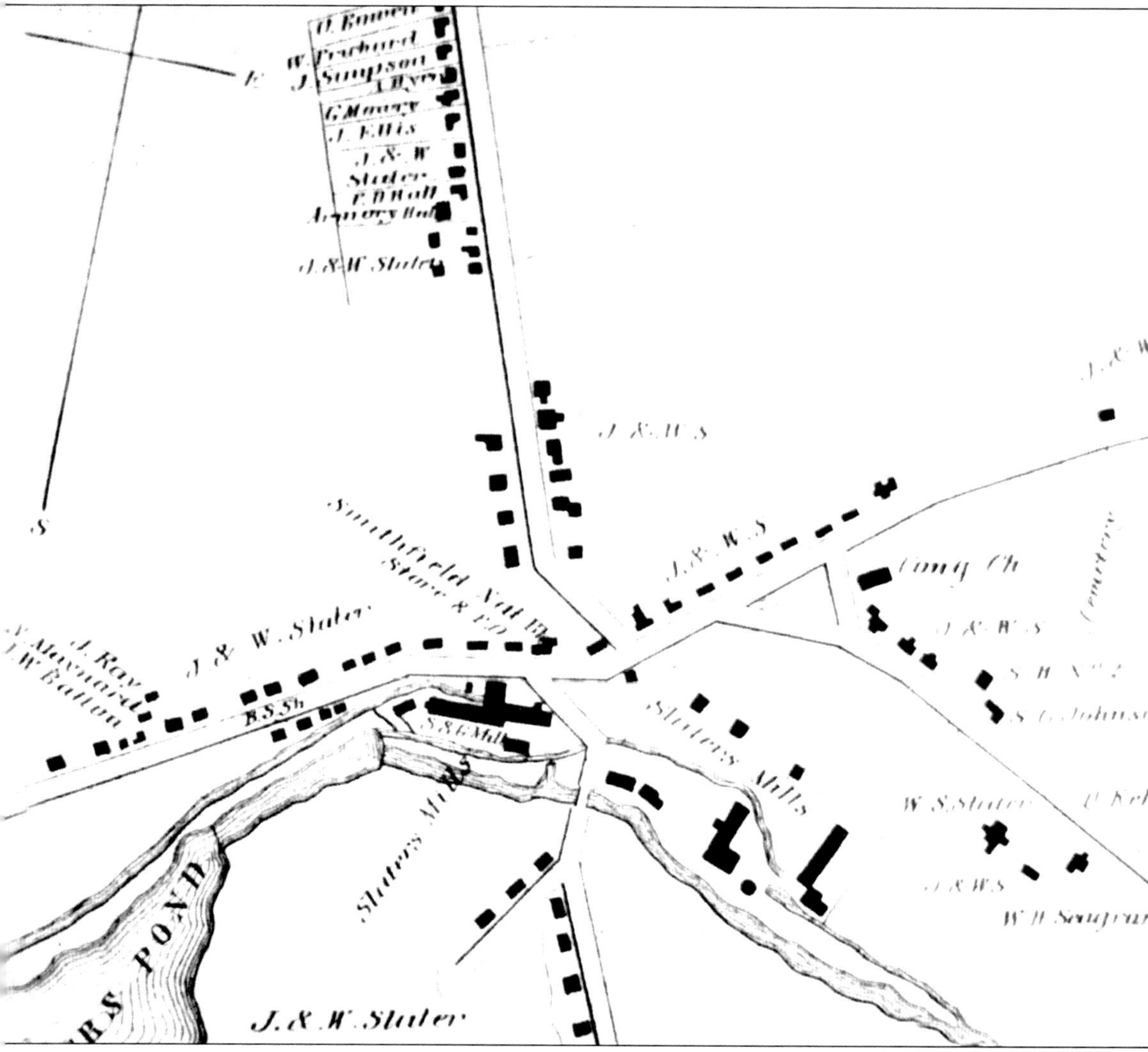

This map of Slatersville in the late 19th century illustrates the extent of the company's land holdings, as well as the spacing of houses in the village center.

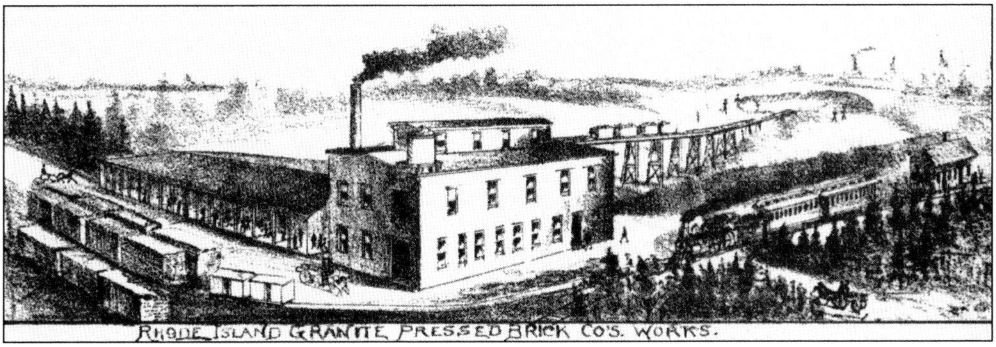

The Rhode Island Granite Pressed Brick Company, on the south side of the Branch River, provided a porous pressed brick for building foundations. A going concern in this 1895 illustration, it made the bricks for the lower level of St. Luke's Mission on Green Street. (NSHA.)

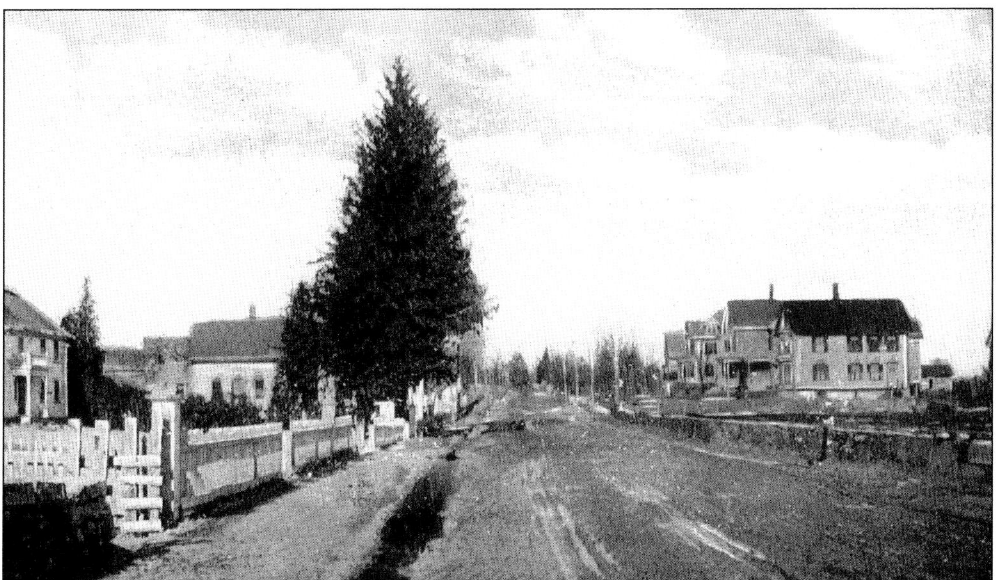

A check with the map on page 66 shows that the impressive houses on the east side of North Main Street were constructed in the late 19th century. The ruts in the dirt roadway suggest the continued difficulties of travel by road.

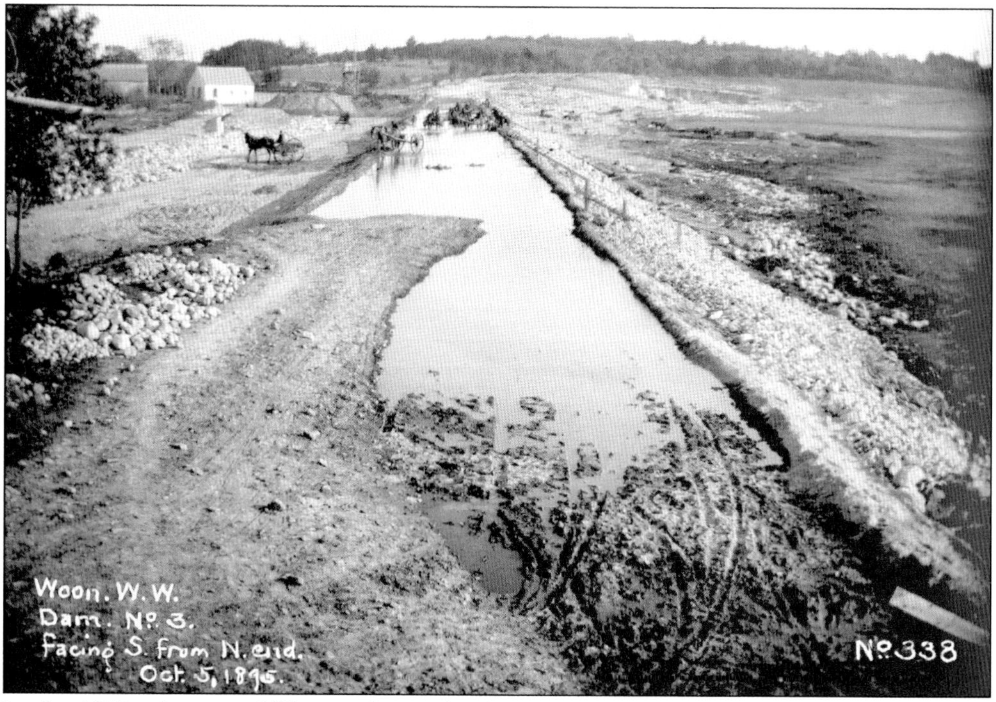

In the 1880s, the city of Woonsocket realized a need for new water supplies. The Crookfall Brook along Rocky Hill Road drained a vast area known as the Island Woods, flowing through the Obed Paine Farm. The city purchased the farm and, by 1895, had constructed a lengthy dam to flood Paine's land and to impound an extensive acreage of water (above). A spillway and gatehouse controlled the flow from the reservoir into the Crookfall Brook (below), which continued its course to the Blackstone. (WHS-SSD.)

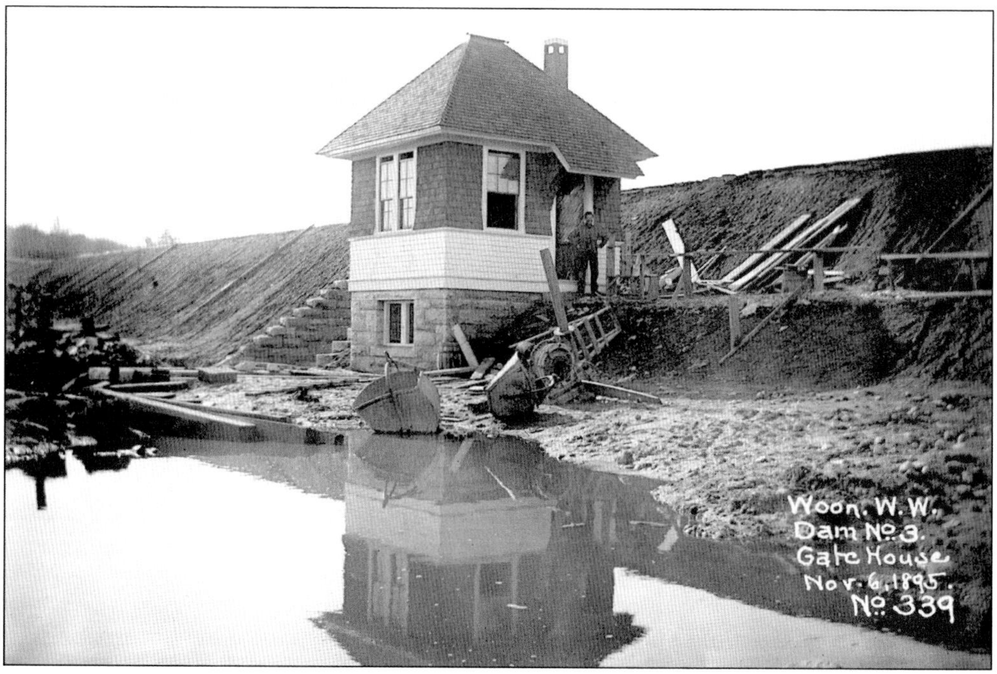

George Maine served the city of Woonsocket for more than 50 years as caretaker of Reservoir No. 3. He helped build the dam impounding the water and went on to plant the surrounding pine groves. An accomplished violinist, violin maker, surveyor, and conservationist, he died at the age of 101 in 1965.

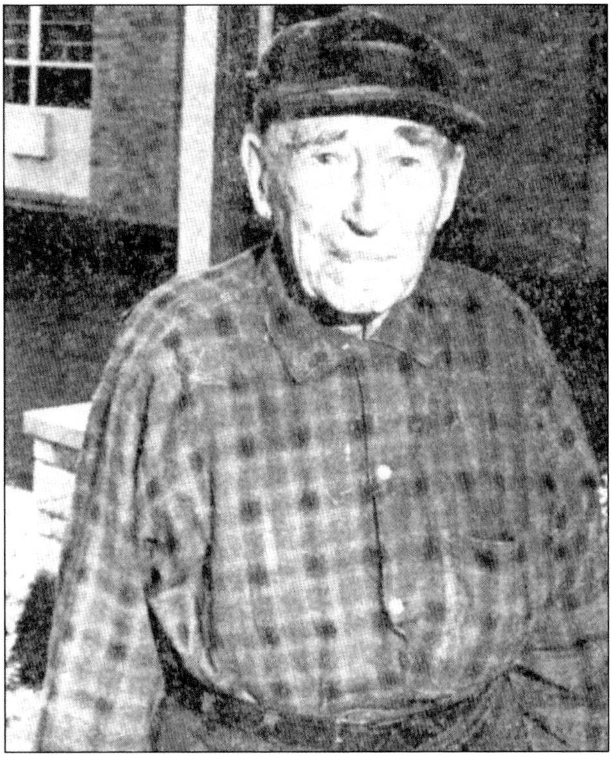

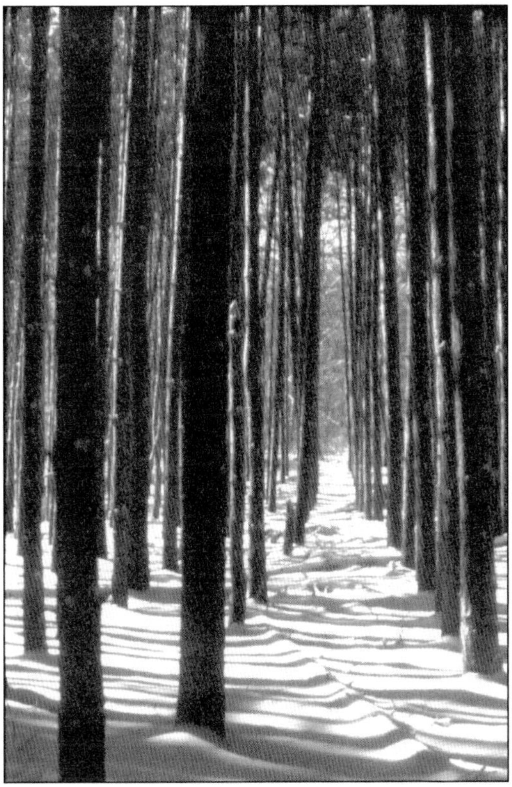

The stately pine trees, whose roots stabilize the soil, rise cathedral-like in several plantations around the reservoir. Charles Purcell was known for pointing out his grandfather's achievements. (WAN.)

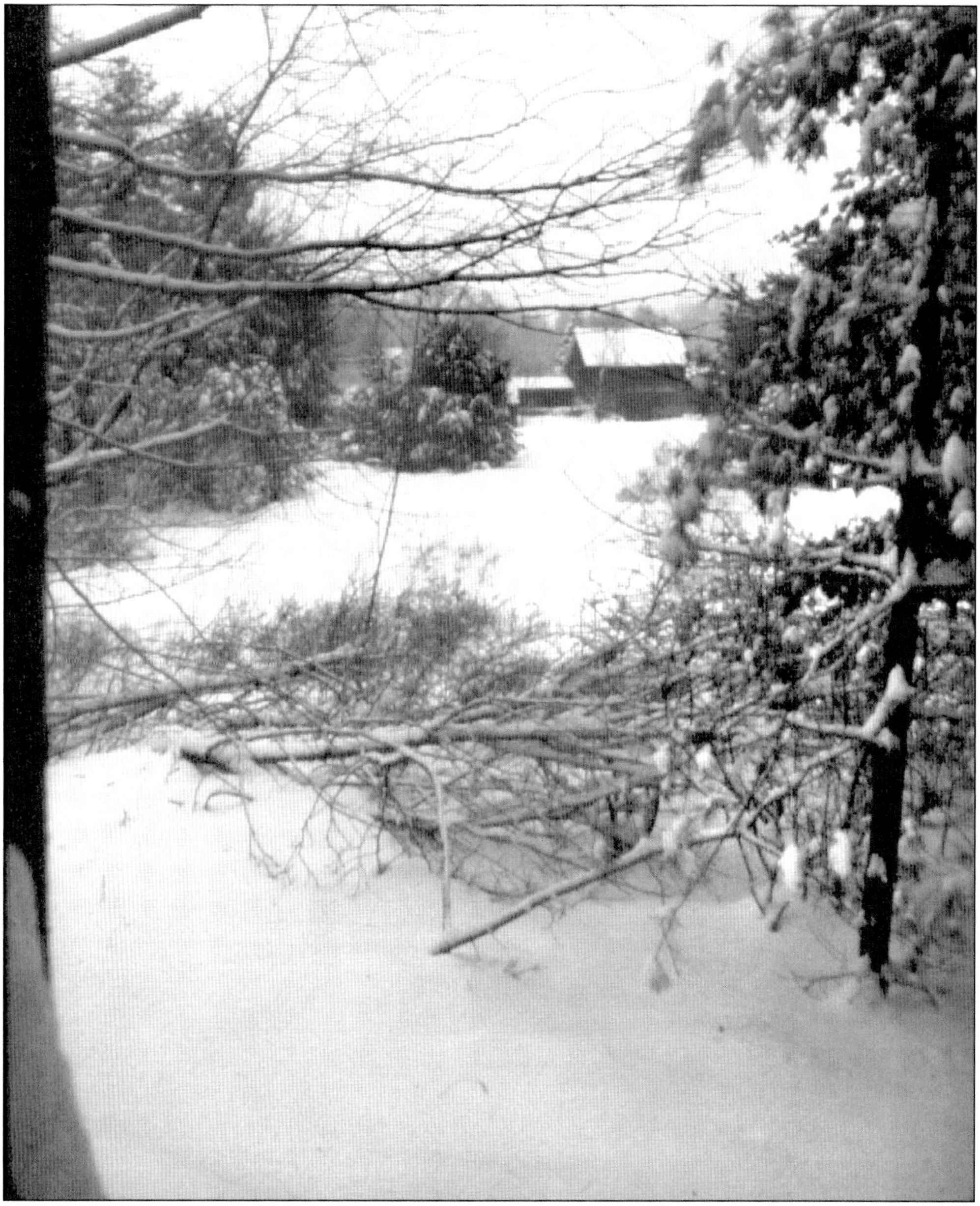

Although the town of North Smithfield had changed greatly in some places during the 19th century, with the development of Slatersville, Forestdale, Branch Village, Union Village, and Waterford, the "outlands" remained the domain of farmers, who wrested their living from the land. (IGN.)

Three

The 20th Century 1901–2000

In the beginning, it was hard to realize that a new century had begun, the last one of the millennium. One day followed another in fairly predictable fashion, but the agents of change were pushing. The Slatersville mills failed, were sold, and reorganized; the process was repeated. With no benefactor, the village was on its own. The population grew, and as housing spread beyond the village edges into the "outlands," open space decreased. The number of working farms declined, leaving formerly cultivated land fallow and open to development. As the automobile became a necessity, trolley and rail lines were abandoned; highways took their place, but not always to the same destination. Schools became fewer but larger. Two world wars and a depression came and went, but North Smithfield endured through it all.

Some of the 20th century is within living memory of everyone. What is remembered is the stuff of history. The images in this chapter represent history lived by many who are alive today.

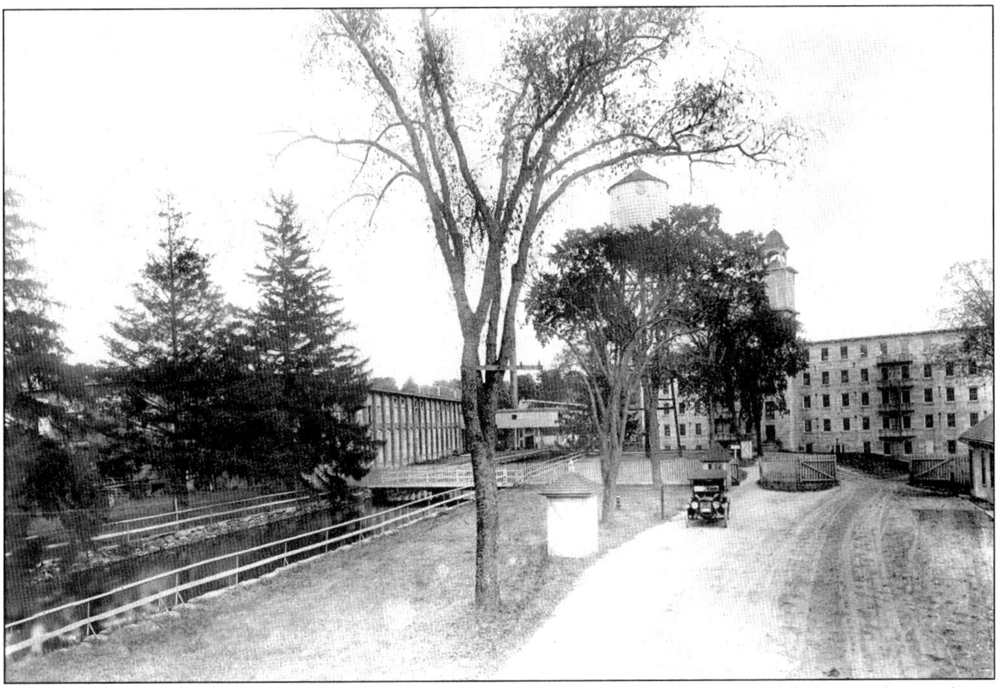

Perhaps the greatest agent of change in the 20th century was the automobile, as shown here in the yard of the Slatersville mills. Even the fate of the mills would be changed after 1900. (NSHA.)

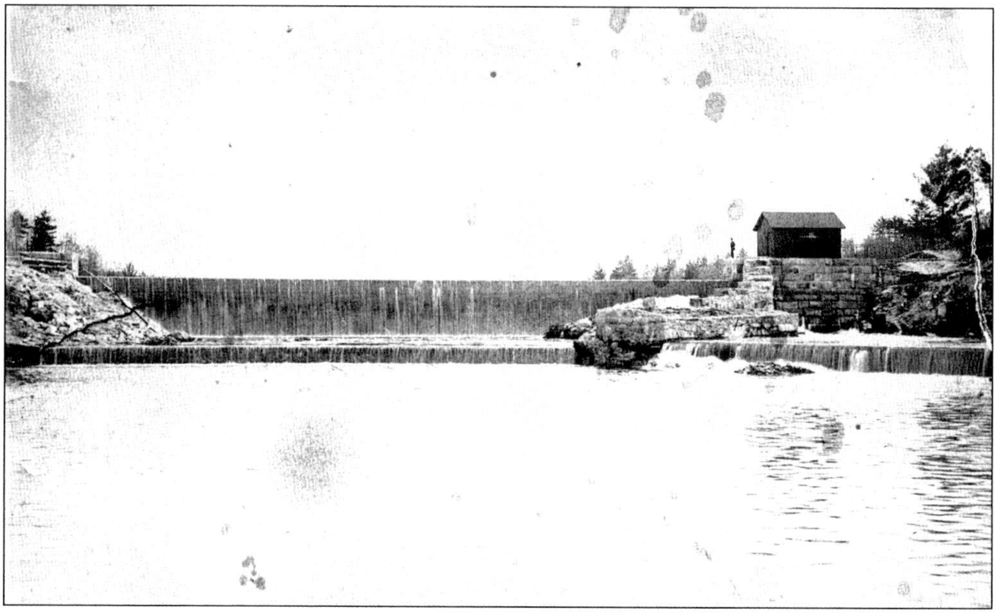

One of the changes to Slatersville came with the construction of the Upper Dam, giving the mills a greater head of water but necessitating the relocation of several buildings to higher ground at the company's expense. The new dam created a deeper reservoir but was a dangerous lure for youthful swimmers. A trench from the dam to the mills extended behind the houses on the south side of Main Street.

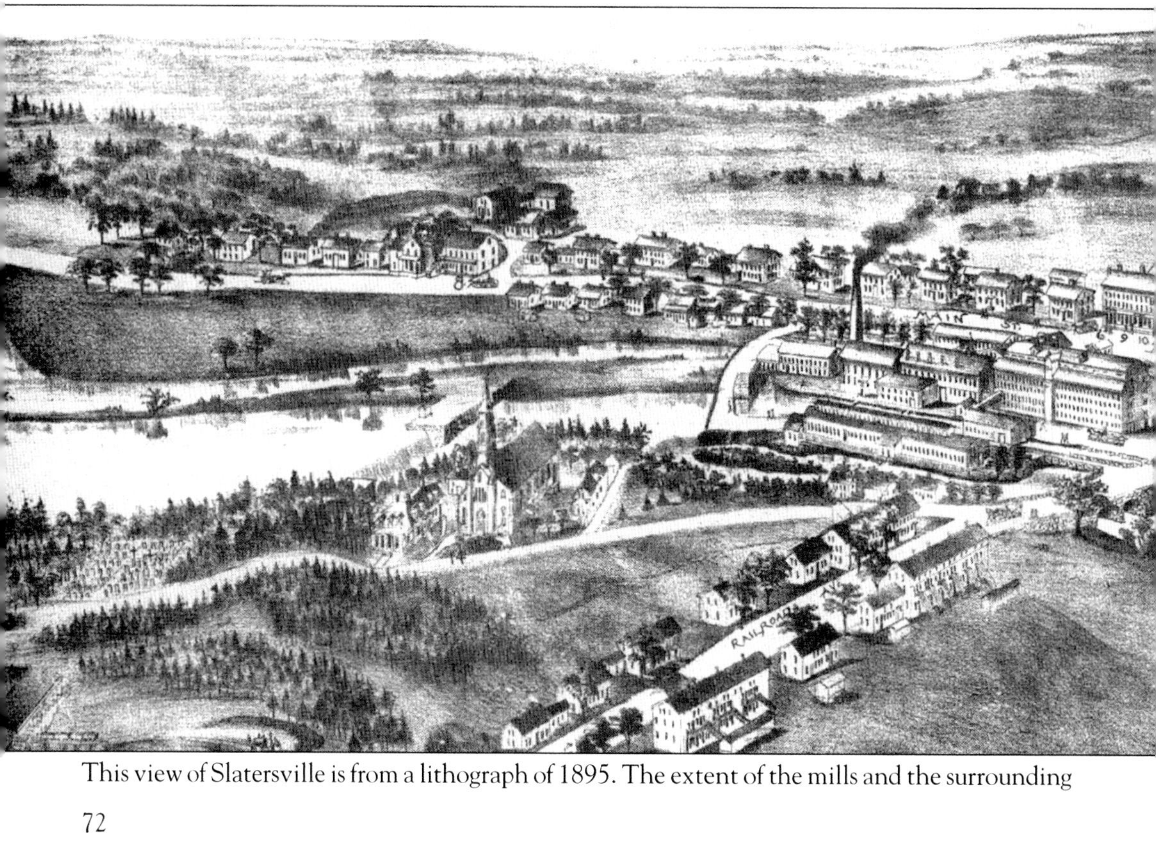

This view of Slatersville is from a lithograph of 1895. The extent of the mills and the surrounding

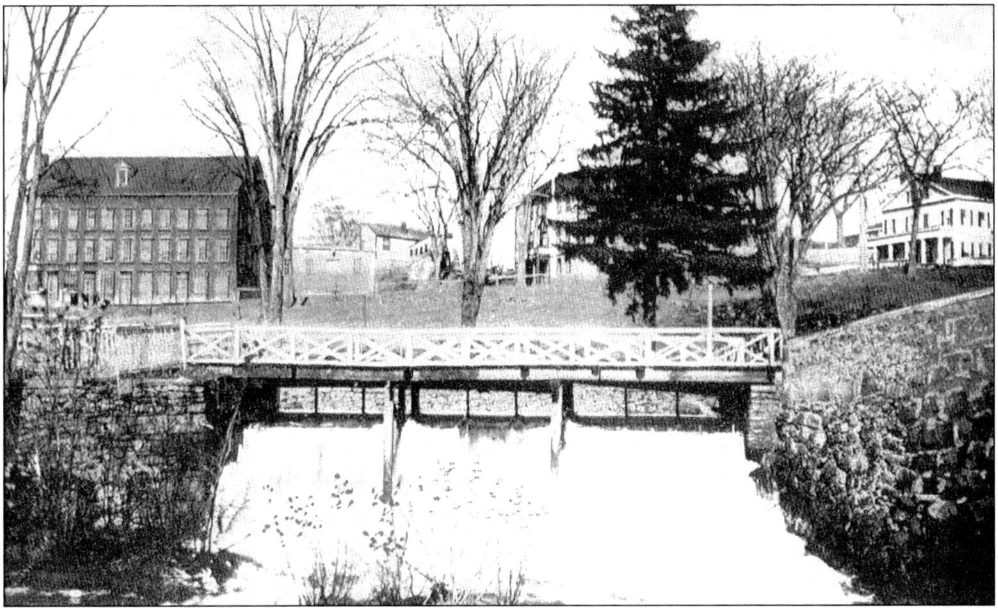

A footbridge across the flume, or trench, powering the Western Mills connected them to the eastern mills. The water in the flume was controlled by a watergate; thus the falls did not always flow so freely.

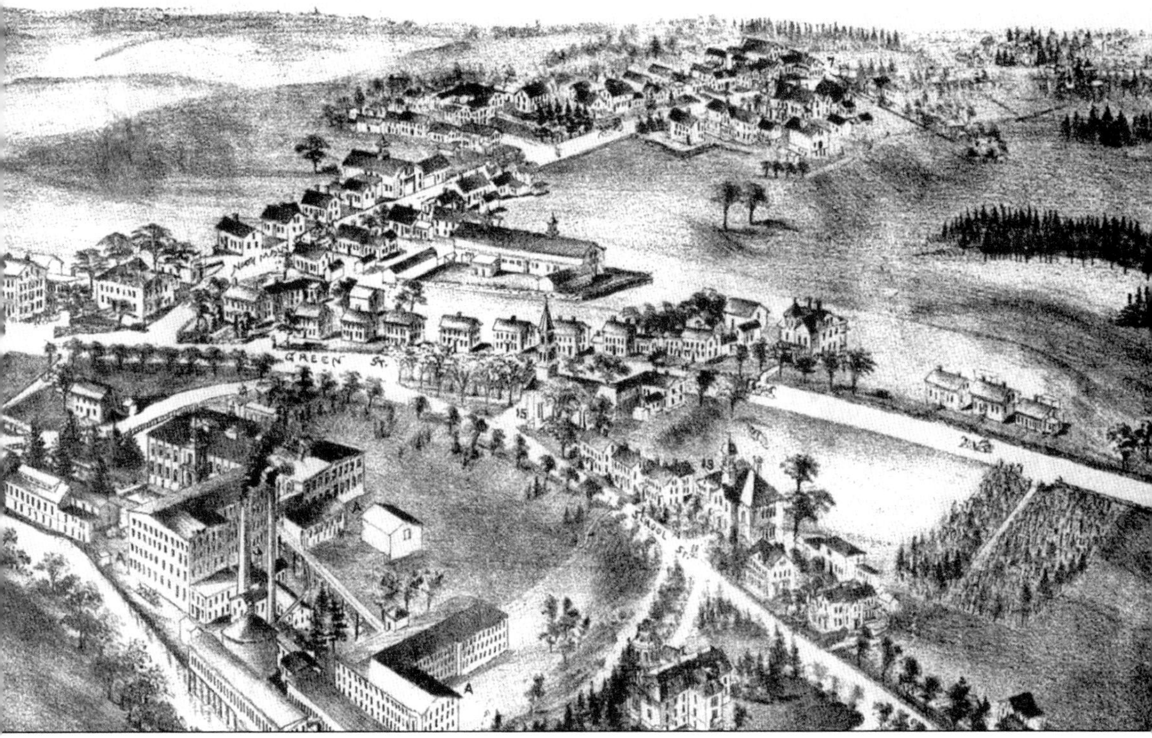

village is clearly shown.

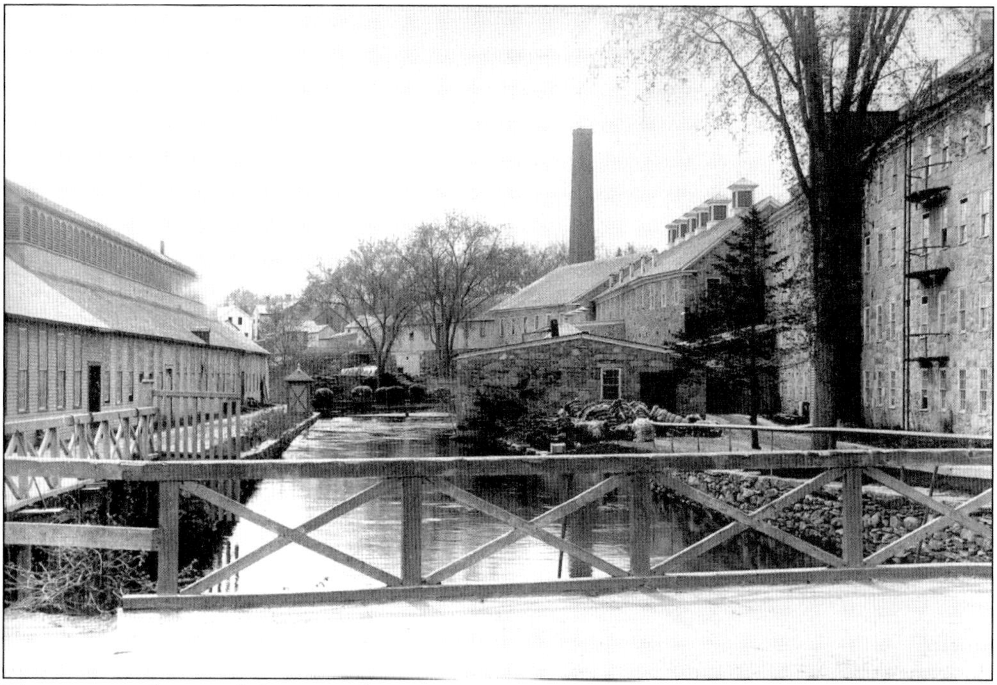

This view up the trench between the Western Mills shows the small machine shop to the right of the trench and the library building, both of which still stand. Beyond the library is a small waterfall where, it is said, in warm weather children armed with their cakes of soap took their Saturday night baths.

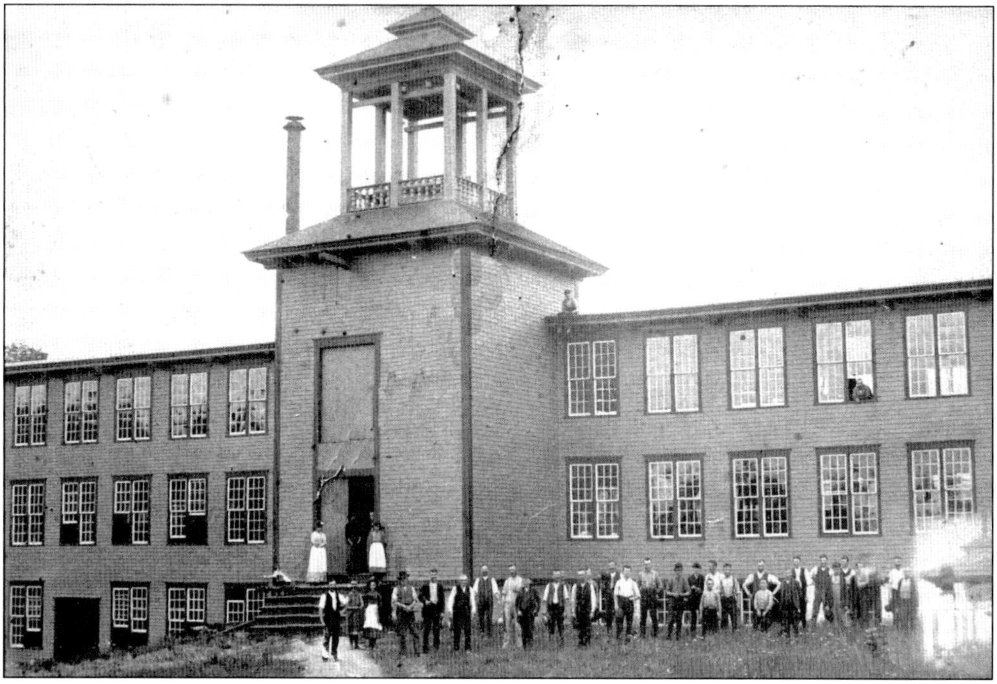

The Western Mills employed a large work force, seen here posing in front of the main building. These mills did much of the dyeing, finishing, and packaging.

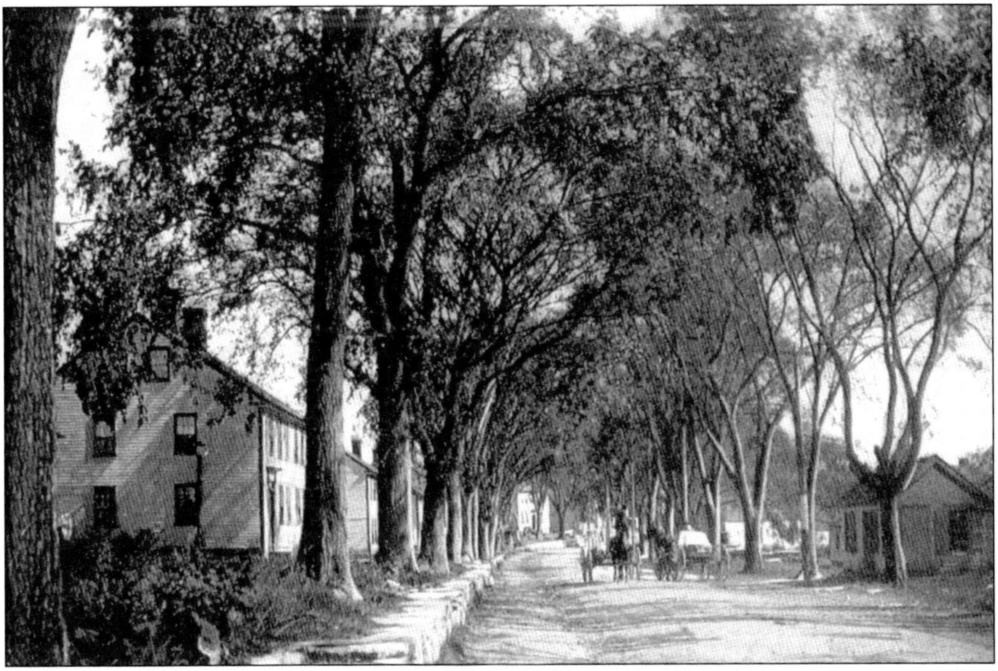

This scene on Main Street, looking east, illustrates the beauty of the elm trees that once arched over the road. Horses and carts still provided transportation.

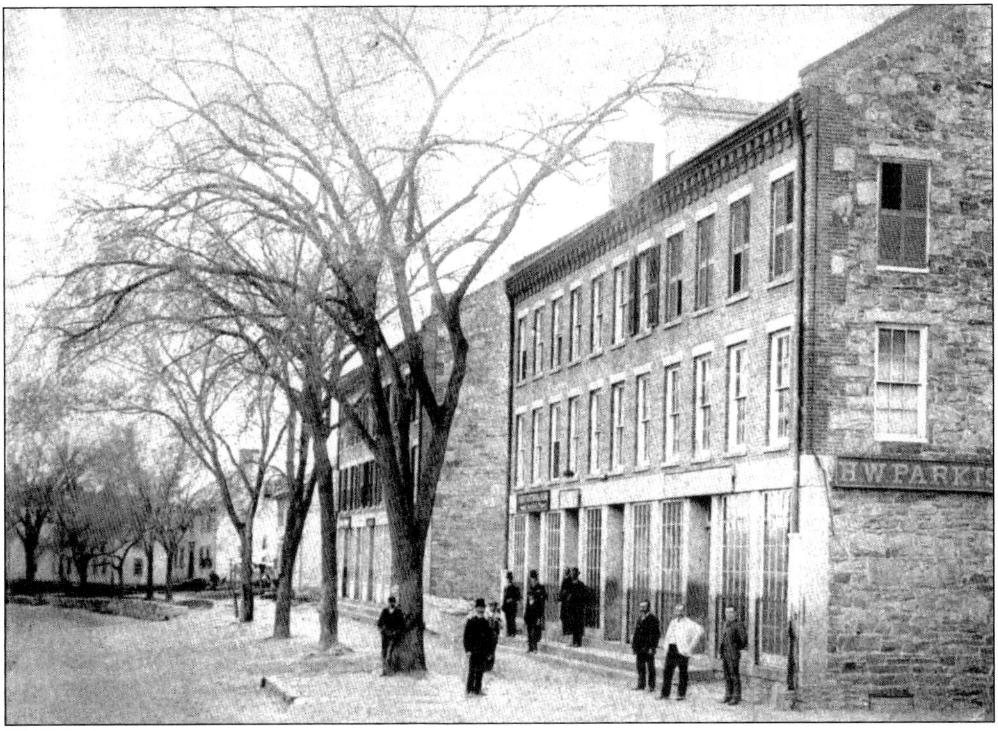

The elms also grace the front of the commercial blocks where the bank and several stores served village residents.

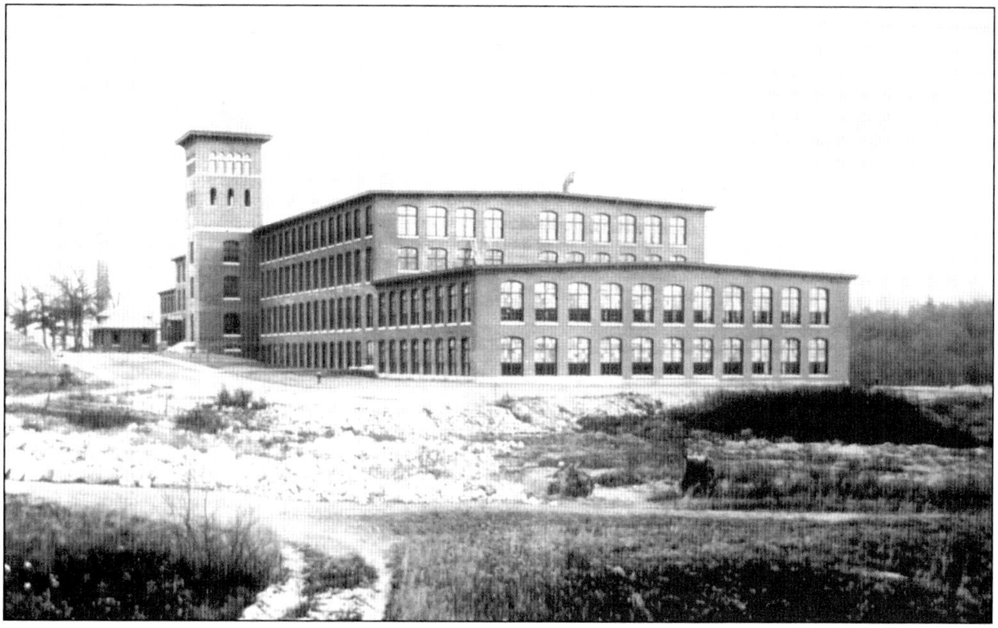

The large buildings of the Blackstone Manufacturing Company were located across the Branch River in Waterford. Later, Tupperware manufactured plastics here.

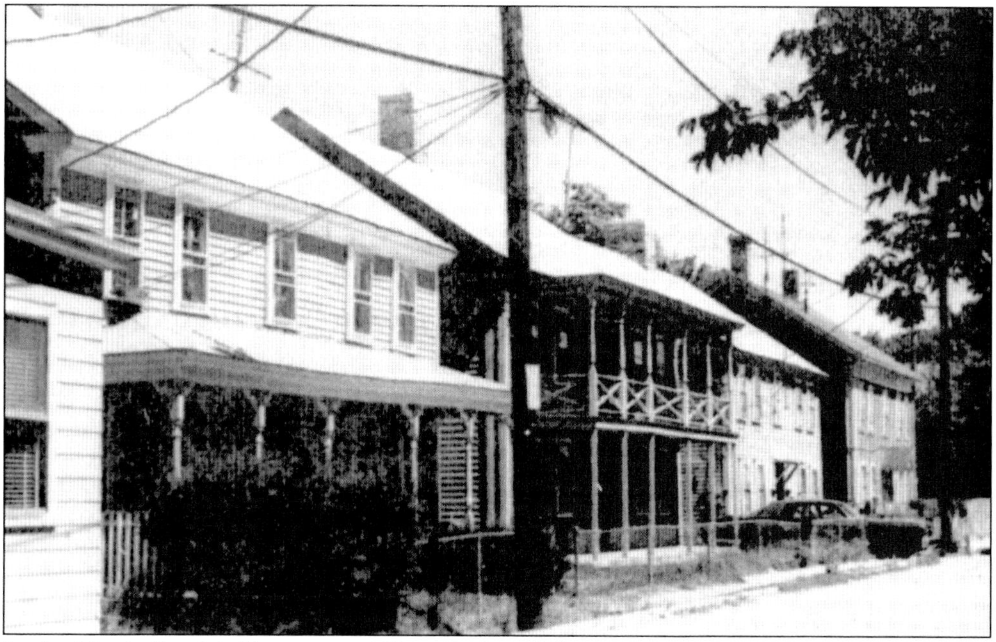

In the North Smithfield portion of Waterford, mill housing was confined to Mill and Canal Streets. The Massachusetts state line ran across some streets; thus, next-door neighbors might live in different states.

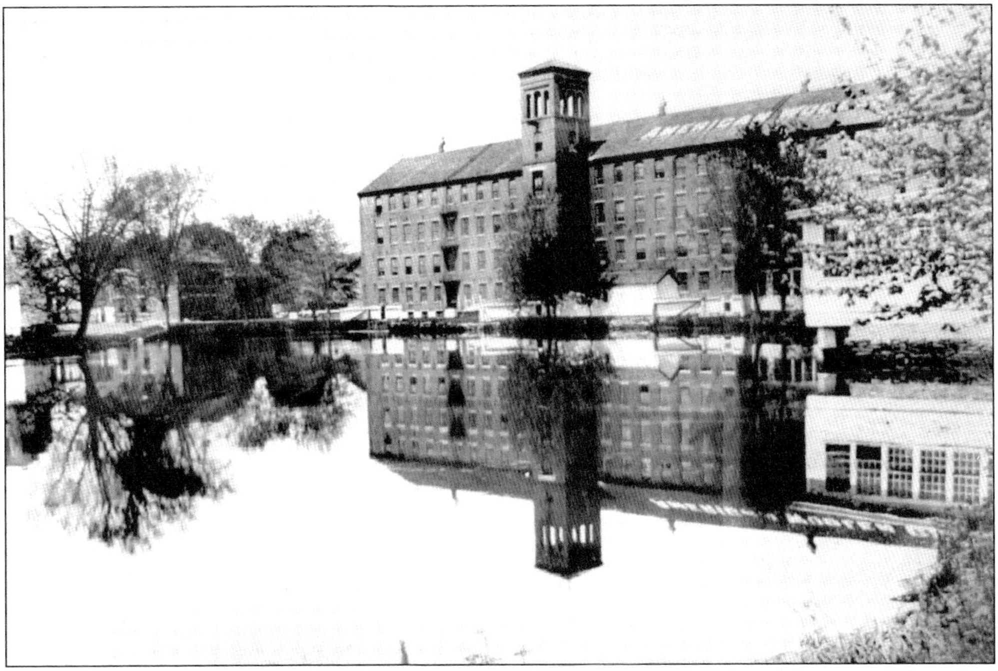

The Mammoth Mill, so called because of its great size, was built off Canal Street in Waterford in 1864. Four stories high and more than 350 feet long, the mill produced woolens. Three trenches carrying water under the mill provided power for three breast wheels.

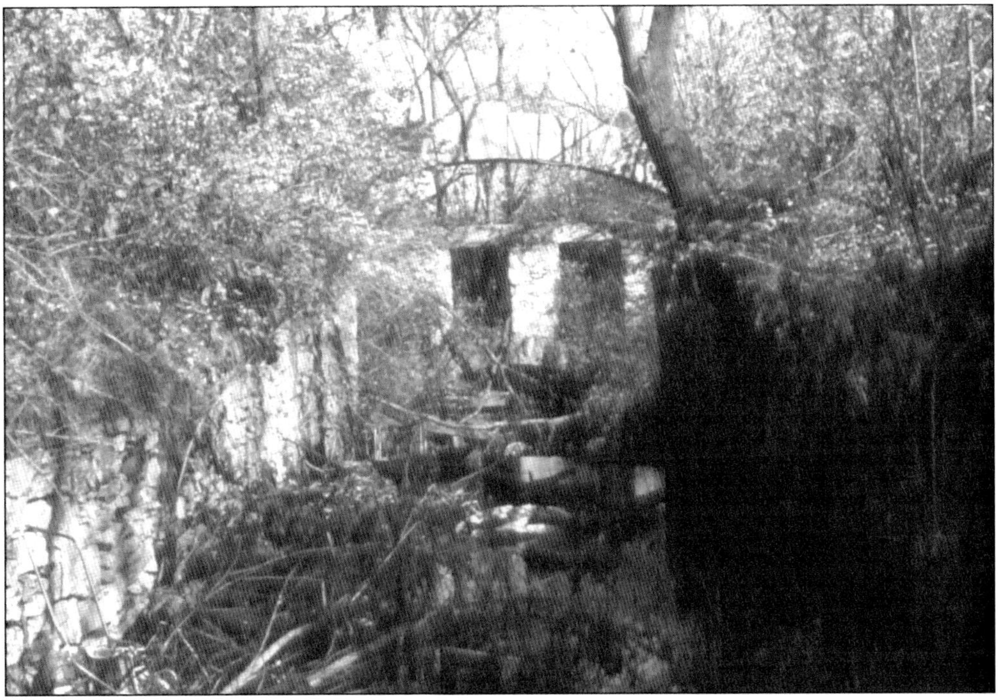

The Mammoth Mill was demolished c. 1930, but remains of the trenches persisted until recently. Sided with cut stone, they were topped by cut stone arches, visible in this photograph. Note the keystone in the arch.

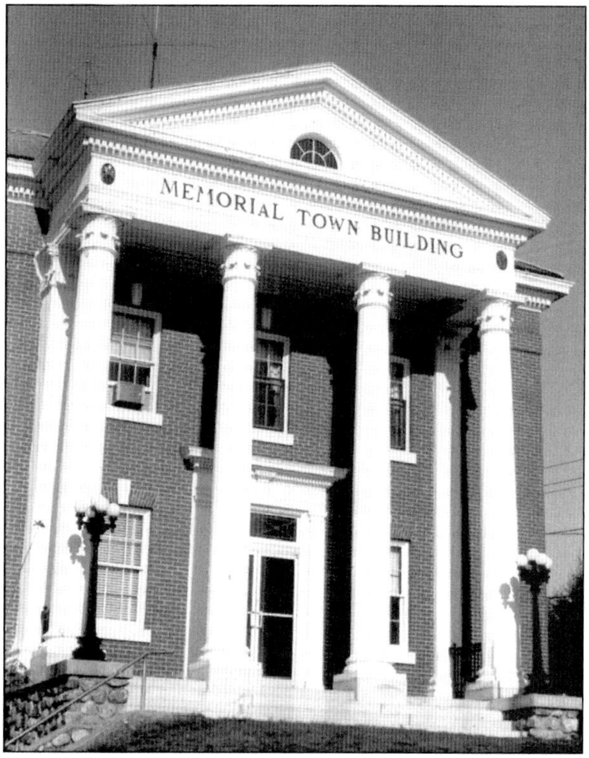

The North Smithfield Town Hall was built in 1912 on the site of the earlier 1830s inn. Commanding a view over the mills to the top of Tabor Hill, and over the reservoir to the west, the building housed all town functions until the closing of Bushee School allowed it to serve as an annex for some services.

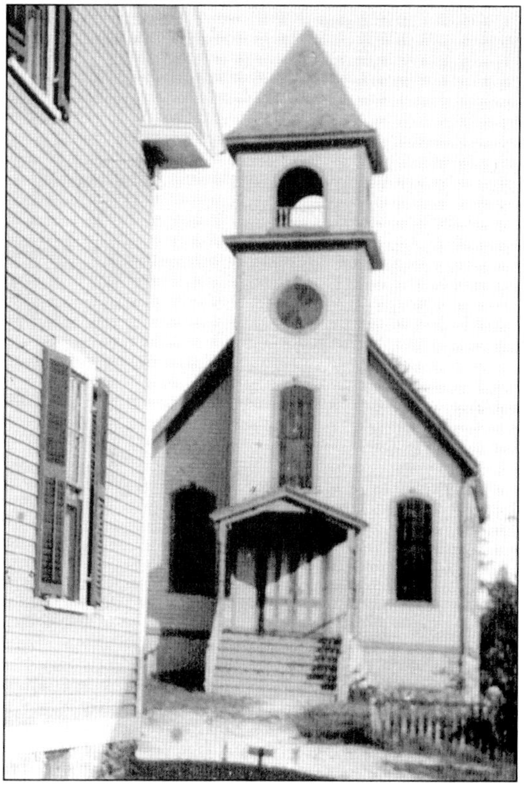

Built in 1897 as St. Luke's Episcopal Mission, this building (upon close of the mission when the mills failed) filled various community roles. As Lincoln Hall, it housed meetings and entertainments. In 1913, it was sold to Union Grange No. 13, Patrons of Husbandry. As Grange Hall, it functioned until 1994, when it was given to the North Smithfield Heritage Association and renamed Heritage Hall. The steeple was a victim of the 1938 hurricane.

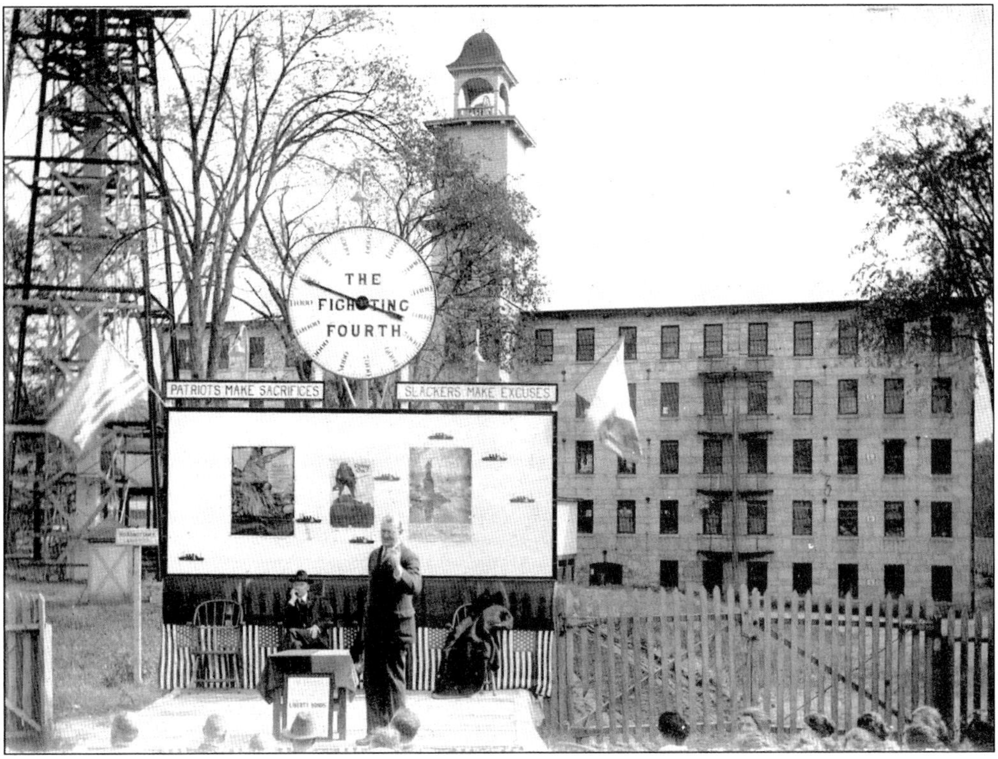

During World War I, the Slatersville mills were busy producing textiles for the war effort. Rallies, such as the one shown here, were held to sell Liberty Bonds to finance the war. Slogans urged citizens to make sacrifices to support the troops. Note the American and French flags.

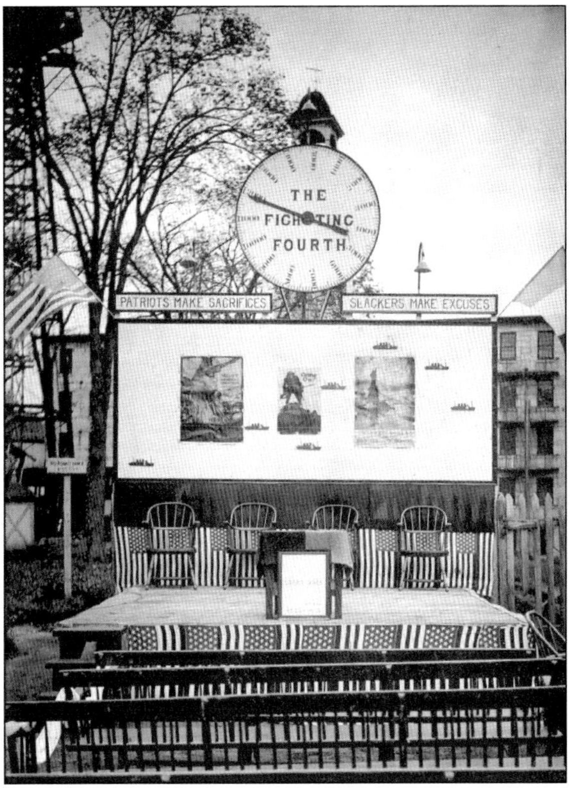

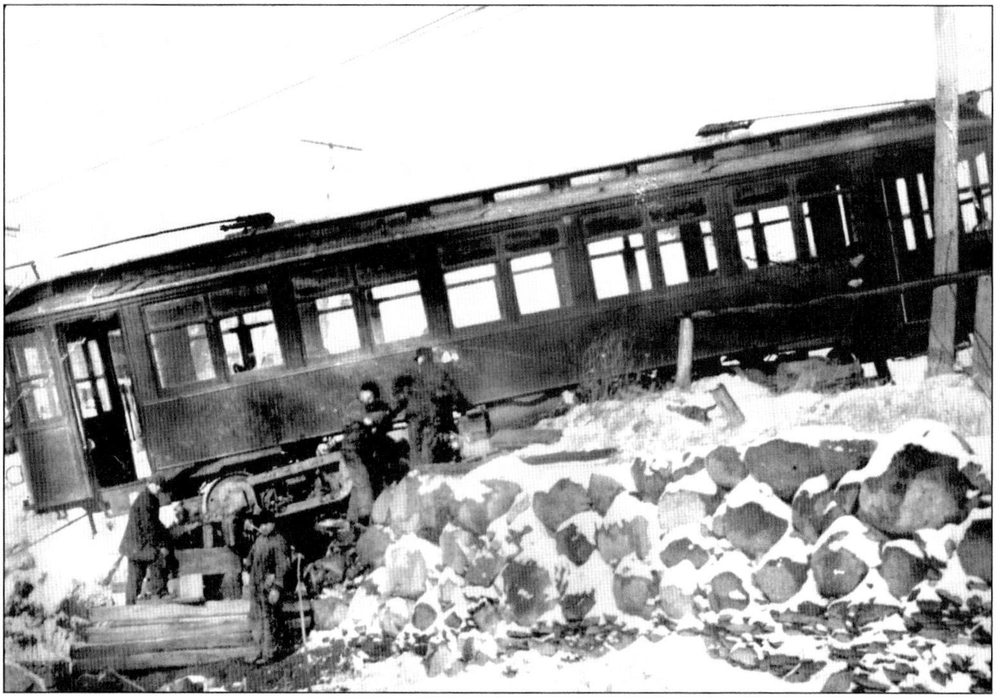

The electric railway was an important link to both Woonsocket and the western towns in Burrillville. In 1925, the "big" trolley took a dive into Cherry Brook beyond the edge of Union Village, evidently just another happening for this particular star-crossed car.

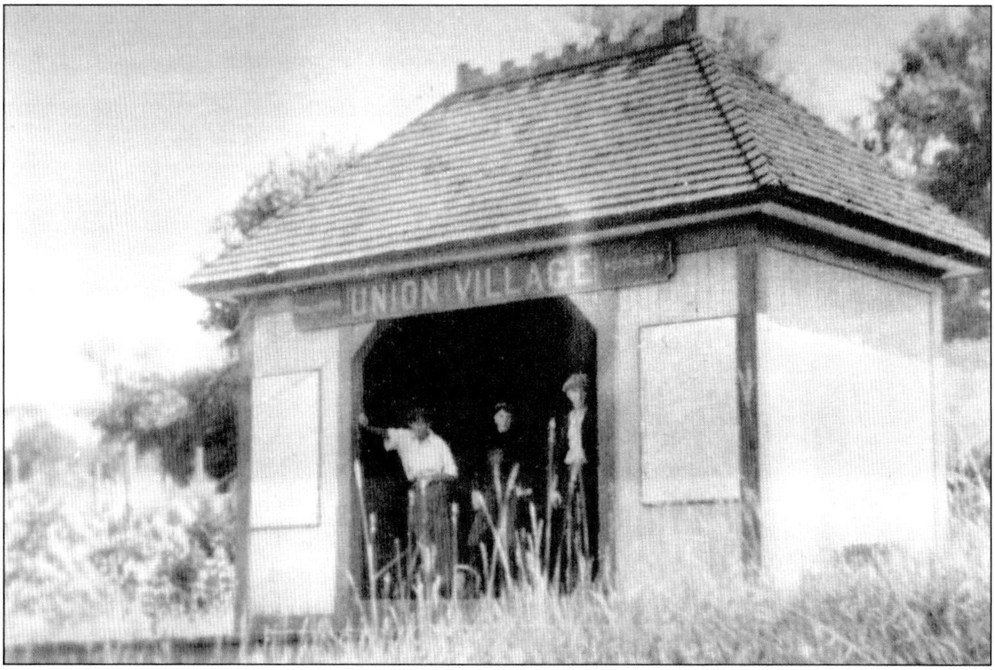

An attractive station near the Paine Farm provided shelter for passengers in Union Village waiting for the train to take them to Pascoag or Boston. There were benches along the three side walls. The train stopped here on signal, as it did at many places along its route. (WHS-SSD.)

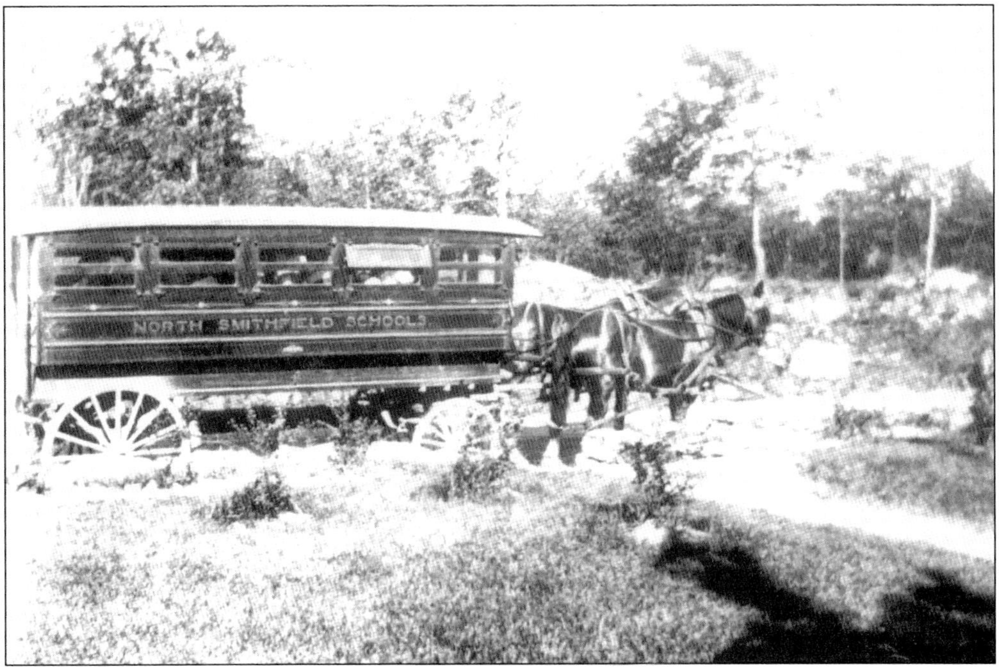

This horse-drawn bus (above) provided transportation to school for some parts of town in 1922, while in the Primrose area, Fred M. Carpenter carried students in his Model T truck (below) with a back roof covering. When he no longer drove the school route, he removed the top to allow use for farm chores, such as haying. (RD.)

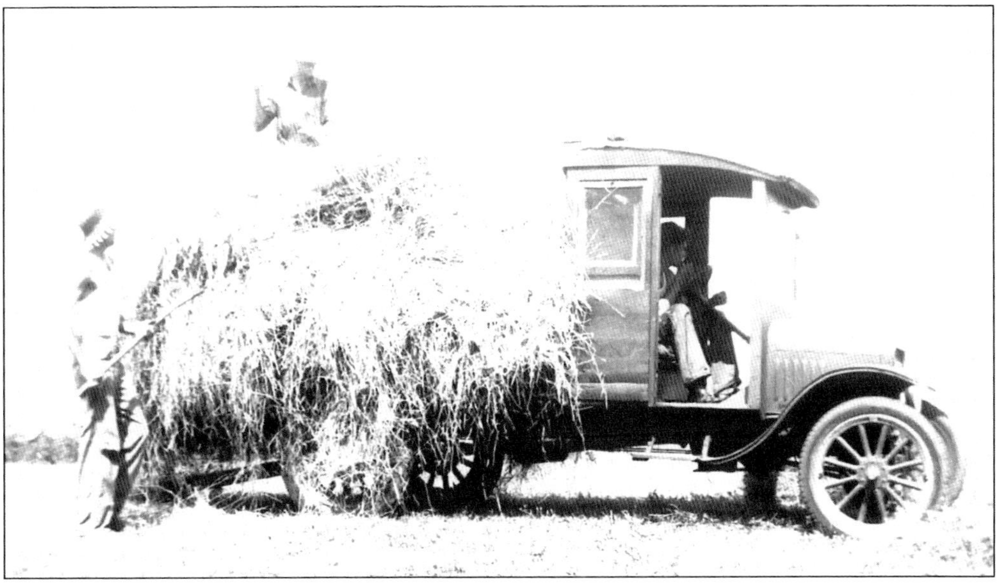

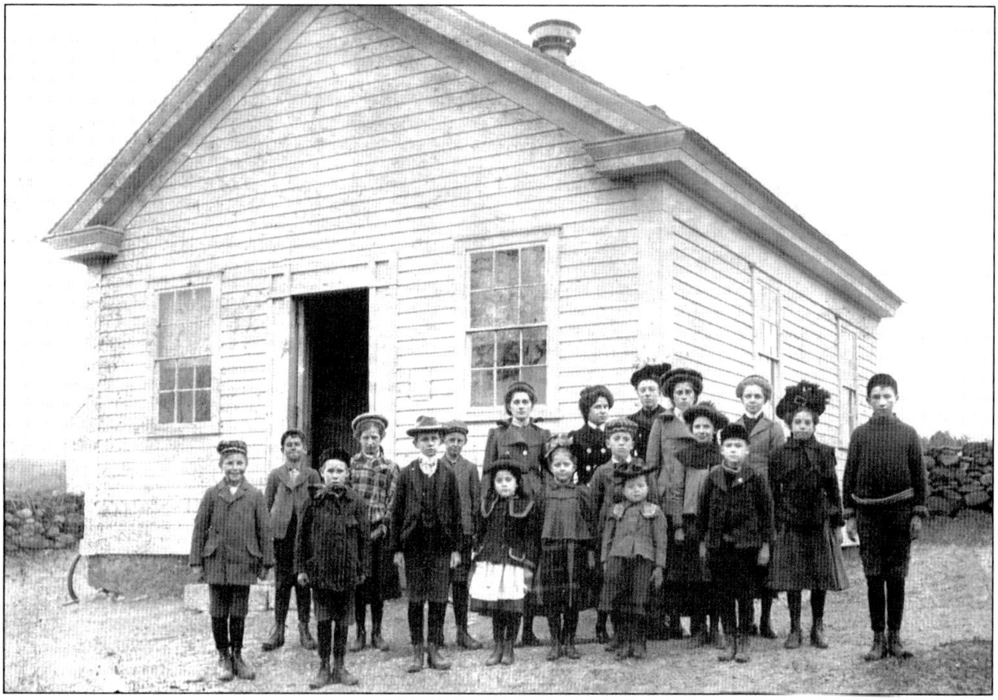

This photograph of students in the Aldrich District School is dated April 1901. The students are members of the Thayer, Ballou, Sayles, Smith, and Bailey families. The school was located on a hill along Great Road, now Eddie Dowling Highway, near the junction with Hanton Road.

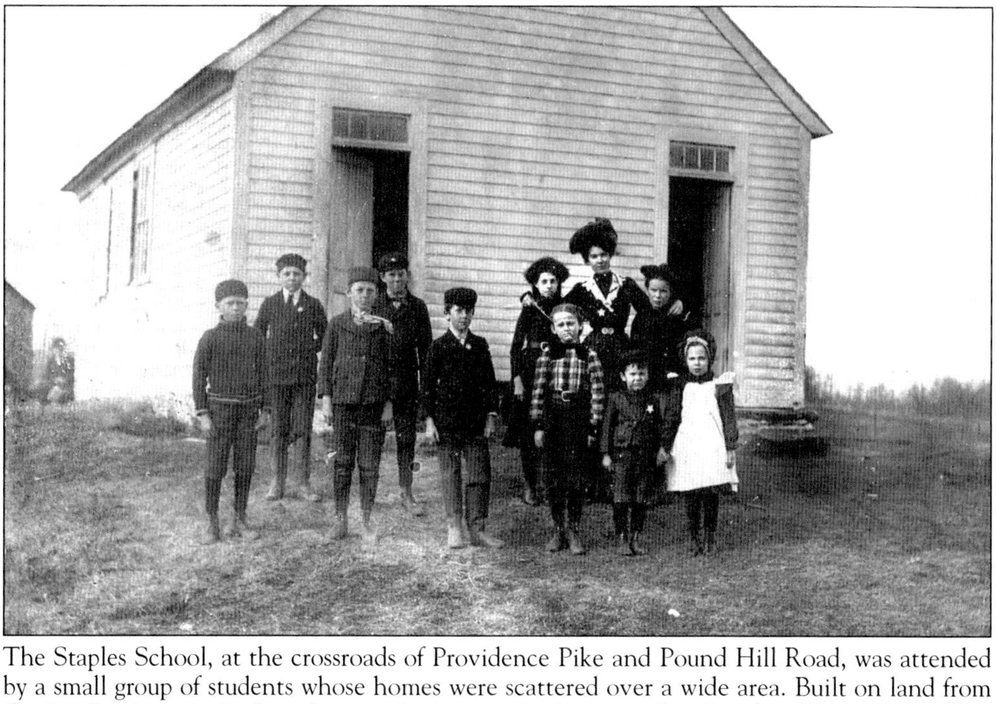

The Staples School, at the crossroads of Providence Pike and Pound Hill Road, was attended by a small group of students whose homes were scattered over a wide area. Built on land from the Staples farm, it displays the two doors typical of separate boys' and girls' entrances. This photograph dates to *c.* 1902.

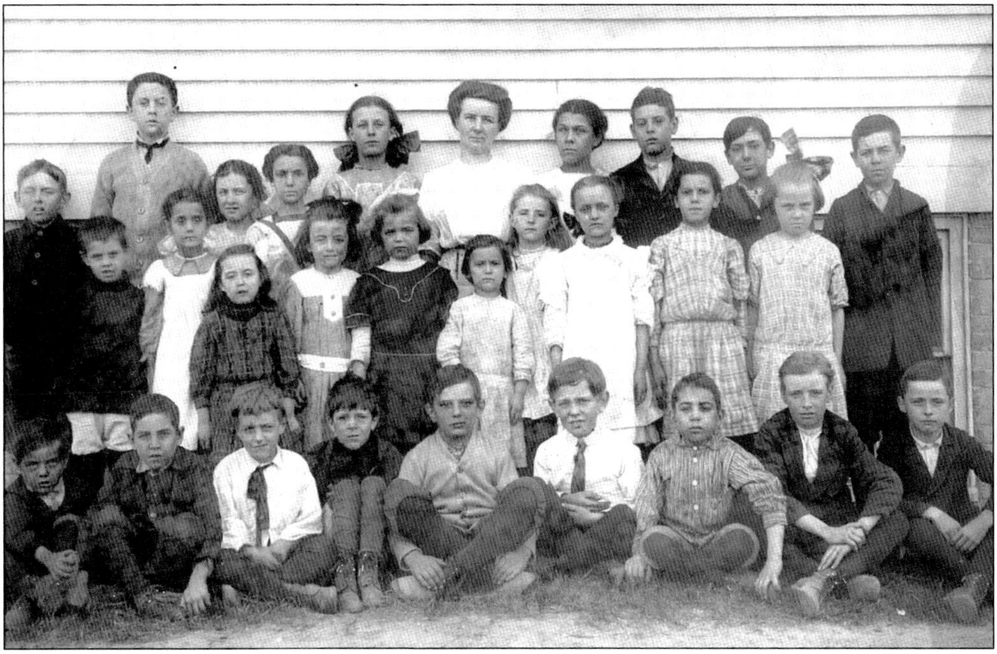

These gatherings of students at the Forestdale School in 1912 (above) and 1916 (below) are larger than those in the small rural schools and suggest the difficulties faced by teachers in some one-room schools. The building was then painted white; for the past few decades, it has been the "Red Schoolhouse." The 1912 photograph includes students from the Tessier, Kogut, Dwyer, Bouley, Perron, Brodeur, Cassie, and Mandeville families. The 1916 students are members of the Desrosier, Stokes, Martin, Dugas, Kogut, Tessier, Bouley, Childs, Tarvis, Oleck, and Mandeville families.

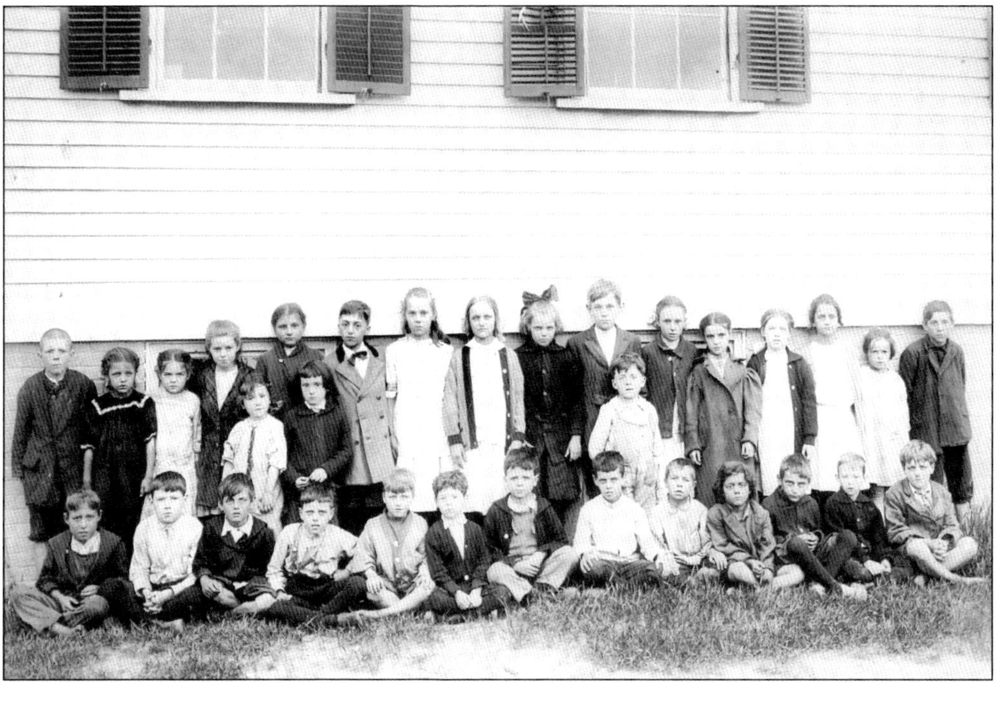

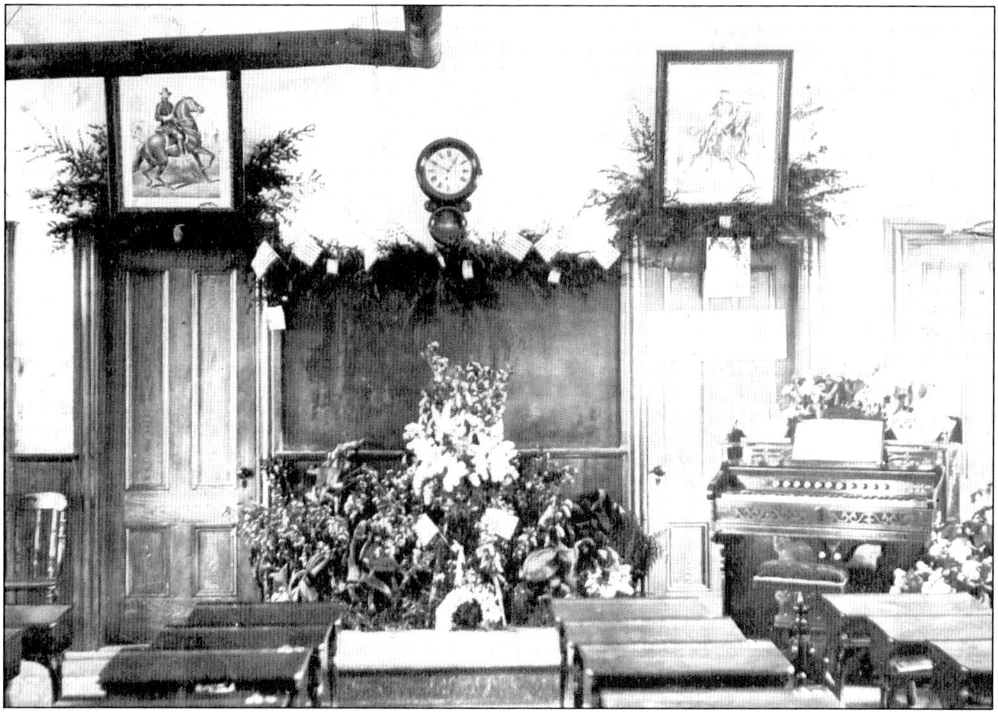

The interior of the Forestdale School is decorated for a special event in May 1895. The flowers, greens, and organ suggest the importance of the occasion. (Tabor.)

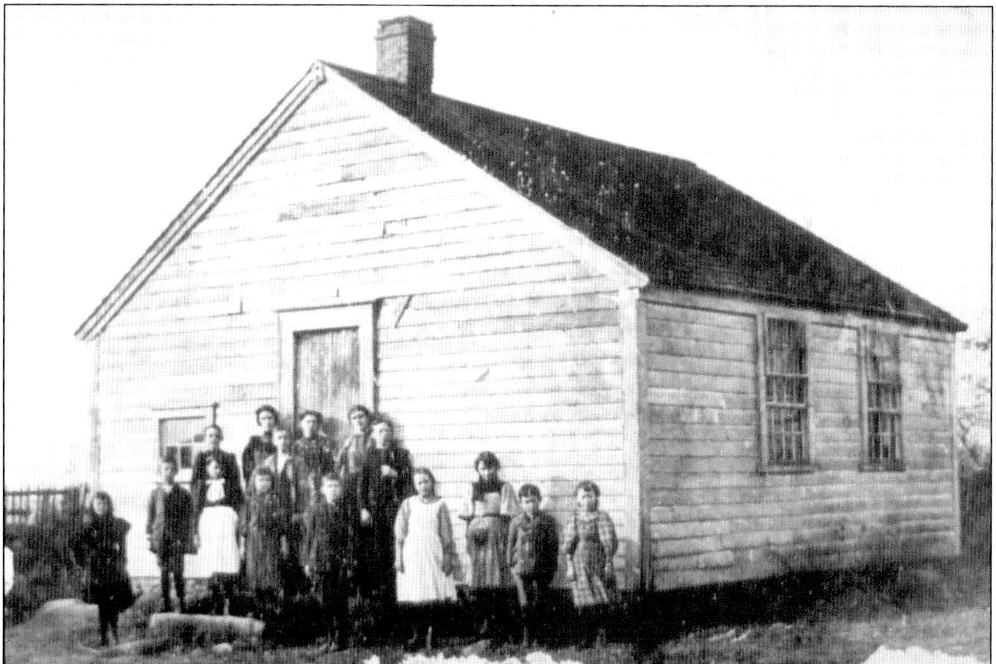

This Andrews School, on Grange Road opposite Rocky Hill Road, was actually the second building on the site, the first having been removed to become an ell on the Goodwin house. This photograph was taken before 1926, possibly even before the Grange was located next door.

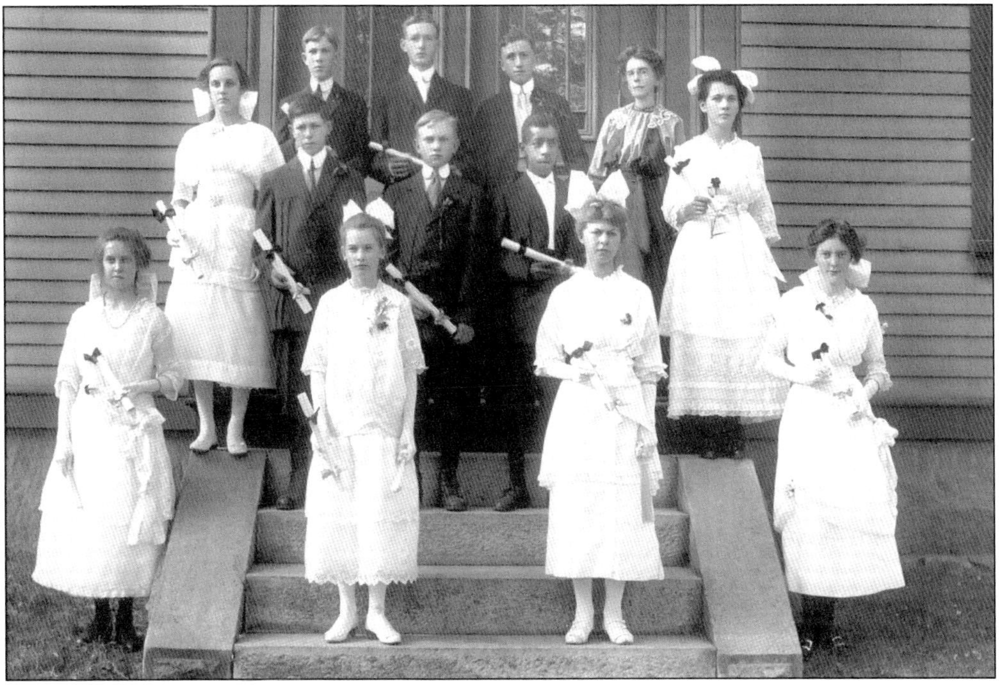

Eighth-grade graduates pose in front of the Slatersville School in this undated photograph. From left to right are the following: (front row) M.E. Follett, L. Estes, N. Carpenter, and unidentified; (middle row) A. Mandeville, ? Miller, E. Christiansen, ? Curliss, and R. Lunn; (back row) unidentified, L.W. Follett Jr., ? Barrows, and teacher ? Parker.

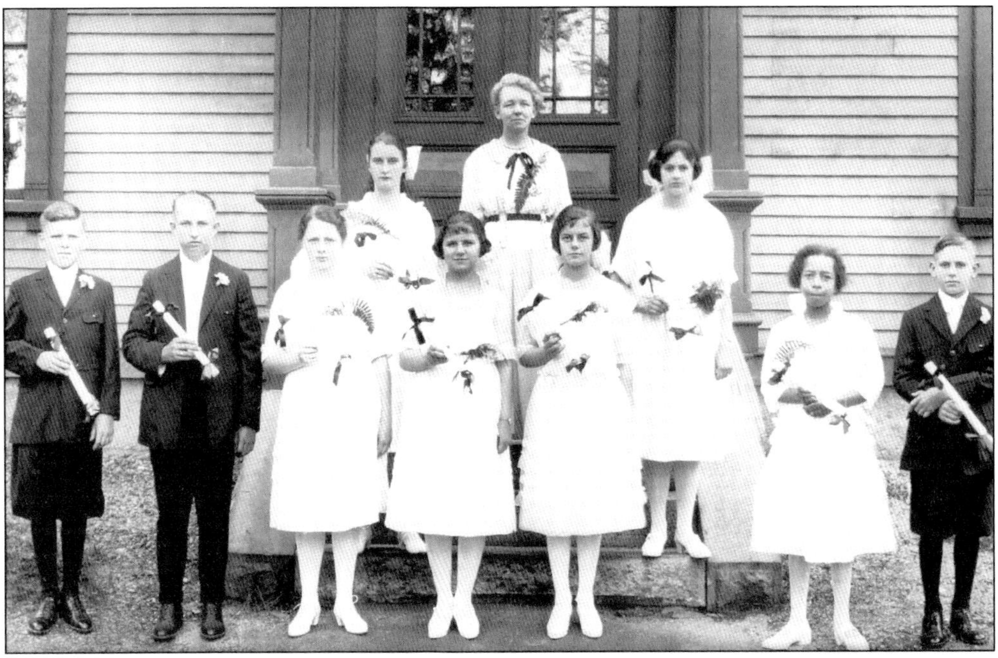

Included in this photograph of the eighth-grade graduates in 1922 are, from left to right, the following: (front row) C.W. Aldrich, A.W. Aldrich, H.M. Wheeler, M. Lyons, I. Broadhead, A. Curliss, and E. Broadhead; (back row) M. Goodwin, principal M. Aldrich, and D. Fogarty.

Graduation Exercises of the

Union Village, Bushee and Waterford Schools

Thursday Evening, June 22, 1933

8:00 o'clock

Bushee School Assembly Room

---

1. "The Siren"
   "American Liberty"
   ORCHESTRA
2. Address of Welcome
   PHYLLIS IRENE HOYLE
3. Song, "When the Roses Bloom Again"
   GRADES VII AND VIII
4. "The Duty of an American" *Theodore Roosevelt*
   ETHEL BEATRICE CROUTEAR
5. Cornet Solo, Elsie Polka"
   FLORENCE IRENE SAYLES
6. Address
   MR. L. METCALFE WALLING
7. March, "Liberty's Sons"
   Waltz, "Dearest"
   ORCHESTRA
8. "Canoe Song"
   GRADES VII AND VIII
9. "Farewell"
   HARVEY CHADWICK PAULEY, JR.
10. Presentation of Diplomas
    MR. SAMUEL FARRON

Orchestra of combined North Smithfield Schools:

Bushee School: Ruth Sayles, Florence Sayles, Ella Sayles, Edward Sayles, Cyril May, Fred Ballou.

Slatersville School: Margaret Finlayson, Albert Laliberte, John Keegan, Ralph Stearns, Charles Baldwin, Asby Jolin.

Union Village School: Fred Clarkson.

Master Gabriel de Calmoutier, leader.

Eighth-grade graduation was an important event for students in the smaller schools. This program

LIST OF GRADUATES

W. H. Titherington

BUSHEE SCHOOL

Ethel Beatrice Croutear
George Aldei Dagesse
Steven William Melnik
Florence Melba Minot
William Howard Titherington
Maurice Patrick O'Donnell
Claire Frances Roddy
Florence Irene Sayles

Class Motto: "Labor Conquers All Things"

Colors: Blue and Gold

UNION VILLAGE SCHOOL

Herbert Pearson Bailey, Jr.
Kent Elwood Fisher
Phyllis Irene Hoyle
Arthur Webster Jones
Josslyn Ames Kelly
Newton Arnold Paine, Jr.
Harvey Chadwick Pauley, Jr.
Meredith Anna Belle Prue

Class Motto: "March On"

Colors: Blue and Gold

WATERFORD SCHOOL

Mary Margaret Misiaszek
Anna Frances Iskierski

was loaned for use here by the family of William Howard Titherington, one of the graduates.

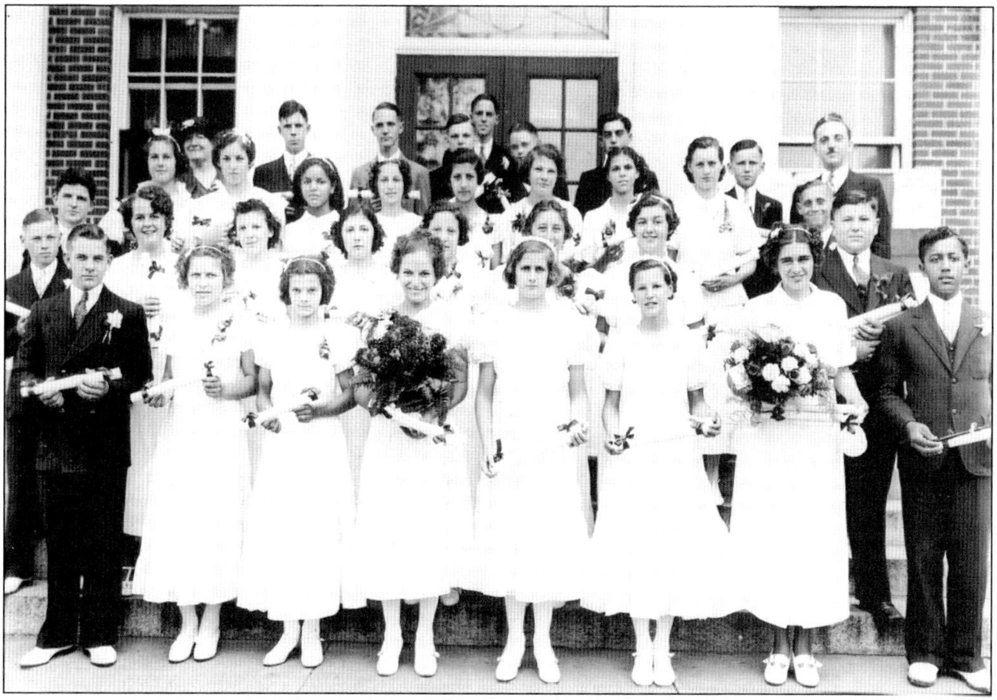

The Class of 1934 poses in front of Kendall-Dean School, which had by then replaced the old Slatersville School. Included in this class is Thomas Mundy (third row, far left).

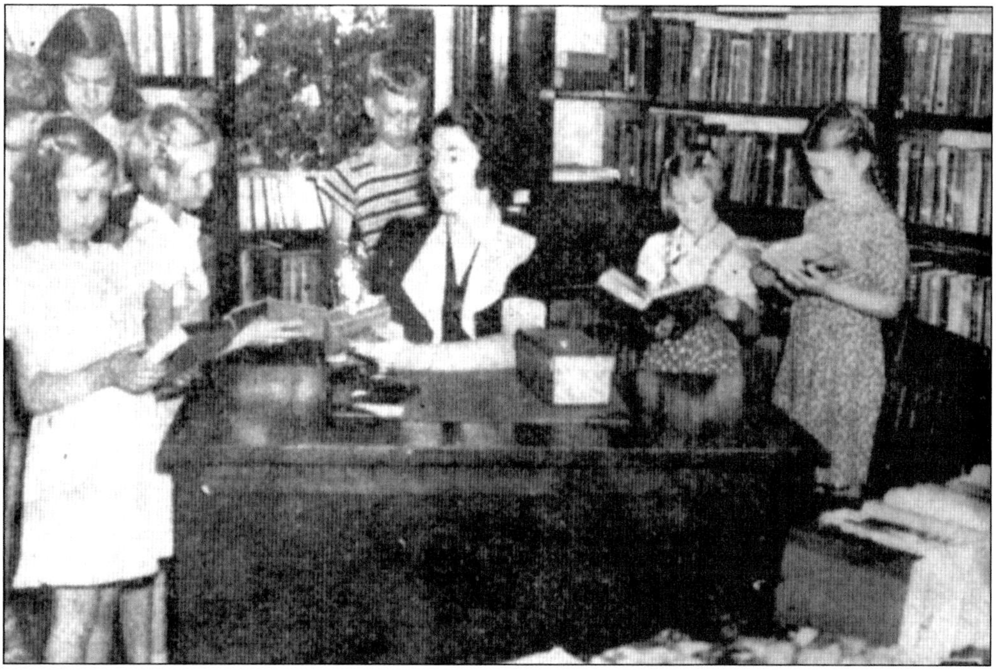

In the 1940s, the library established by teacher Mary Foley Potenza in the little center front room of the Forestdale School was a lively place. The children paying attention to Potenza here are, from left to right, Constance Gurski, Daryl Gove, Wanda Gurski, Alan Morrison, Alice Ferrier, and Margaret Wilkinson.

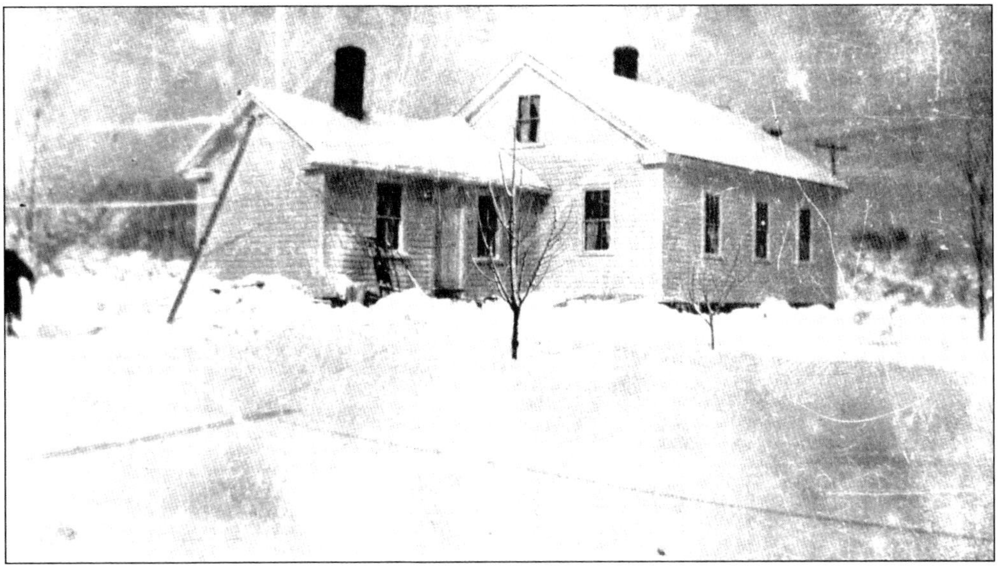

The larger section of this house, the Mowry School, was bought by Fred B. Carpenter *c.* 1920 and moved from Greenville Road across Douglas Pike to its present location on Route 104, where he added an ell to provide space for his growing family. A second story was added in the 1970s. (RD.)

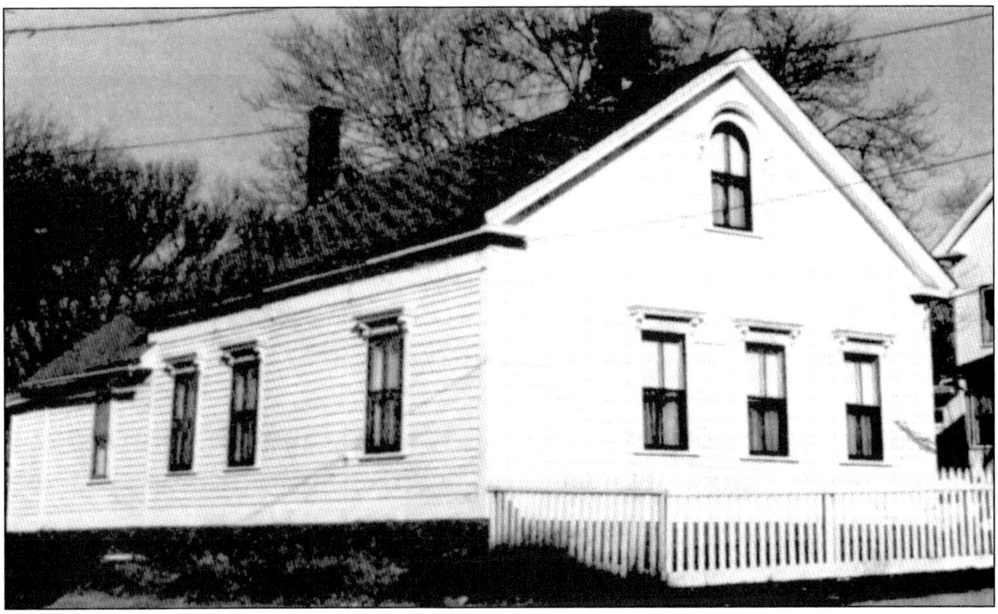

The Waterford School was moved downhill from its Mendon Road location to form an extension for this house on St. Paul Street.

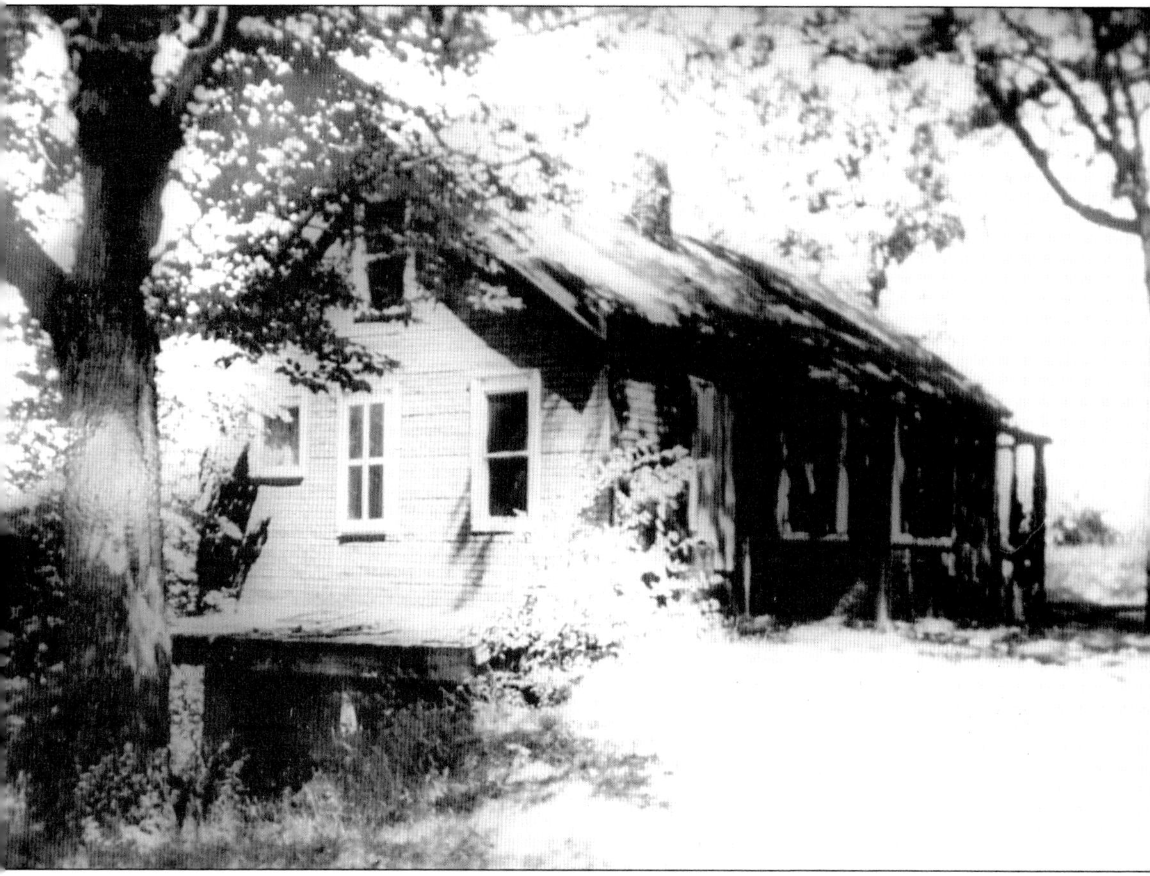

This simple house, at one time used as a cider mill, was located on the Paul Smith property. It also served as a family home, where a small dairy was located in the lower area. A spring across Greenville Road was used to keep the milk cool.

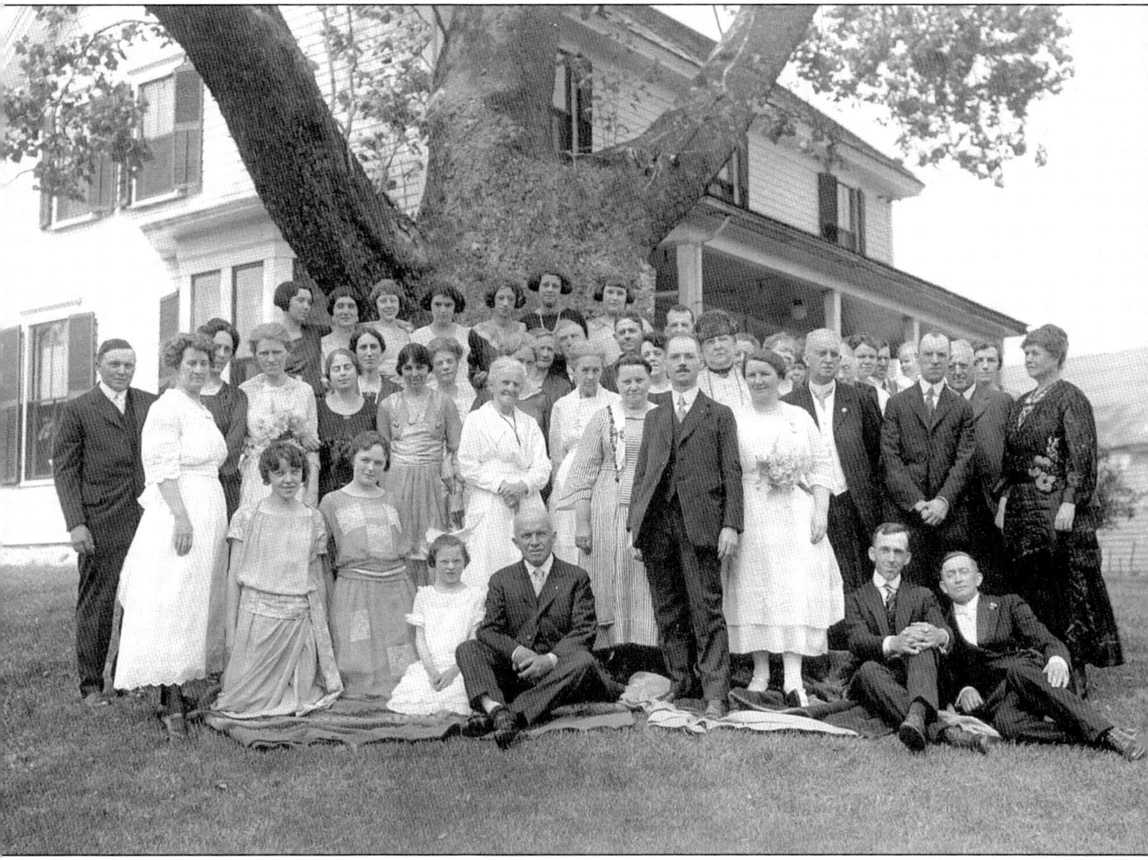

This photograph, described as a "family portrait," was taken on the Henry Green farm on Pound Hill Road. (DG.)

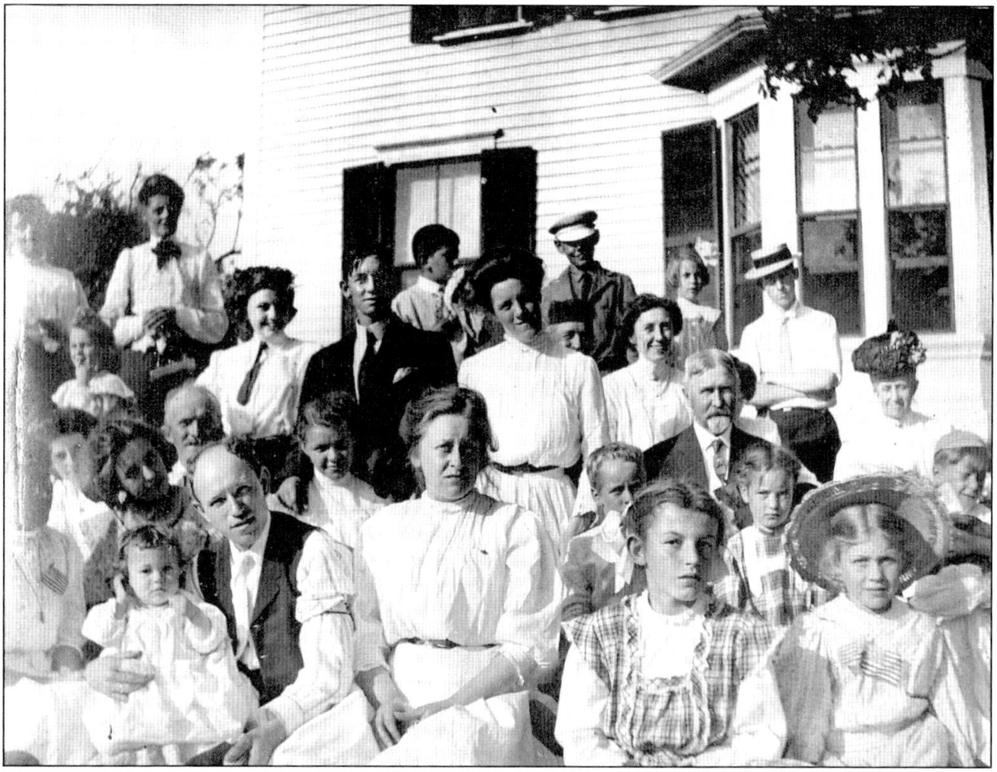

The Henry Green farm was a favorite for outings. Here, a large group poses for a picture. (DG.)

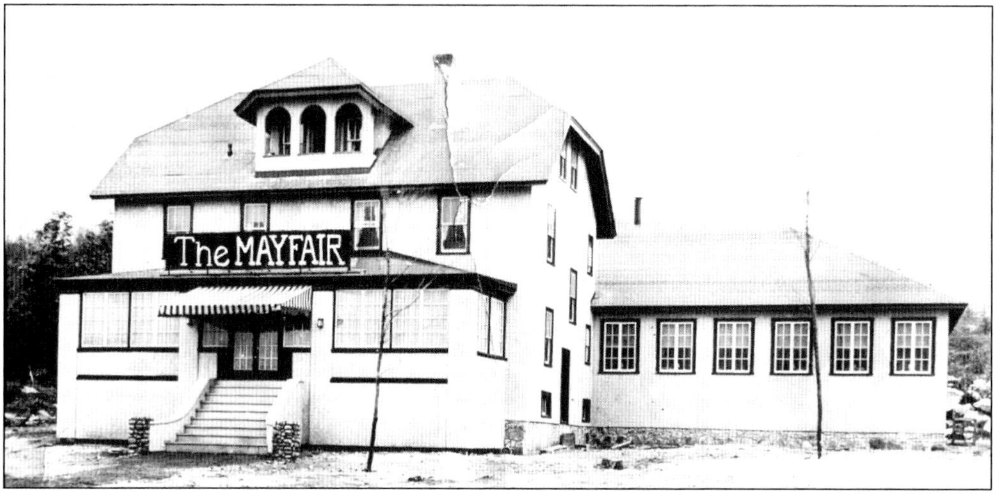

A few decades later, another popular place, more formal than the Green farm, was the Mayfair restaurant, on Eddie Dowling Highway at the corner of Sayles Hill Road. It was replaced by the Friendly Club.

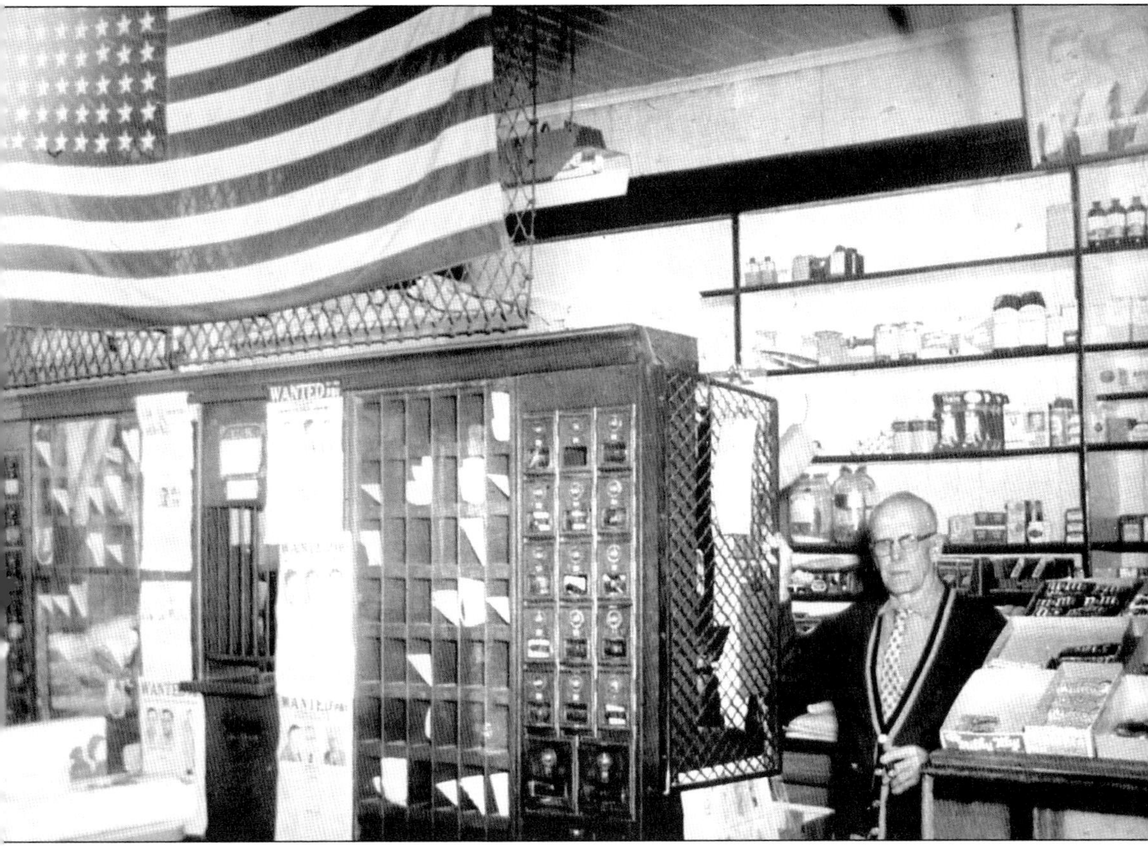

In the commercial block in Forestdale, a post office and general store flourished for many years, with postmaster Arthur Stokes doing double duty as he managed both jobs for 30 years, starting in 1915.

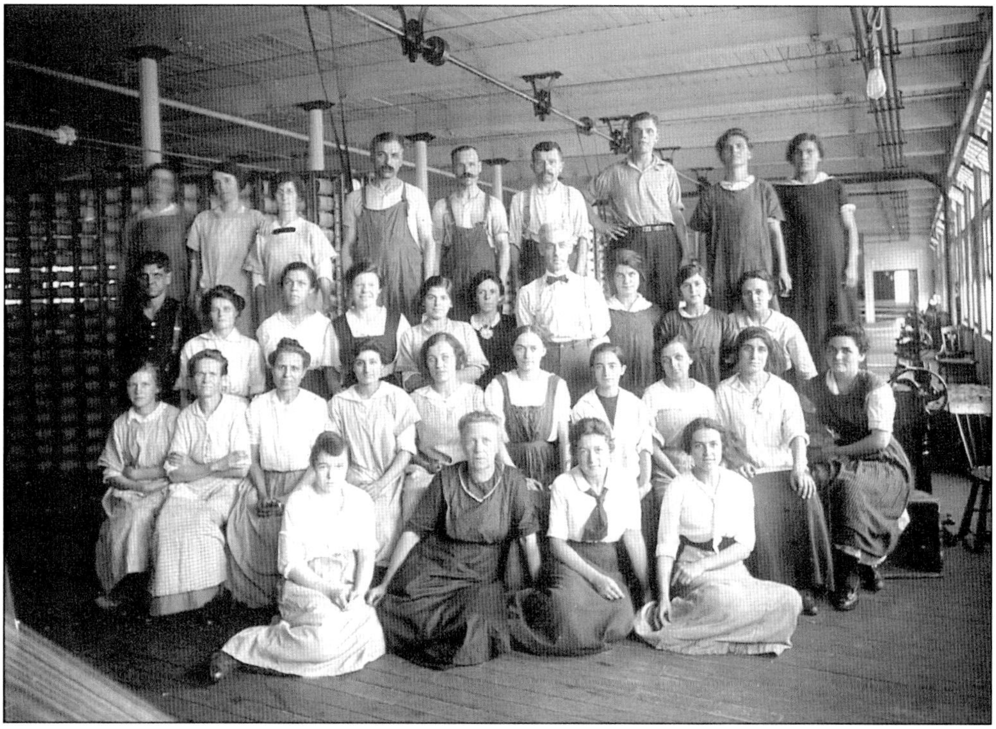

In Room 2 in the "new part" of the Forestdale Mill, warpers gathered for a group picture in the 1930s (above). The warpers worked in the stone mill, where they posed by their machines, which spread the warp threads on the looms (below).

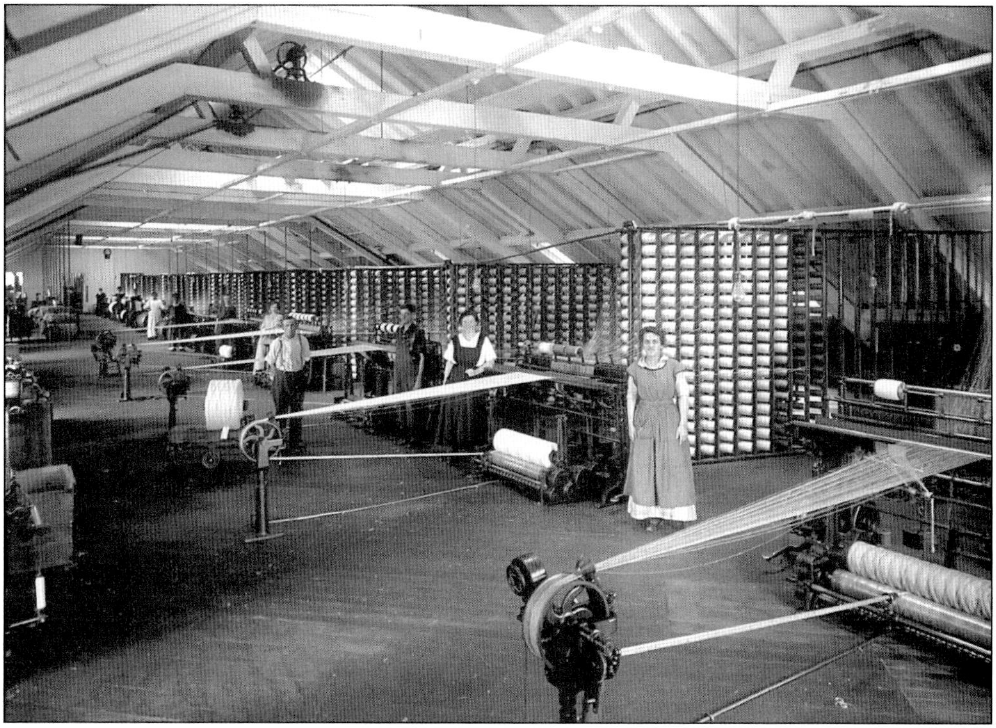

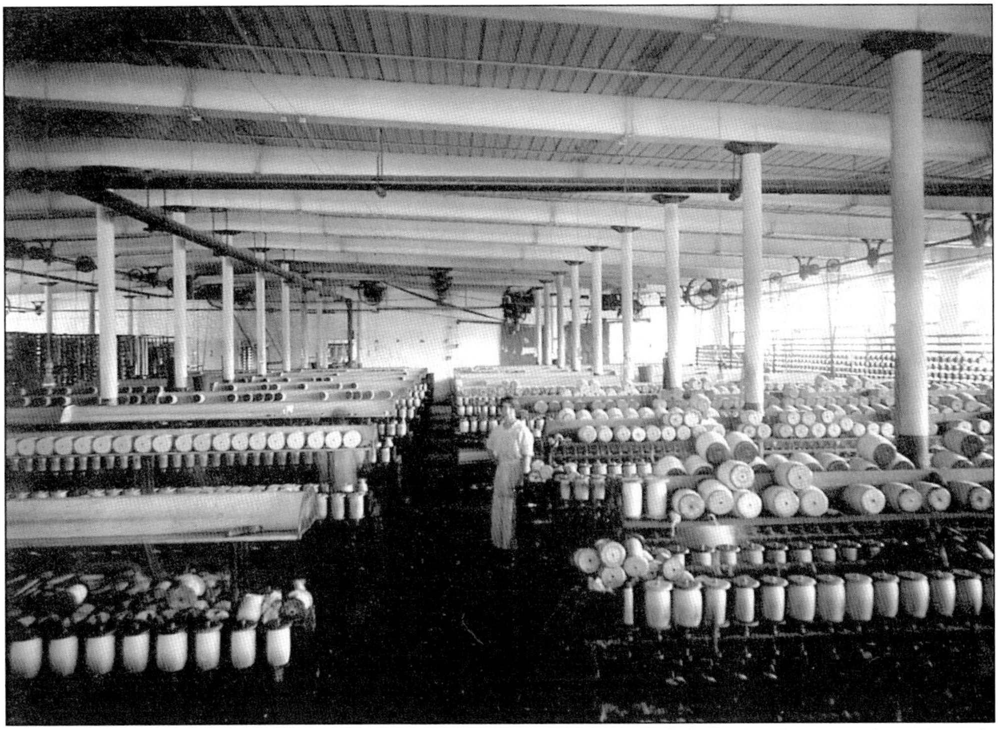

In the new part of the mill, the brick building, spoolers tended to the large racks of spools (above), while the twisters in the same building worked to fill the bobbins to be used in the shuttles for the looms (below).

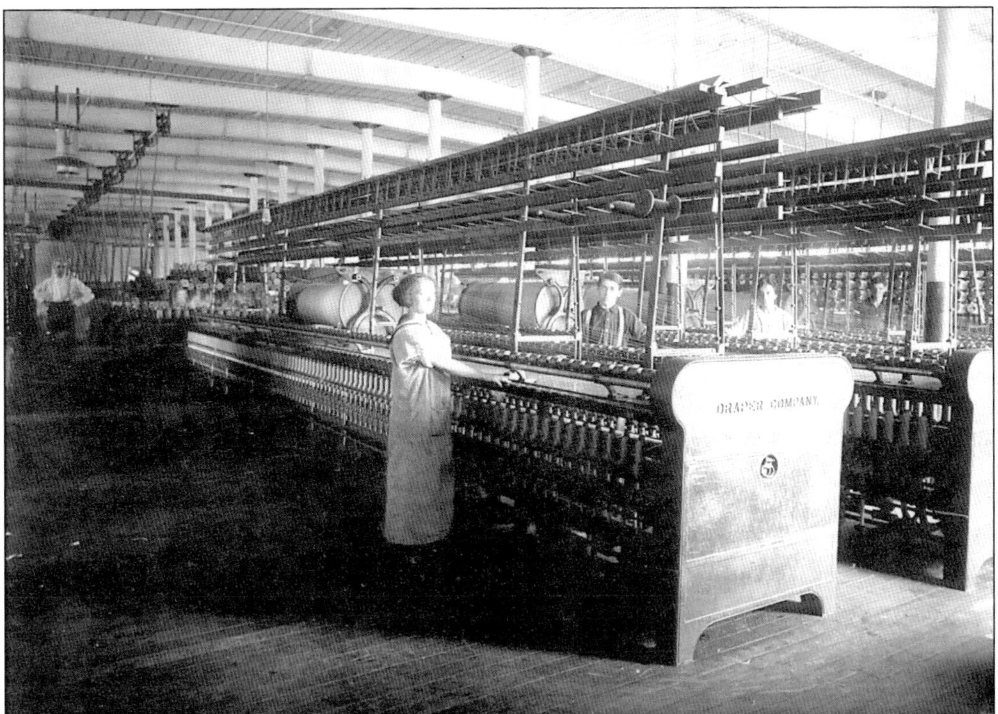

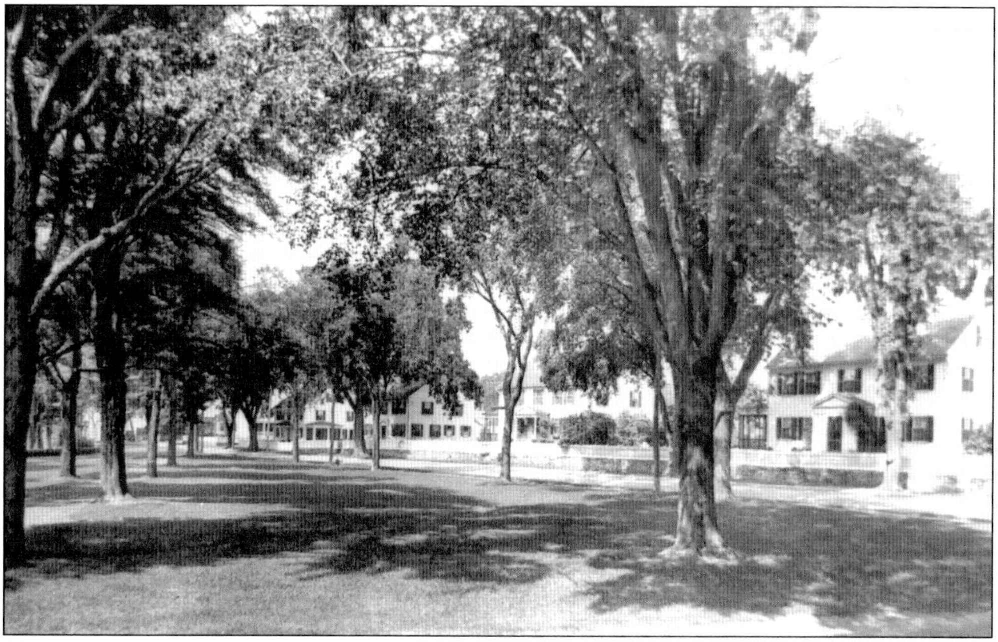

The grassy common in Slatersville, shaded by stately elms (Amos Lockwood's fortuitous vision), continued to grace the center of the village through the mid-20th century.

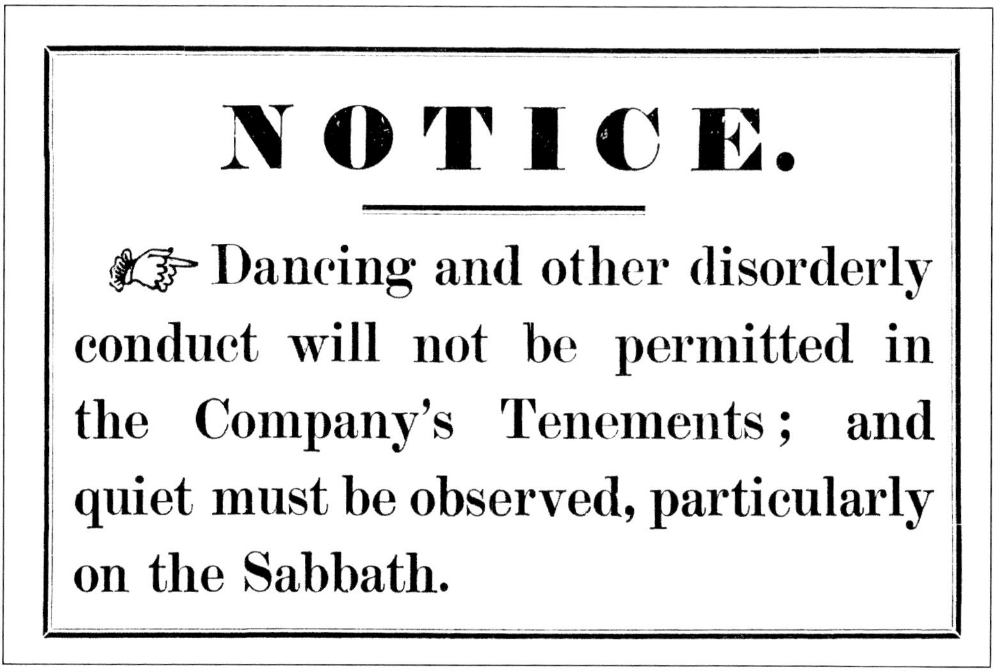

NOTICE.

☞ Dancing and other disorderly conduct will not be permitted in the Company's Tenements; and quiet must be observed, particularly on the Sabbath.

The values of civility and decorum were encouraged by signs, such as the one shown here, displayed in all the Slater tenements.

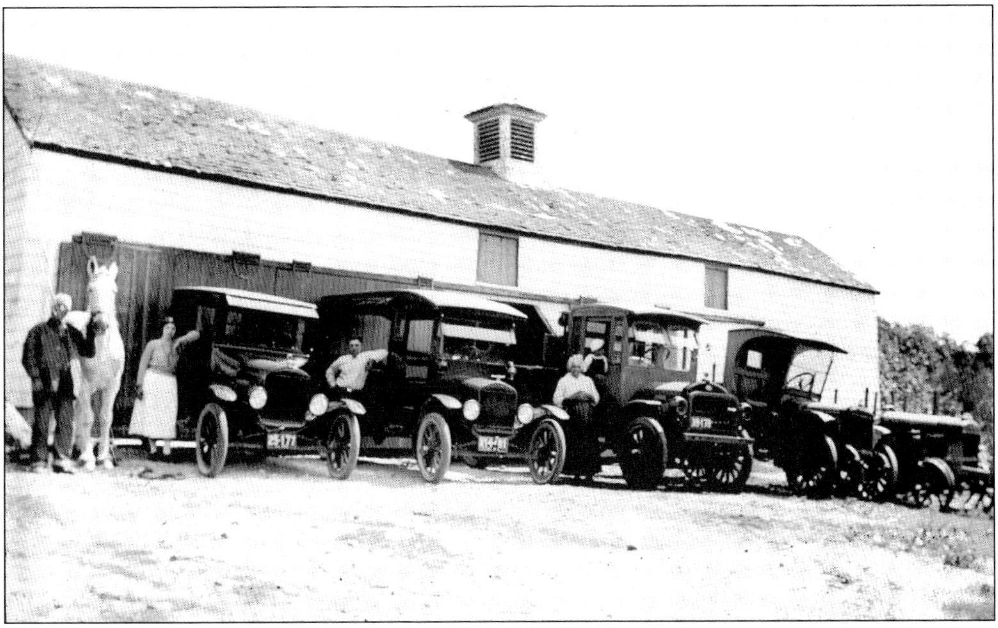

Near Primrose Pond, Joseph Cesario farmed the land and raised fruit in his orchard. In 1918, he displayed his fleet of trucks along with his favorite horse. Pictured, from left to right, are an unidentified man, Theresa Scotto, Joseph P. Cesario, and Joseph's wife, Elizabeth. (EC.)

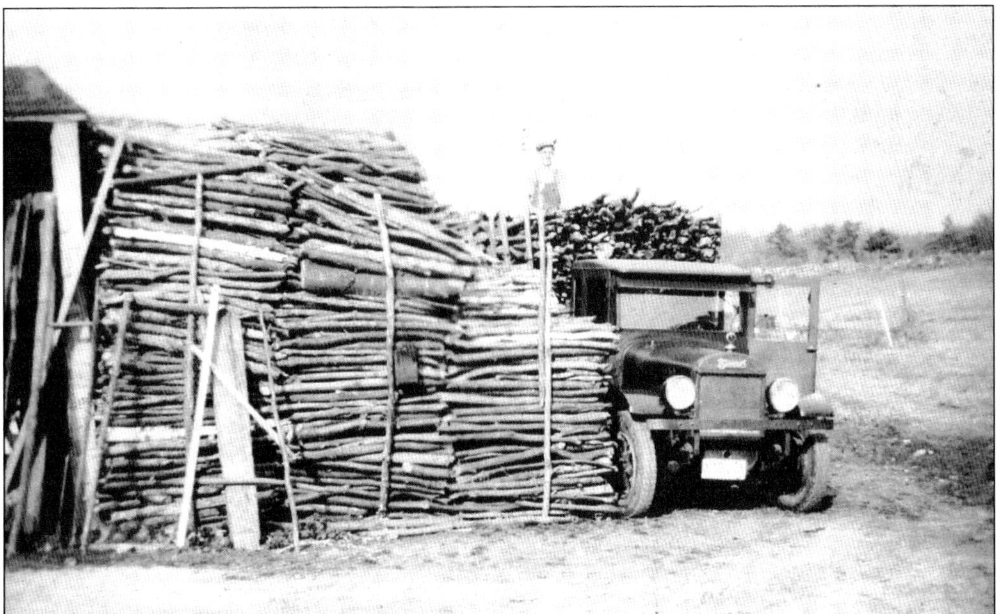

One of the Cesario enterprises was the cutting and sale of wood, which is shown stacked for delivery to customers by truck in 1920. (EC.)

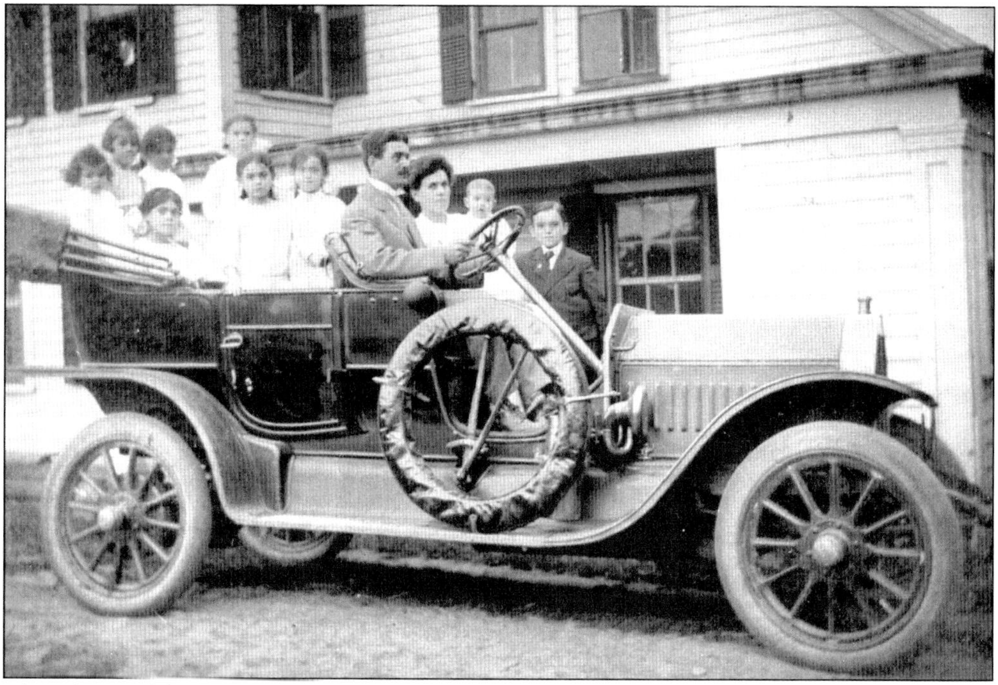

The advent of the automobile presented another form of outing. Family drives in large touring cars became the fashion. Here, a family on Buxton Street fills every space in their automobile, even the running board. Note that the spare tire is carefully wrapped and not mounted.

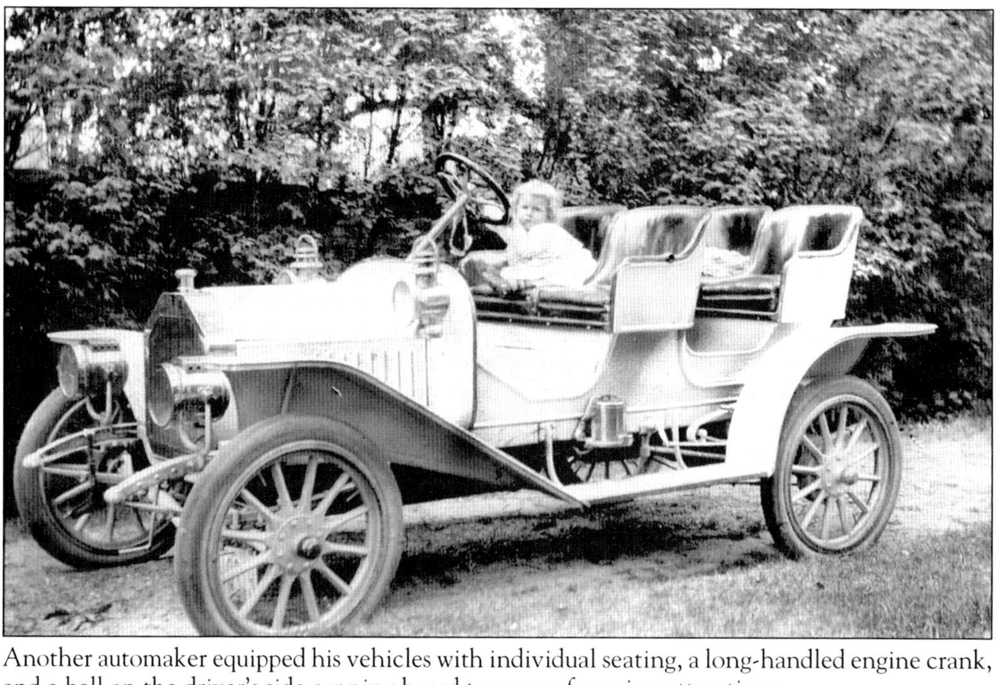

Another automaker equipped his vehicles with individual seating, a long-handled engine crank, and a bell on the driver's side running board to warn of coming attractions.

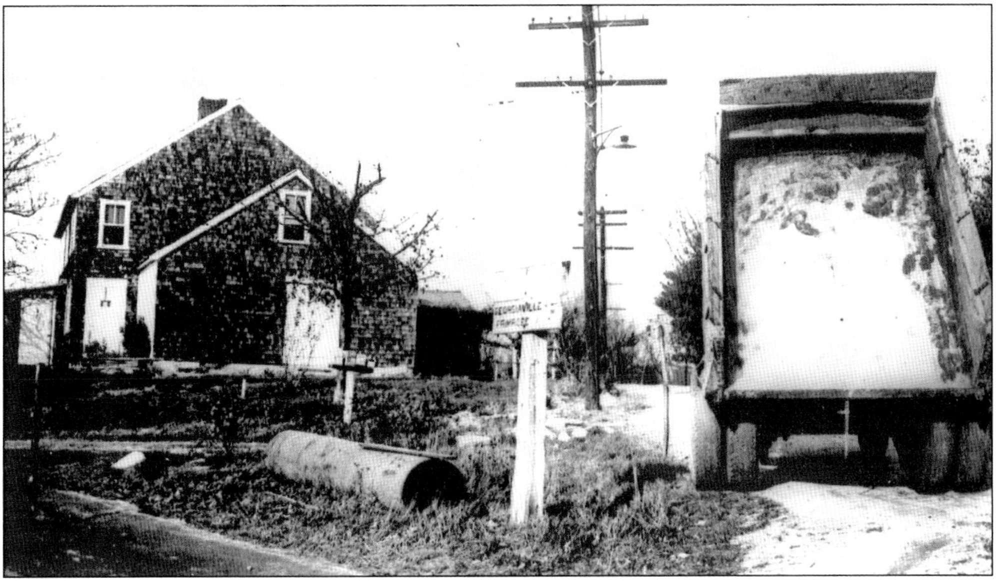

Improvements to the road surfaces were imperative. Here, a dump truck applies base material at the intersection of Grange Road and Providence Pike in the first efforts to pave the pike in 1932. (DPM.)

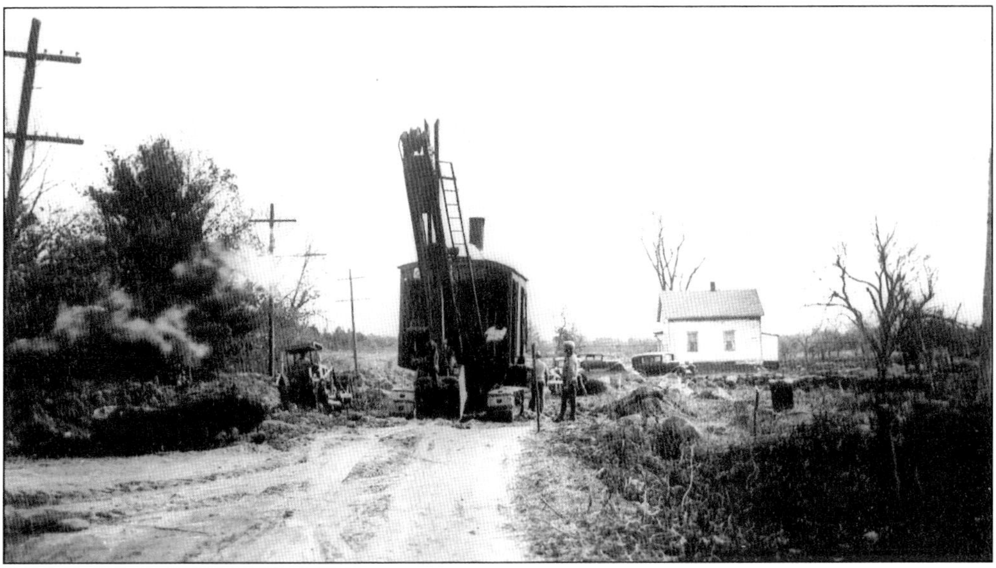

A steam shovel works its way near the Union Chapel just over the Smithfield line, in the process of paving the pike opposite the Harris farm. A toll road, Branch (or Providence) Pike, was constructed in the early 1800s to connect Slatersville with Providence via Douglas Pike. There was a toll booth at the intersection with Douglas Pike. (DPM.)

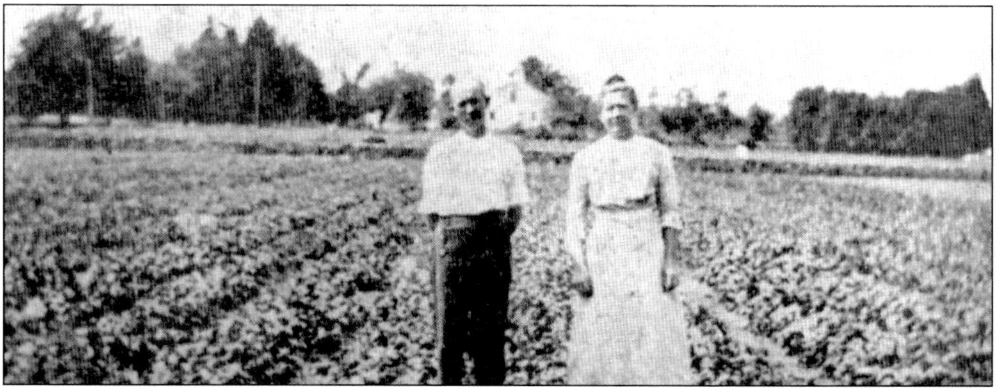

Agriculture still prevailed in parts of the town at midcentury. At Carpenter's Corners, the Carpenter family cultivated a large strawberry patch.

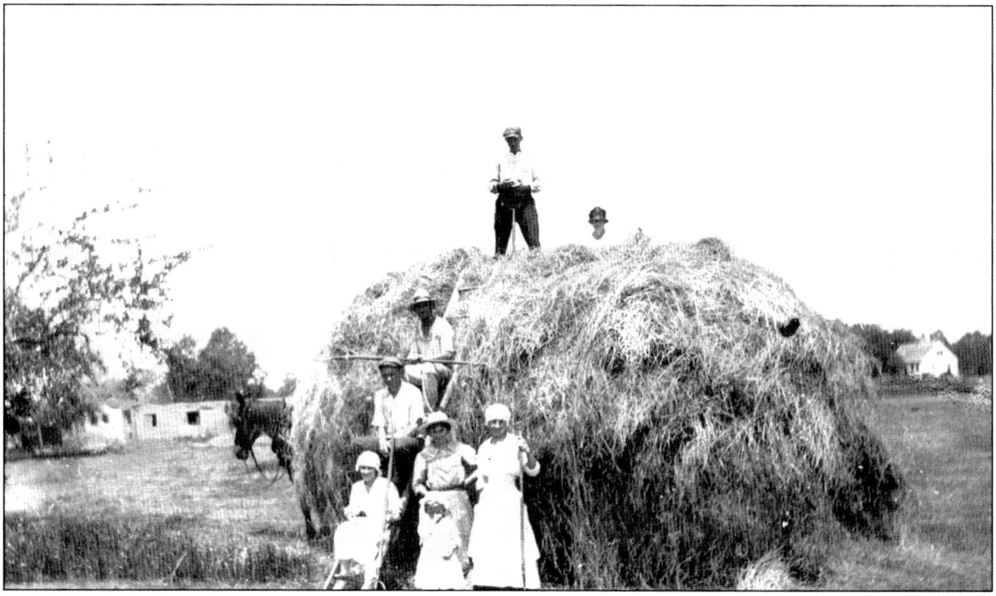

At the Smith farm, haying involved everyone, young and old. The hay wagon was great for climbing and jumping in an era before the baler became common. (GS.)

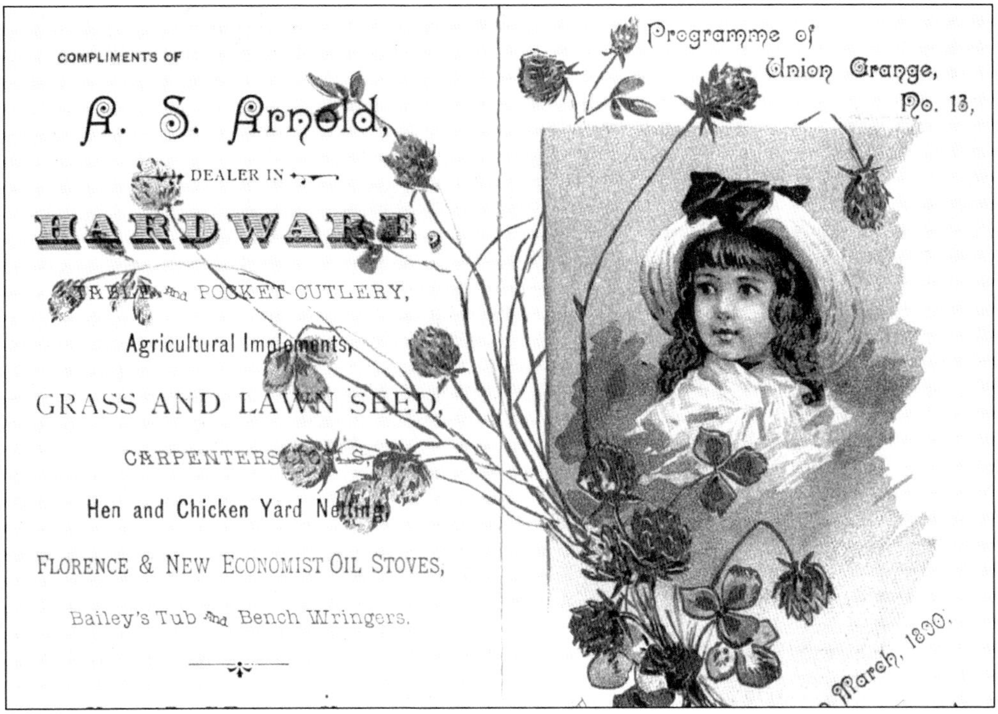

The Grange was a powerful organization in the rural areas, providing up-to-date information on agriculture and home economics, politics, and state and national affairs, as this 1930–1931 program for Union Grange illustrates.

Regular Meetings held the second and fourth Thursdays of each month, at A. O. U. W. Hall, Slatersville, commencing 7:30 p. m.

MASTER, METCALF B. MARSH.
OVERSEER, GEORGE E. TABOR.
LECTURER, EMMA F. ALDRICH.
SECRETARY, CHARLES A. TABOR.
TREASURER, HENRY ALDRICH.

MARCH 13.—Ensilage v. Steamed Fodder. What grains to be fed.

MARCH 27.—Which pays best: Special or Mixed Farming?

Grange Quarterly.

APRIL 10.—Bird Protection. Trespassers' law talks.

APRIL 24.—Potatoes. Best varieties to plant.

MAY 8.—Best Methods of Cultivating Corn.

MAY 22.—Domestic Partnership. Law Talks.

JUNE 12.—Children's Evening.

JUNE 26.—Matron's Meeting. Grange Quarterly.

JULY 24.—Social Life Among the Farmers.

AUG. 14.—How can the home be made more attractive for the rising sons and daughters.

AUG. 28.—Festival of Pomona, Floras and Ceres.

SEPT. 11.—Quotations and selections from Browning.

SEPT. 25.—How can the Grange be made made more useful and elevating.

Grange Quarterly.

OCT. 9.—Little Leaks on the Farm and in the Household.

OCT. 23.—Gentlemen's Meeting.

NOV. 13.---Immigration; its effects socially, morally, and financially.

NOV. 27.---Quotations and Selections from Favorite Authors.

Roll Call. Grange Quarterly.

DEC. 11.---Economical Production of Milk.

DEC. 25.---Election of Officers.

At each meeting in connection with the above, will be music, readings and recitations. Some specialities have been arranged.

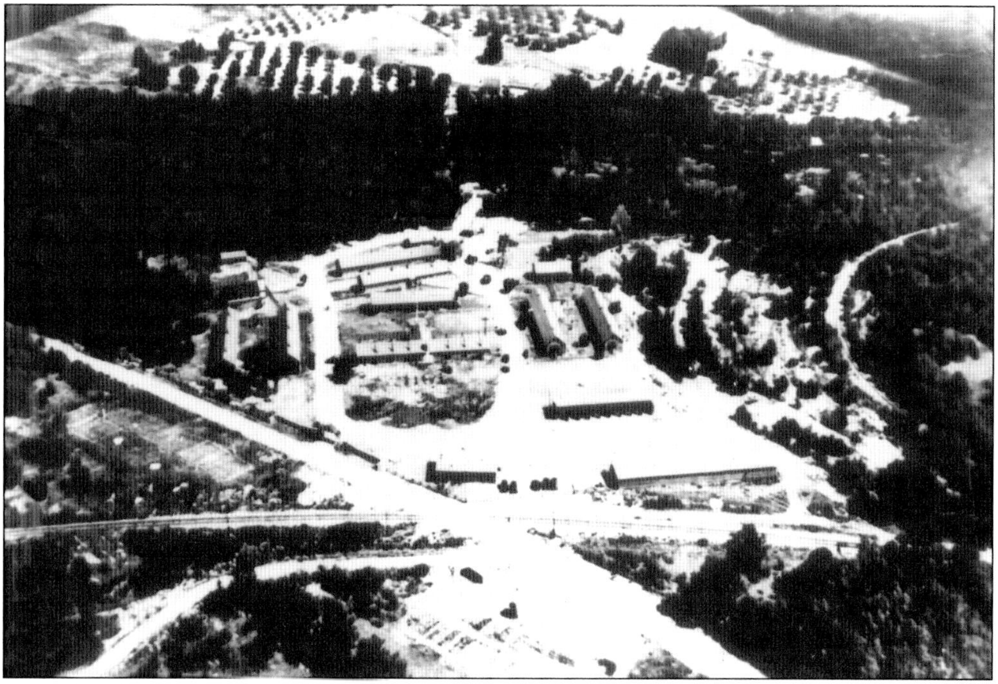

Pres. Franklin Roosevelt's domestic programs of the 1930s were represented in town by the Civilian Conservation Corps, which maintained a large camp on the hill between Primrose Pond and Black Plain Road. The dormitories and common buildings are shown in this aerial view. Primrose Pond and the Cesario orchards are in the background. (EC.)

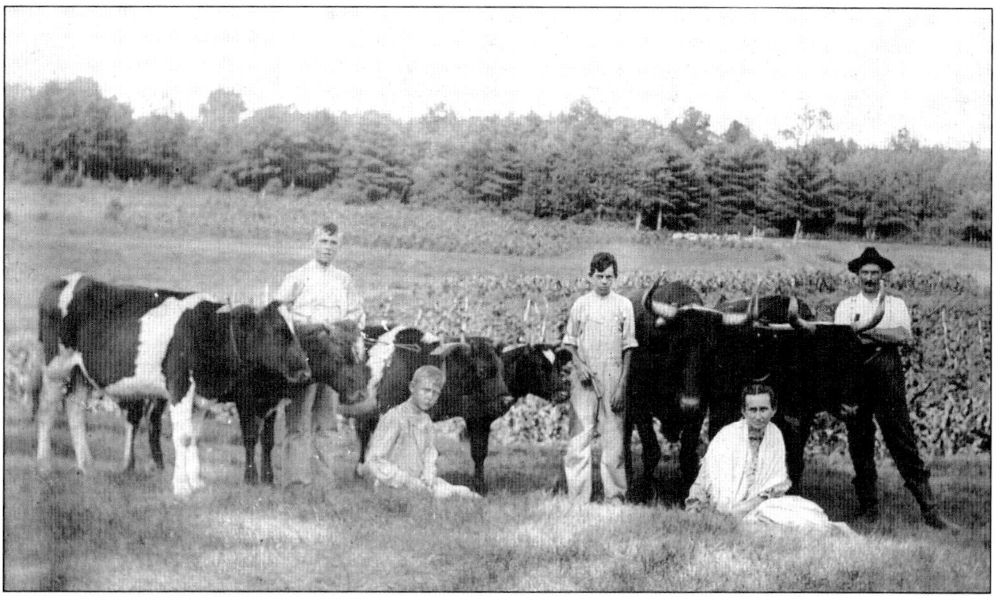

Cows and oxen still had their places on the farms.

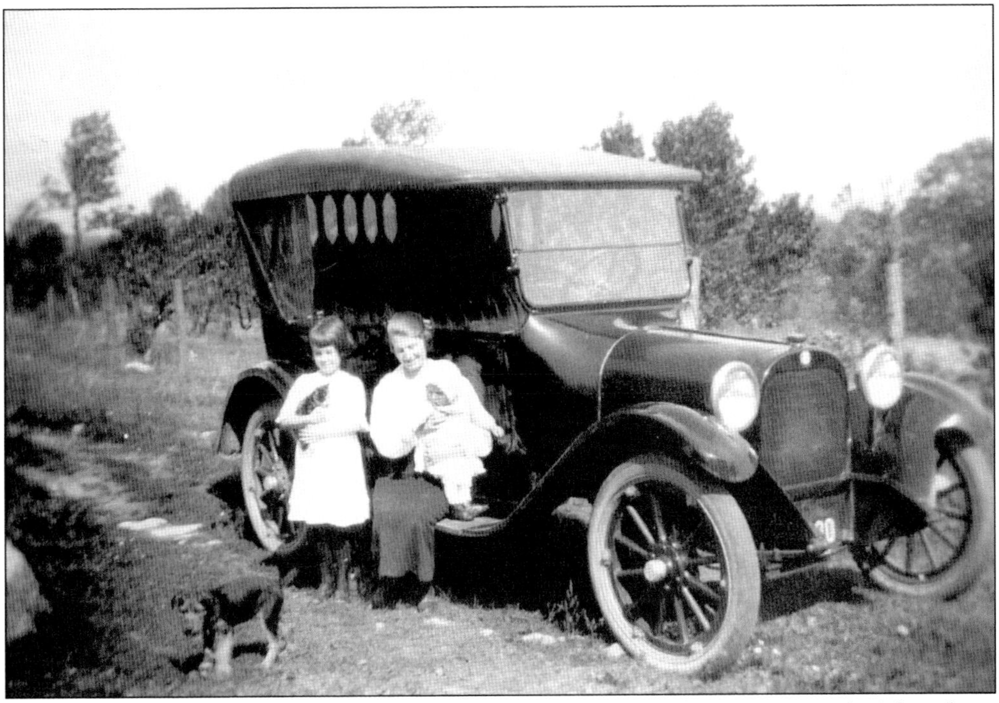

Members of the Titherington family pose by the family car in the 1920s, proud of the tilting windshield and the handsome wooden wheel spokes. (MT.)

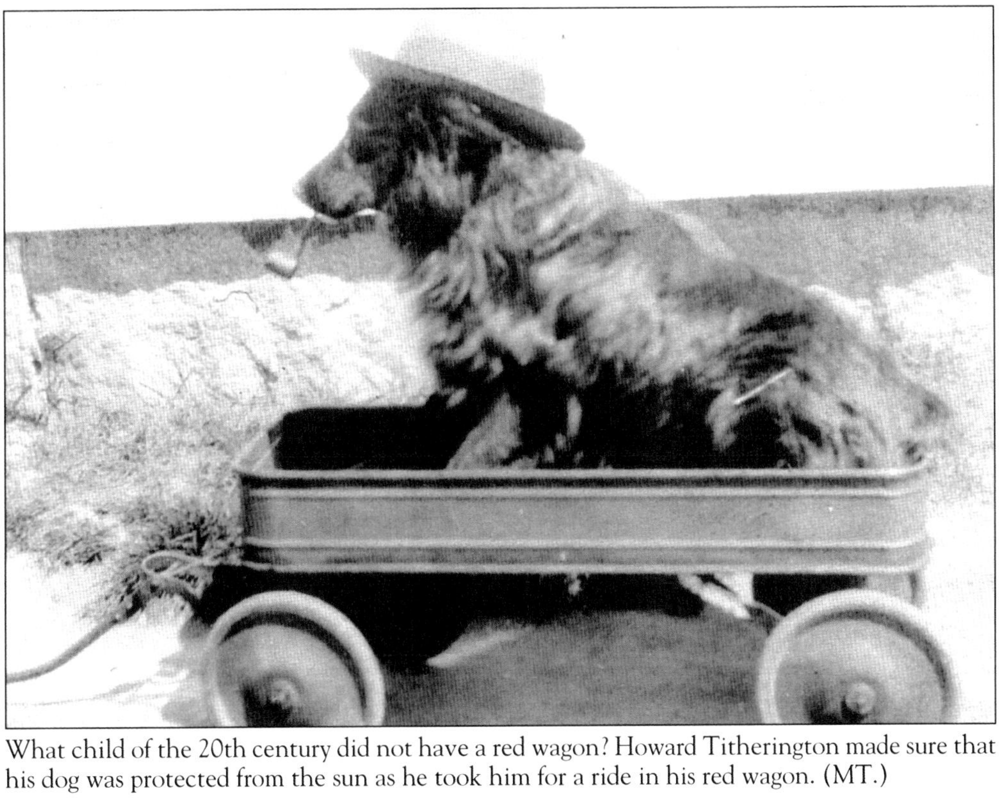

What child of the 20th century did not have a red wagon? Howard Titherington made sure that his dog was protected from the sun as he took him for a ride in his red wagon. (MT.)

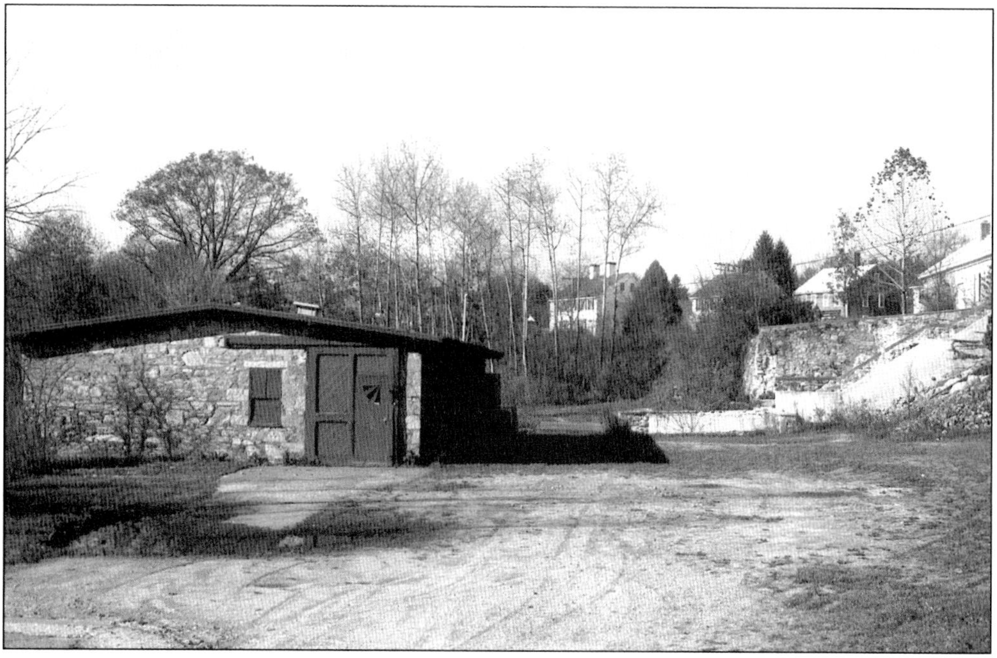

One of the few buildings remaining after the Western Mills were demolished c. 1900 is the stone mill shed along the trench, still in use today.

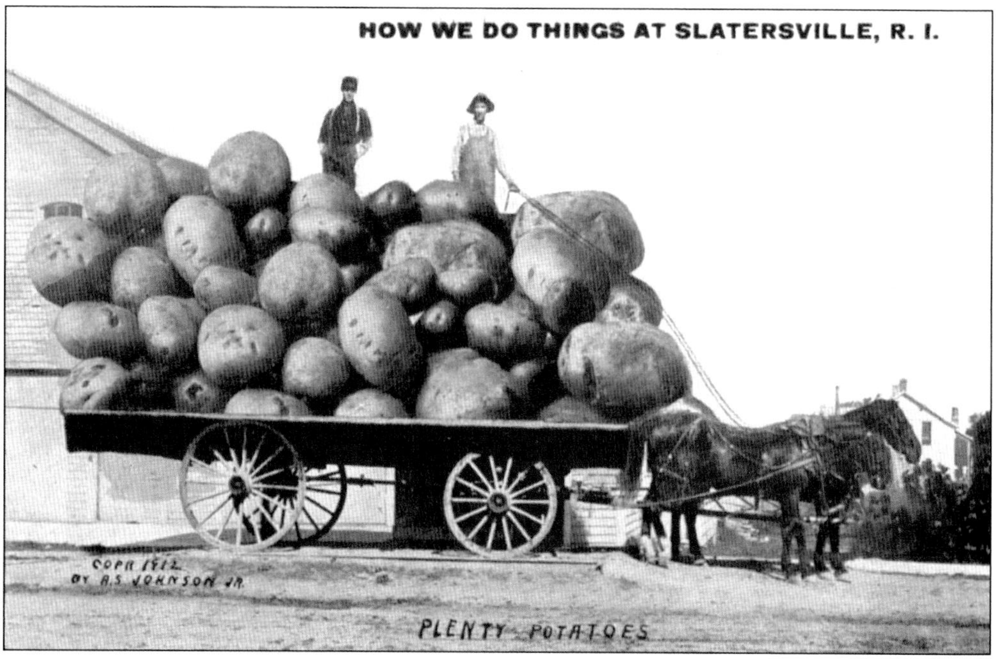

For the smallest state in the nation, this is a lot of potatoes. (RA.)

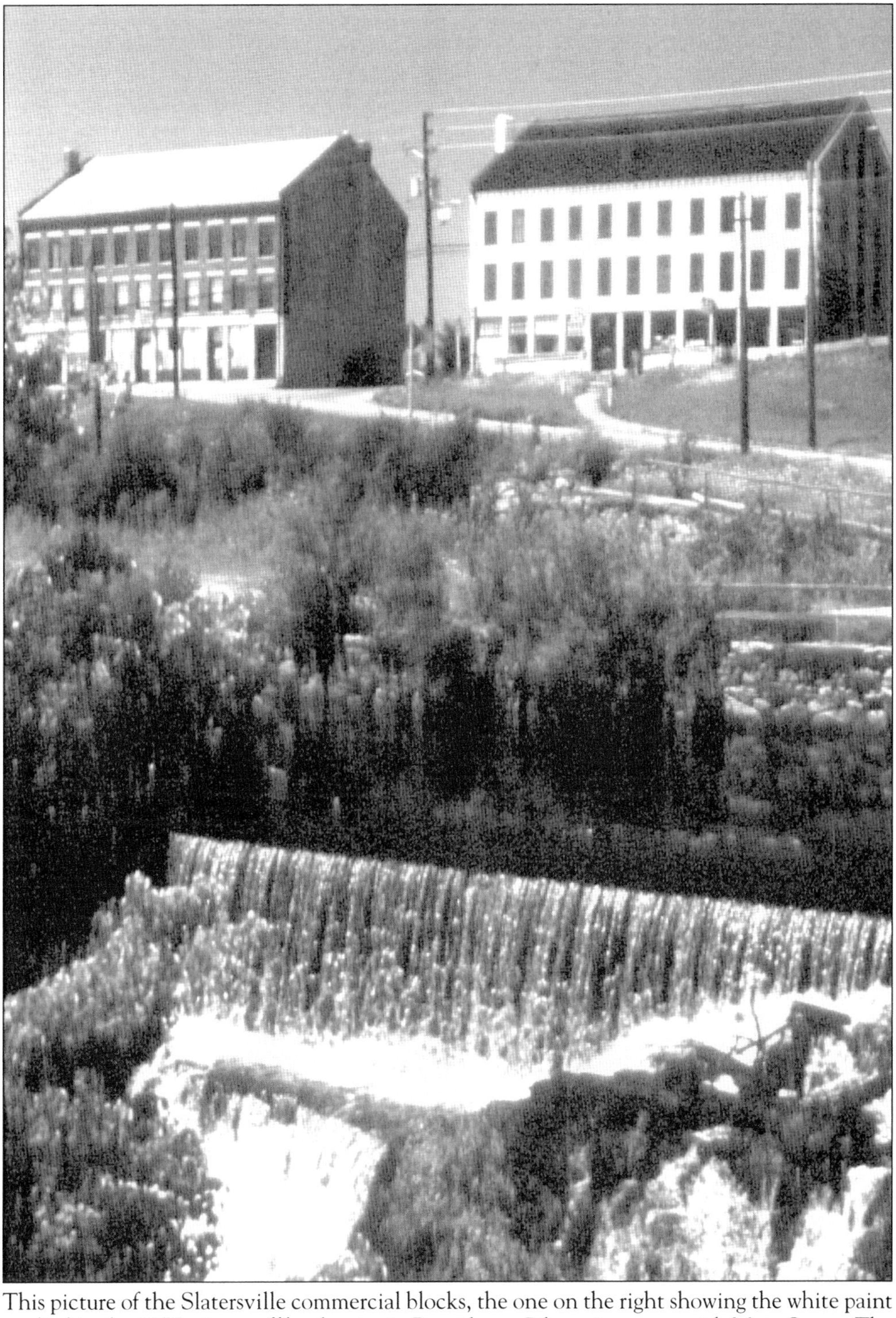

This picture of the Slatersville commercial blocks, the one on the right showing the white paint applied in the 1970s, is set off by the rise in Providence Pike as it merges with Main Street. The falls from the trench, no longer spanned by the wooden footbridge or used for power, splash on the rocks below. (WAN.)

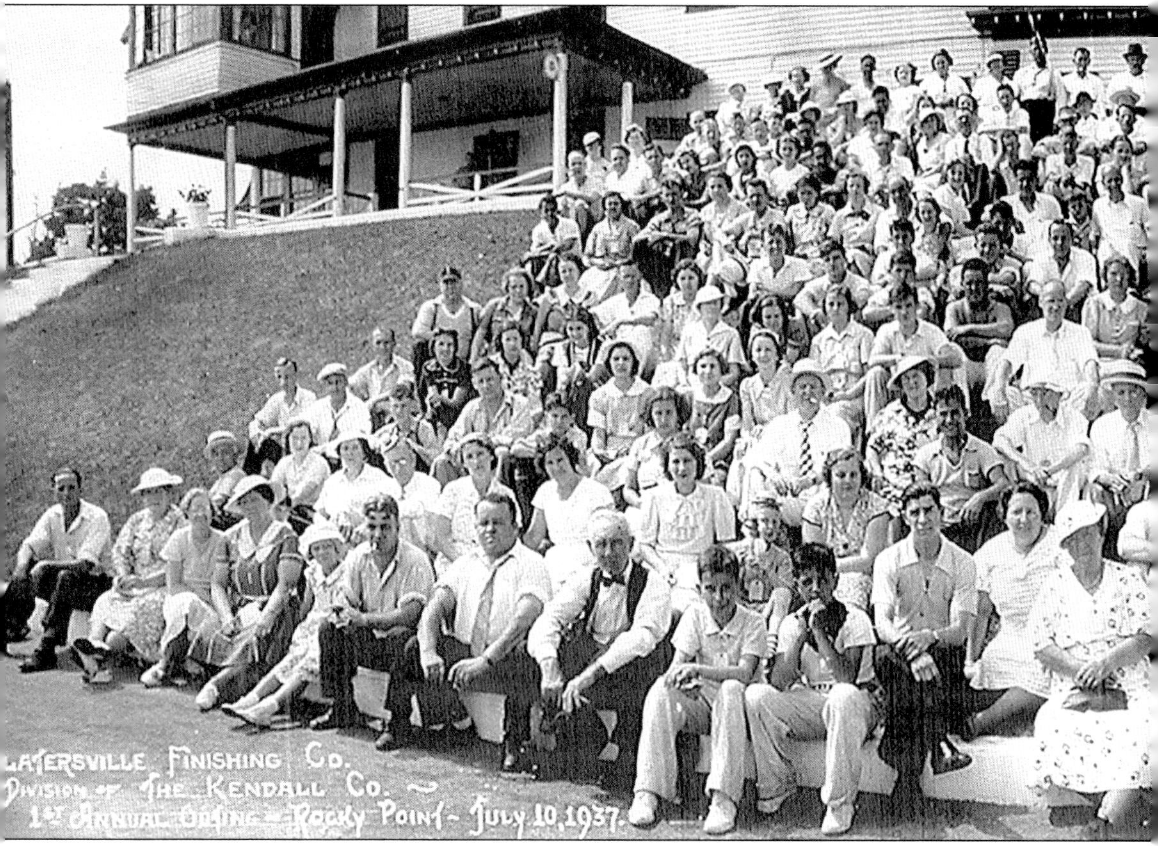

The first annual outing of the Slatersville Finishing Company employees was celebrated at

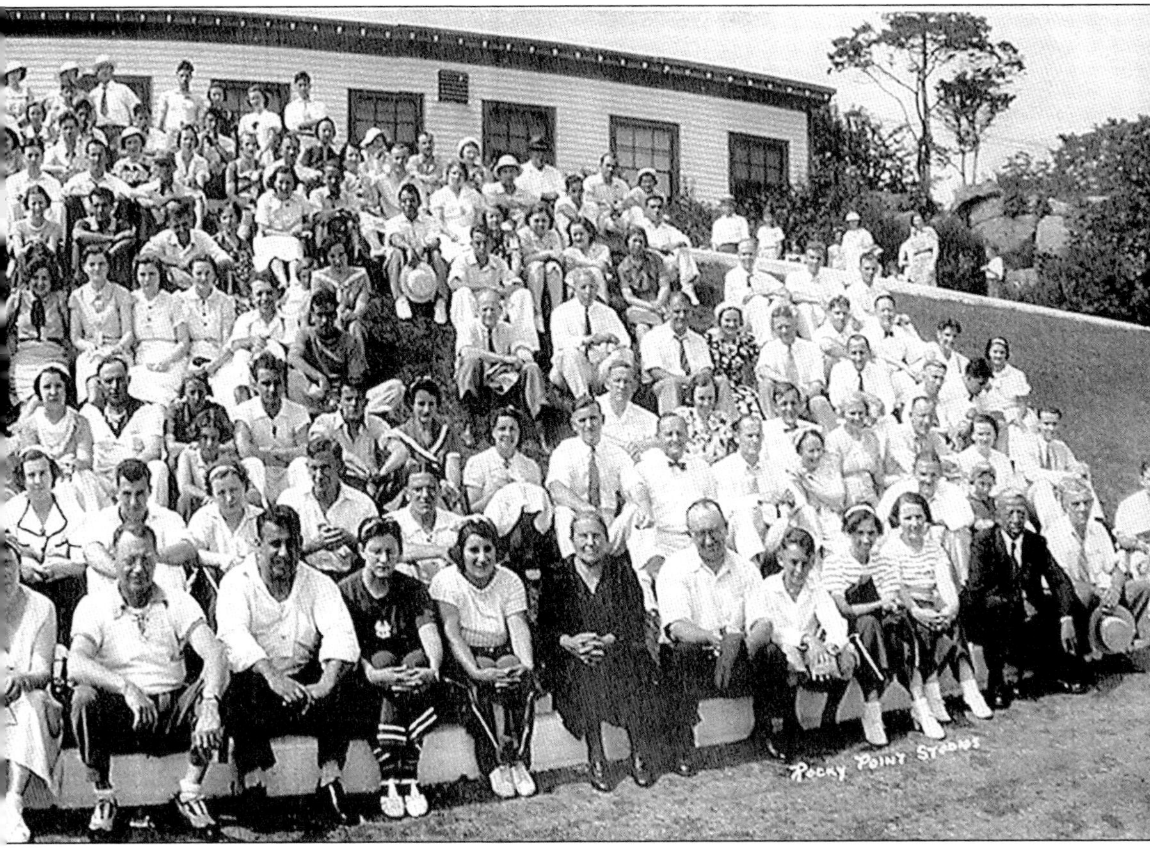

Rocky Point, where this group photograph was taken on July 10, 1937.

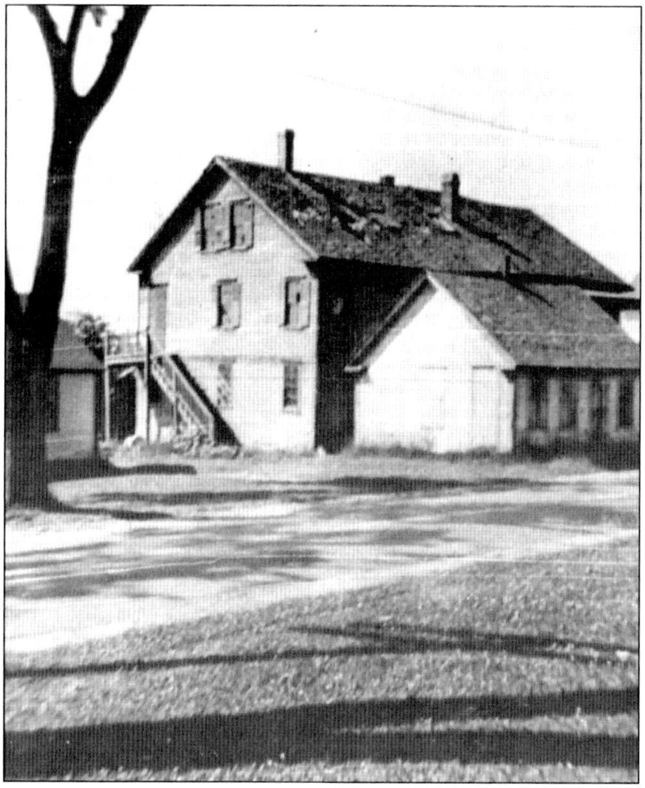

West of the Slatersville Library, near where the post office is today, stood the blacksmith shop shown here. Later, it was converted to an automotive repair business before being demolished.

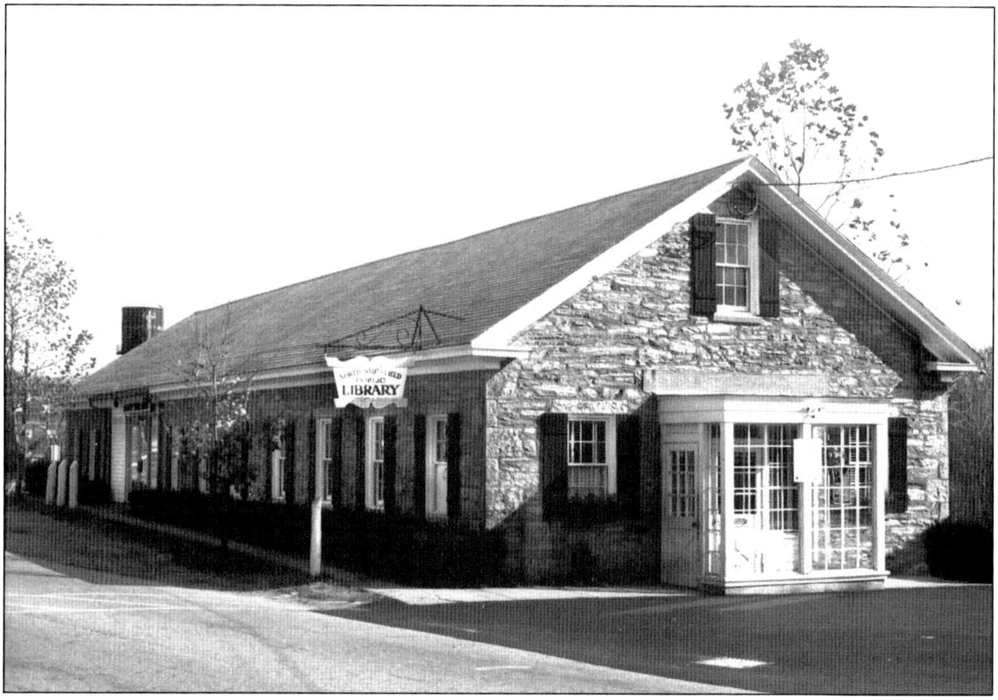

Like the mill shed shown on page 104, the present Slatersville Library is a relic of the Western Mills. Refurbished and later enlarged, it has enhanced Main Street for decades.

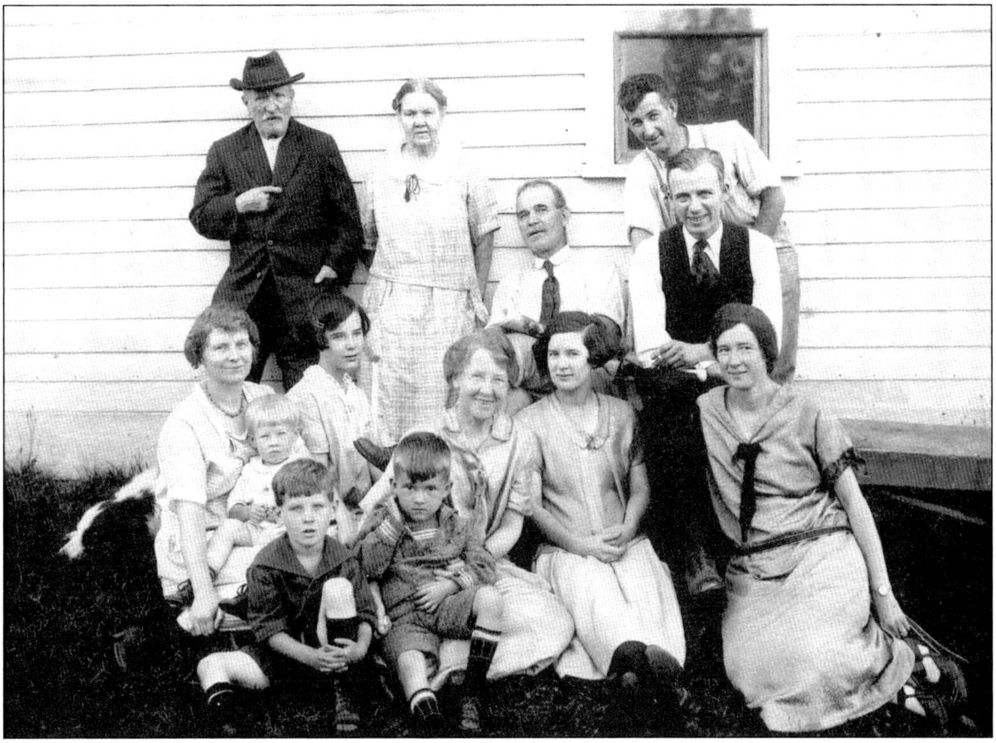

This gathering of the Burnside and Titherington families took place probably *c.* 1930. (MT.)

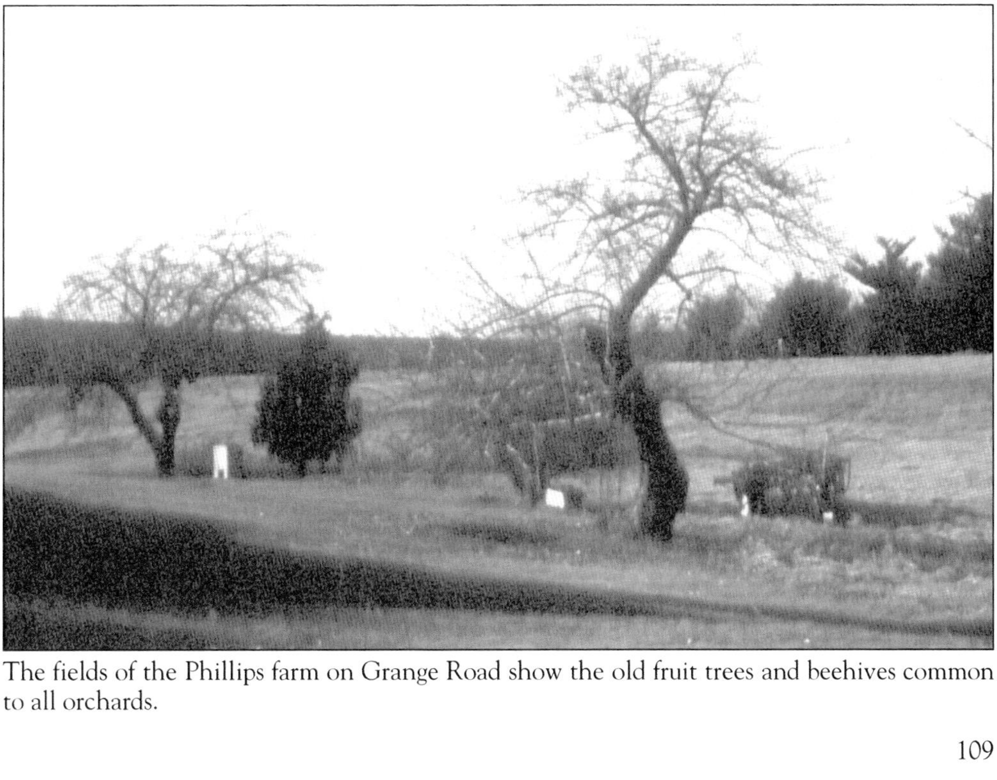

The fields of the Phillips farm on Grange Road show the old fruit trees and beehives common to all orchards.

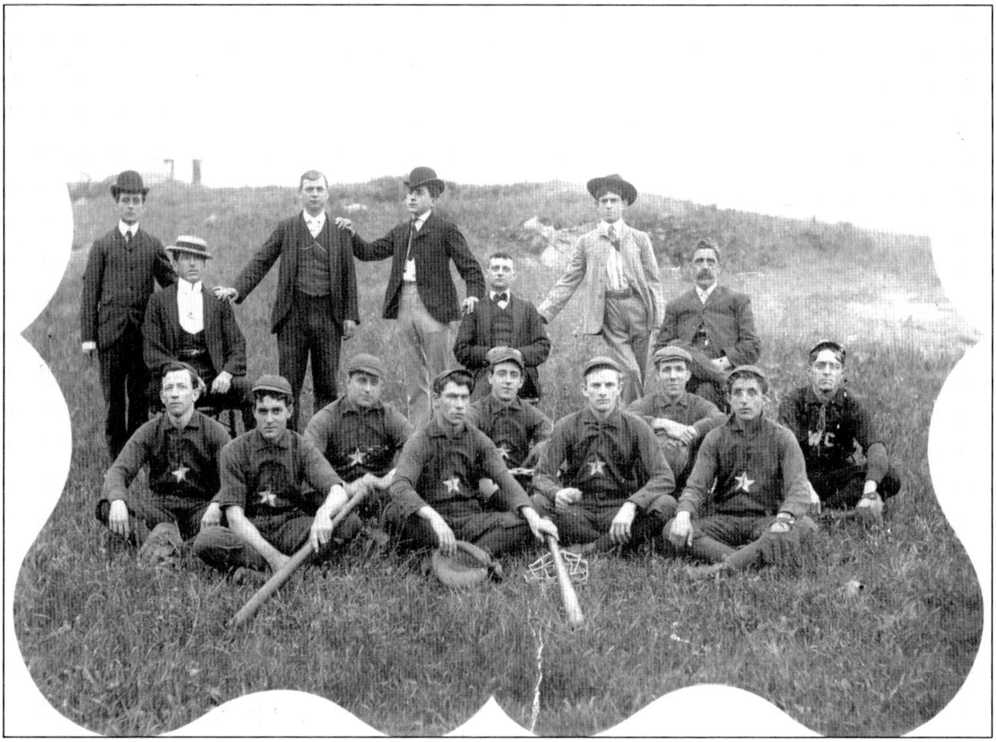

Organized athletics always involved some groups of town youth throughout the 20th century. This baseball team, complete with the star symbol on their uniforms, is an early example of this trend. (EA.)

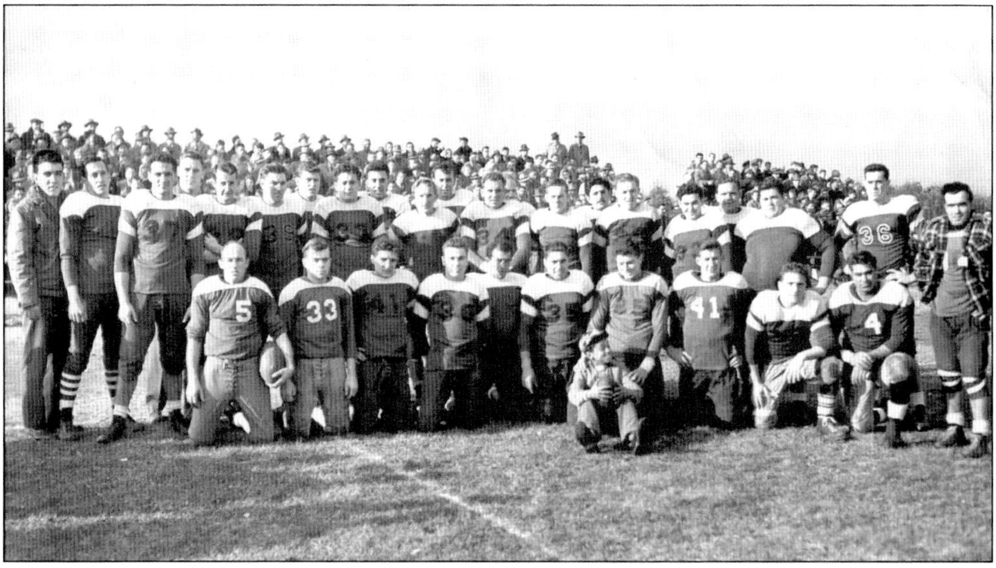

The Slatersville Red Raiders football team proved themselves capable of attracting a large crowd of spectators when they played at Woonsocket's Barry Field in the 1930s and 1940s. (EA.)

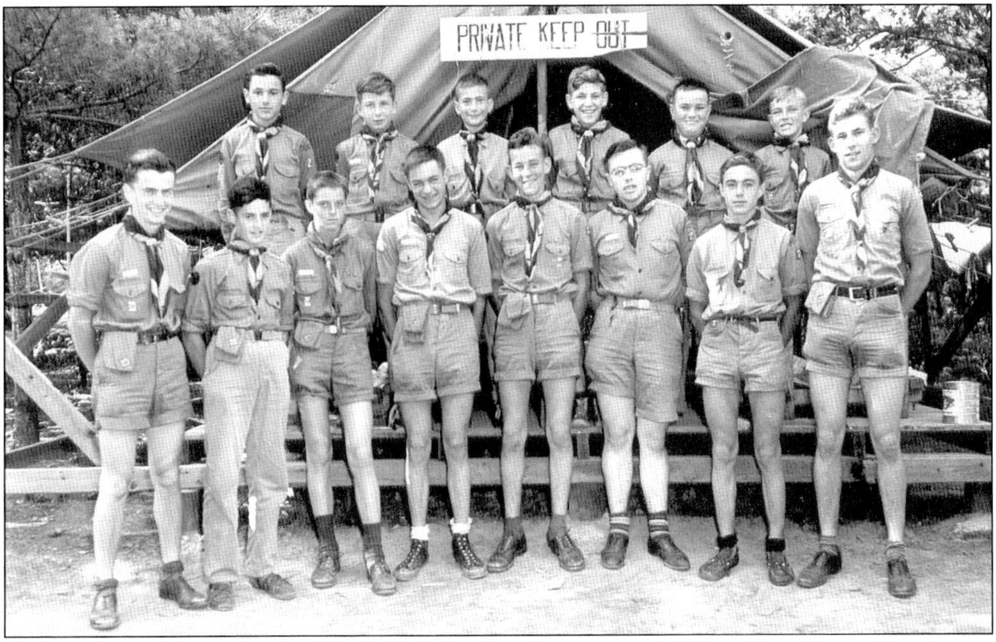

Boy Scout Troop 2, sponsored by St. John's Church, poses in 1948 at Tent Camp Manchosie, Camp Yawgoo, Rockville. From left to right are the following: (front row) J. McGarrigle, H. Poudrier, E. Poznanski, S. Adams, C. Duffy, R. Roy, R. Marceau, and W. Dumais (scoutmaster); (back row) L. Brodeur, R. Anderson, T. Roberts, M. Dandeneau, C. Robinson, and R. Duffy. (WD.)

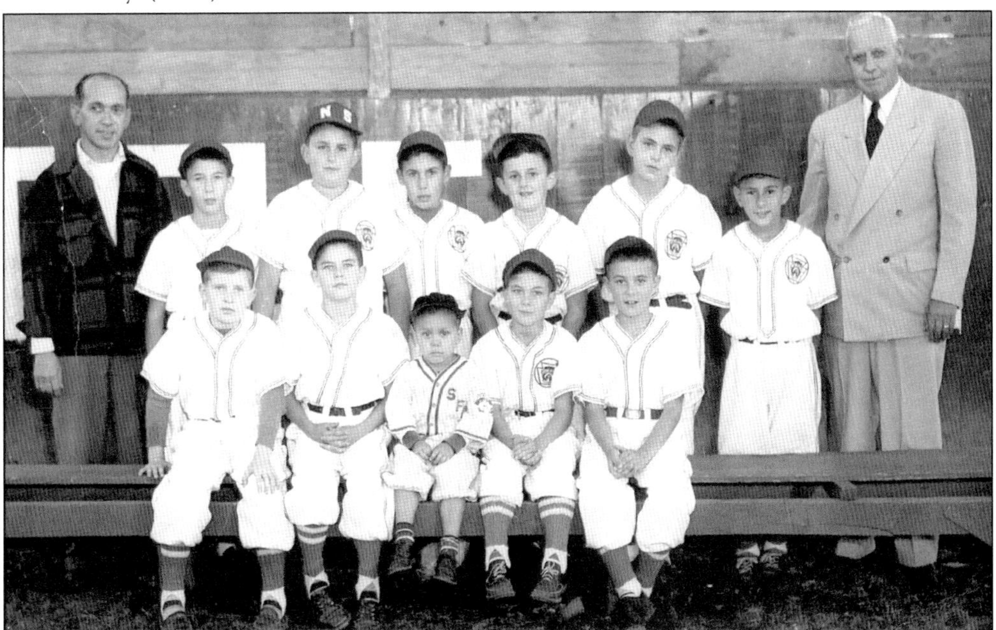

The first Little League in town, sponsored by the Slatersville Finishing Company, is shown in this 1950s photograph. From left to right are the following: (front row) T. Lemieux, ? Charpentier, A. DeVaudreuil, ? Charpentier, D. Pacheco; (back row) coach ? Costa, ? Charpentier, E. Allard, B. Dupointe, E. Lema, D. Hart, R. Costa, and unidentified. (EA.)

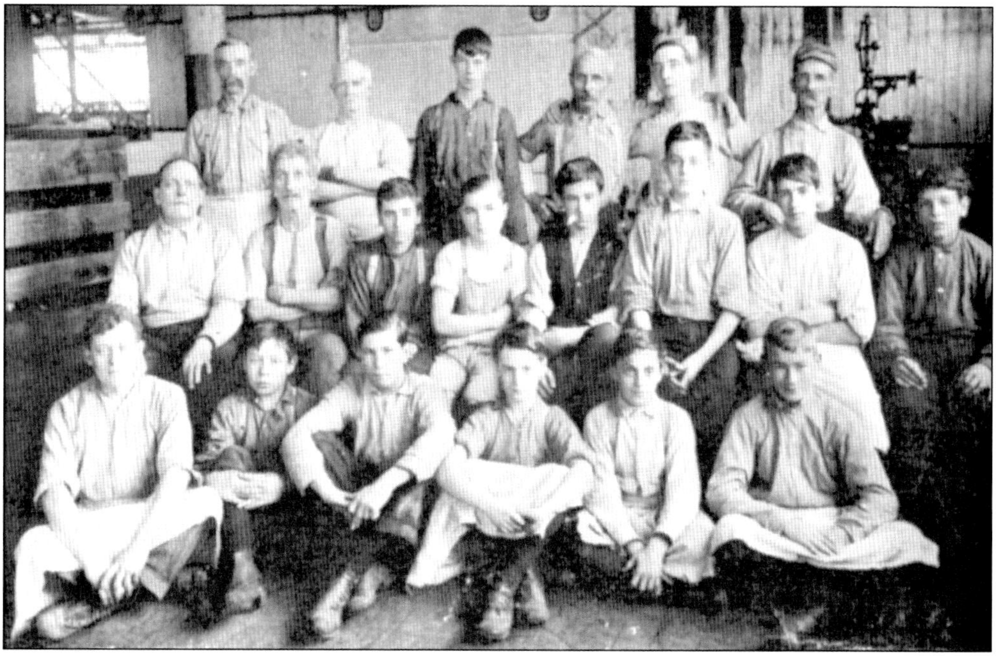

A group of youthful workers at the Slatersville Finishing Company poses for an undated photograph. (TM.)

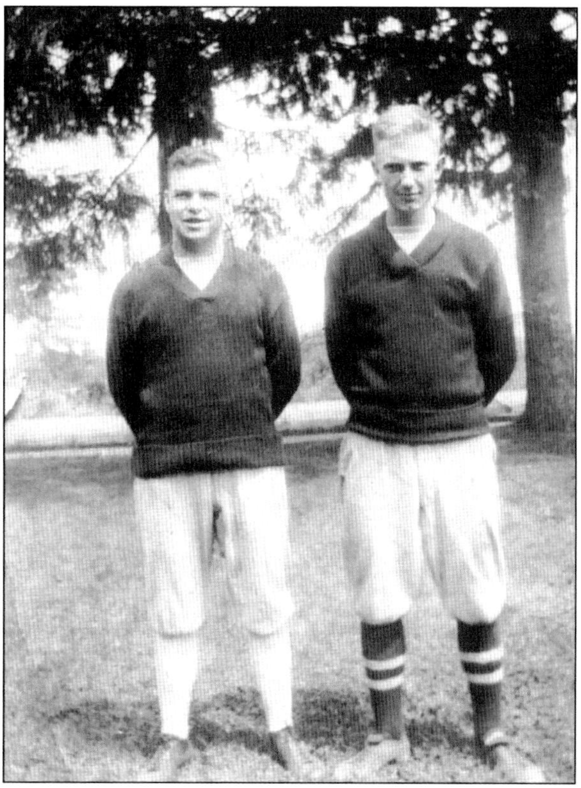

Harris Quinley (left) and Ellery Christiansen of the Slatersville baseball team of 1929 show off their sweaters and knickers. (TM.)

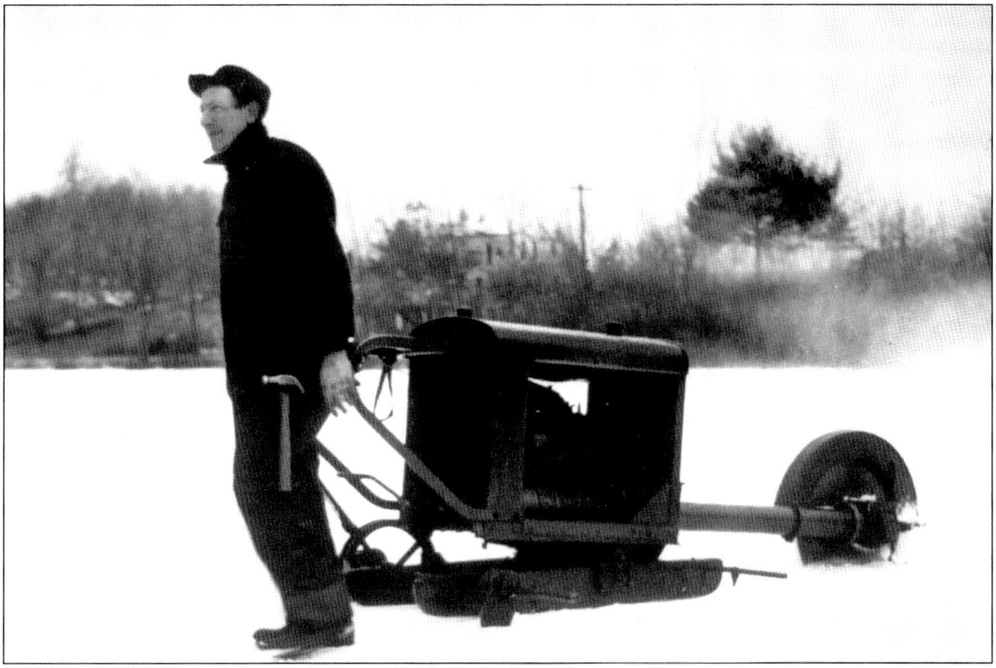

Before the electric refrigerator became part of the family home, ice was the common means of keeping food fresh. Along the west side of Primrose Pond was an icehouse, where ice was stored in the winter to be removed as customers needed it throughout the year. In these scenes from 1946, a mechanical ice cutter scores the ice on the pond (above), and a long pole is being used to move ice floes (below). Snow is piled high along the shores of the pond. (GS.)

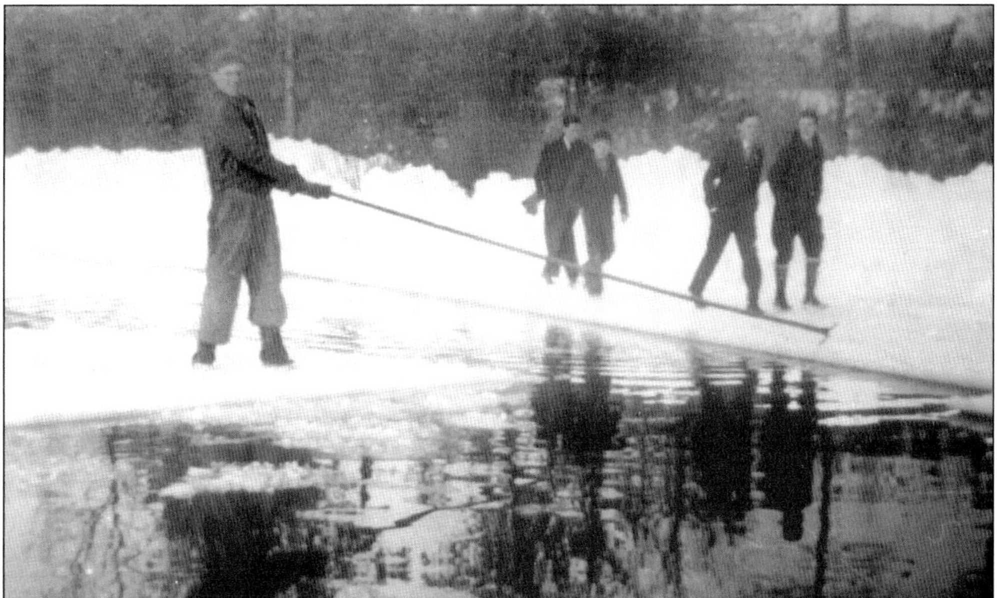

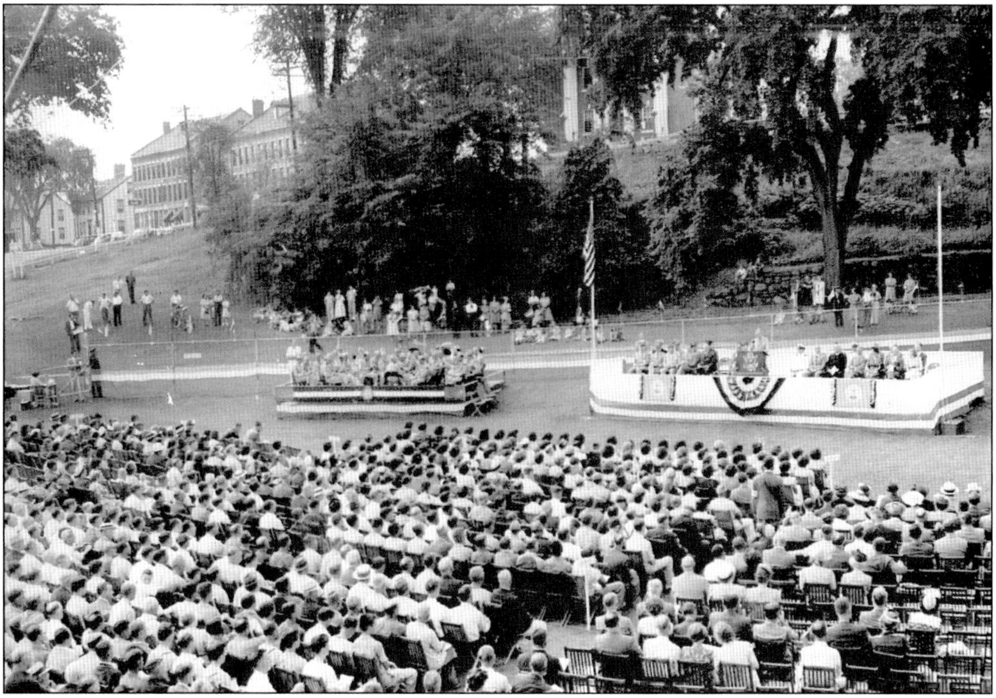

As in World War I, the mills in Slatersville were intensely involved in textile production for the World War II effort, earning the coveted E for excellence. The speakers are on the platform, and the audience is in place for ceremonies in front of the mill (above), while in another location an audience awaits (below).

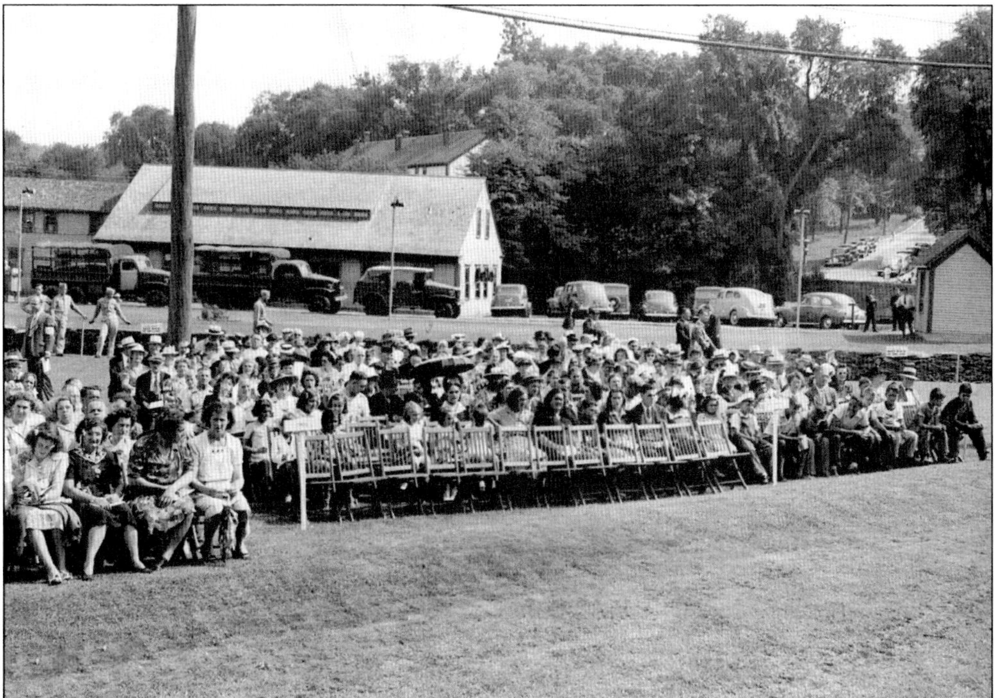

The Mal Hallett Orchestra toured New England in the 1930s, their usual one-nighters featuring swing music a decade before the big bands. Hallett was a six-foot-six-inch musician trained at the Boston Conservatory. His bands at one time or another included Gene Krupa on drums, Jack Teagarden on trombone, and Frankie Carle on piano, among others. Hallett's great height, wavy hair, waxed moustache, and superb musicianship contributed to his popularity.

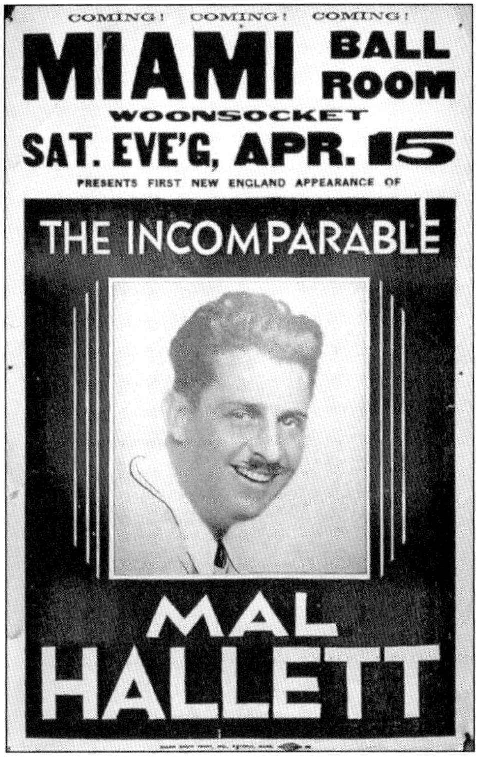

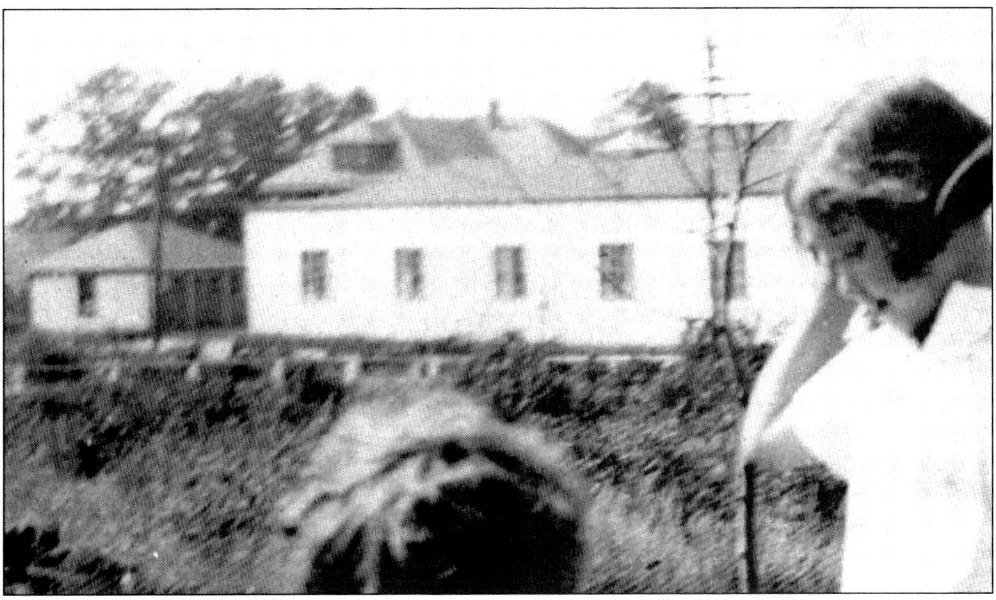

The Miami Ballroom, located at the corner of Lamoureaux Boulevard and Greenville Road, was well known for attracting smooth dance music. In use until midcentury, the building collapsed under the weight of rain-drenched heavy snow on the roof. The ballroom's outline can be seen on the lawn across from the little store.

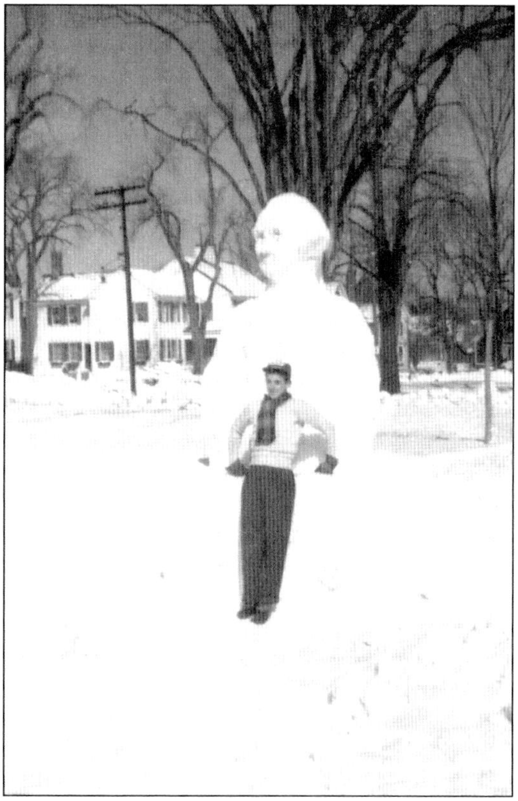

A young Tom Mundy poses on Slatersville Common in front of his snow sculpture of George Washington after a plentiful snowfall in 1937. (TM.)

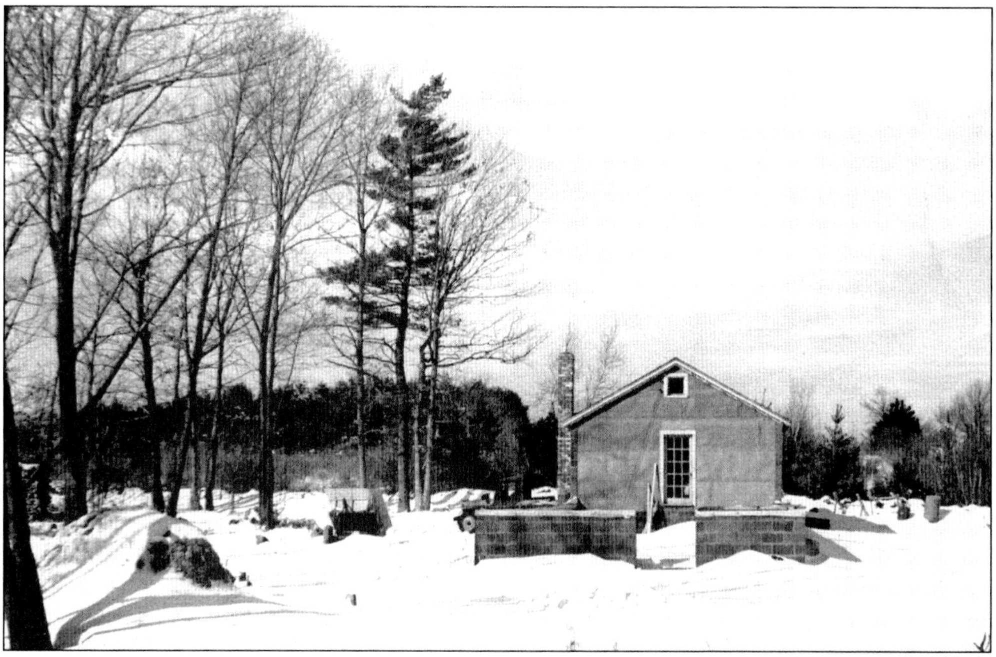

When he returned from World War II, Tom Mundy began his greenhouse in 1946 with this modest building. He used the frame and other components from a Massachusetts greenhouse that he took apart and reassembled on the Slatersville site. (TM.)

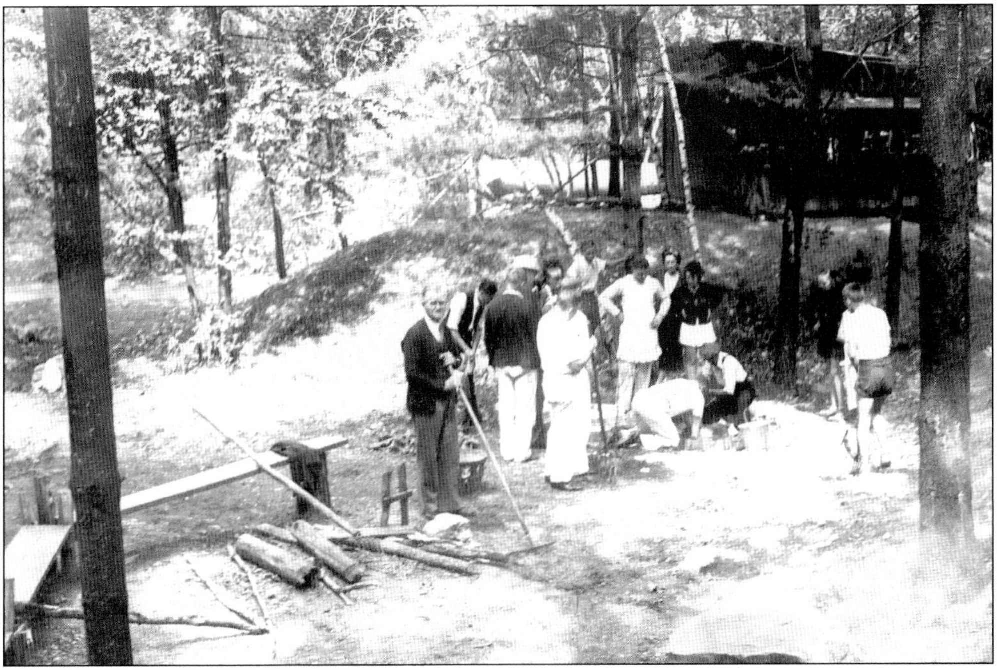

In the late 1920s, Camp Toonerville was established by the Eastman family of the Congregational church. Located along the shores of the Lower Reservoir, it functioned as a day camp for the youth of Slatersville, offering activities and games, swimming, and campfires. During the summer, Rev. Harvey M. Eastman and his wife lived in a cabin at the camp, providing residential supervision. Adults and families also enjoyed good times at the campground until shortly after World War II. (TM.)

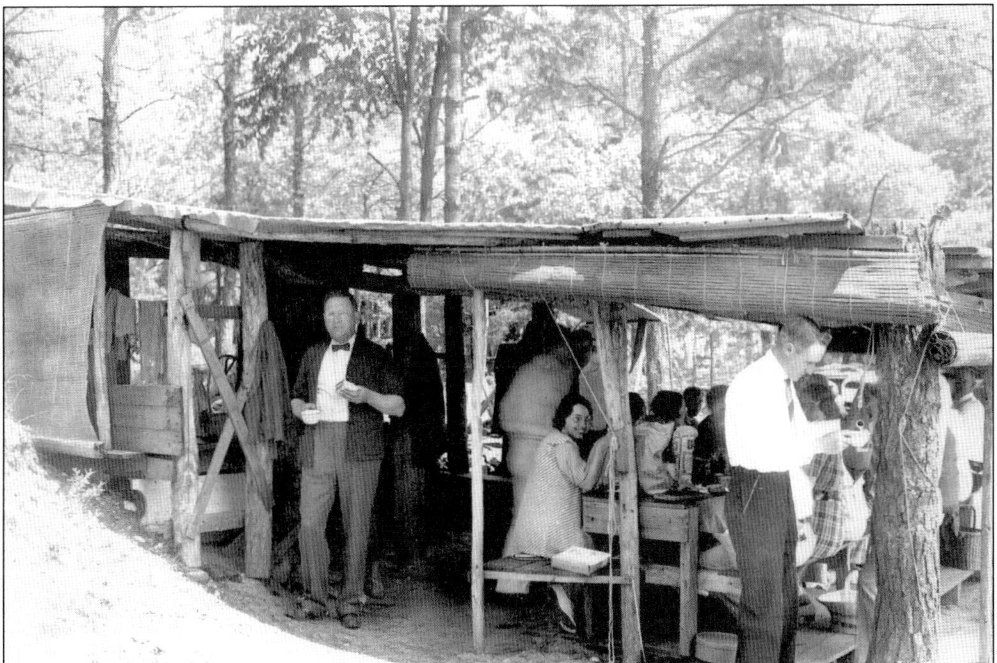

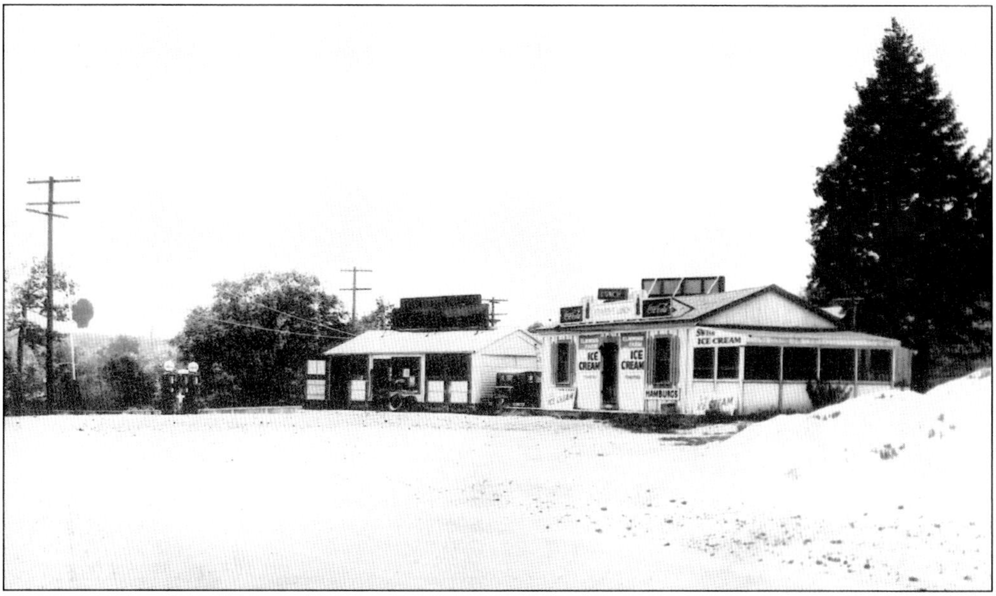

Kennedy's Lunch and the adjacent gas station were longtime fixtures at the corner of Great Road and St. Paul Street. It still serves customers from before dawn to early afternoon. (SR.)

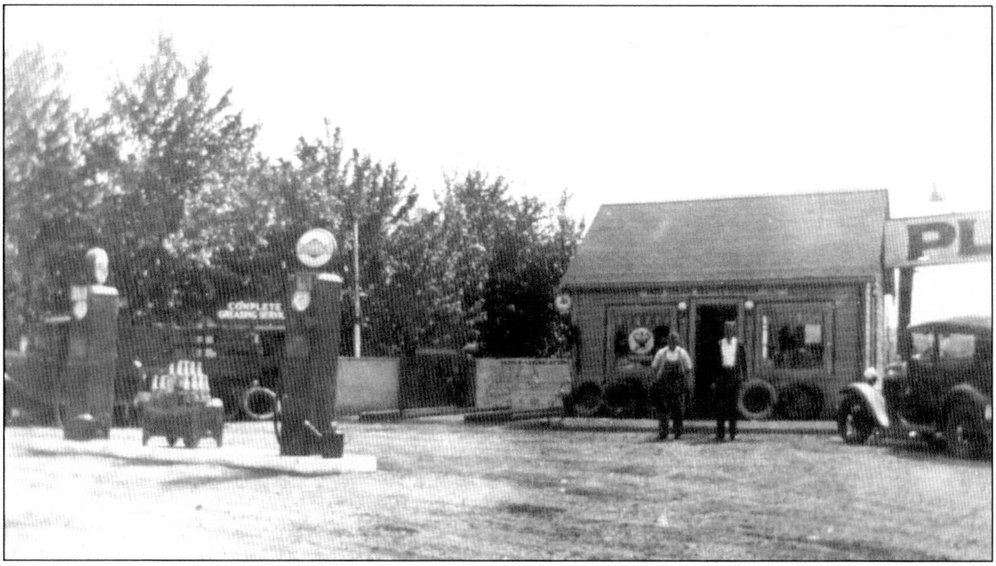

The Park Square service station opposite Park Avenue was operated by "Pop" Legare and his family for many years. Shown here c. 1930, the building still remains behind the newer Mobil station.

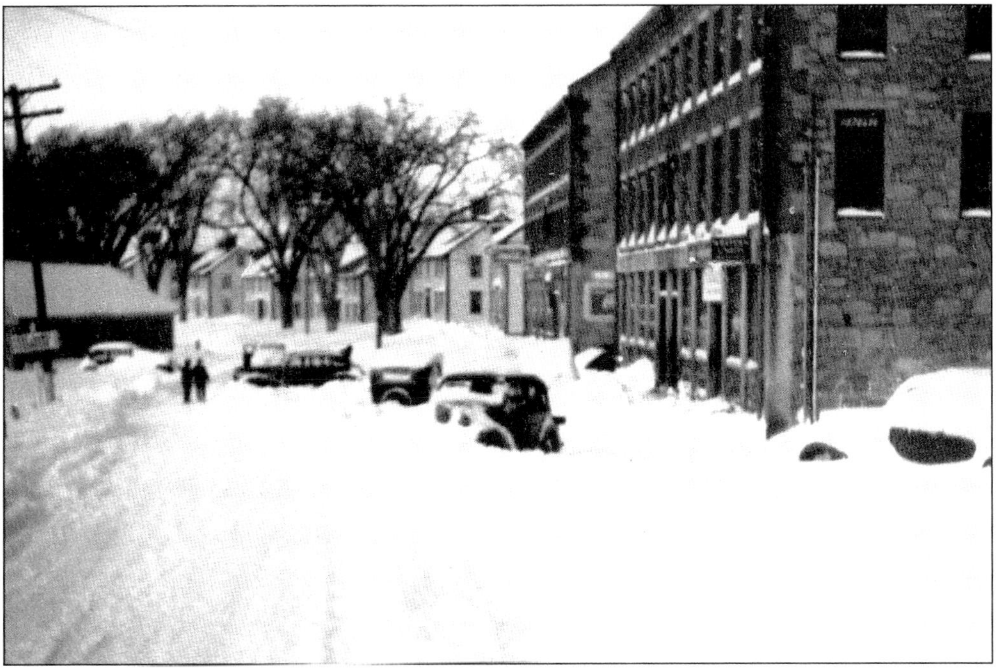

Heavy snow in 1936 buried cars and made traffic impossible on Main Street in Slatersville. (LW.)

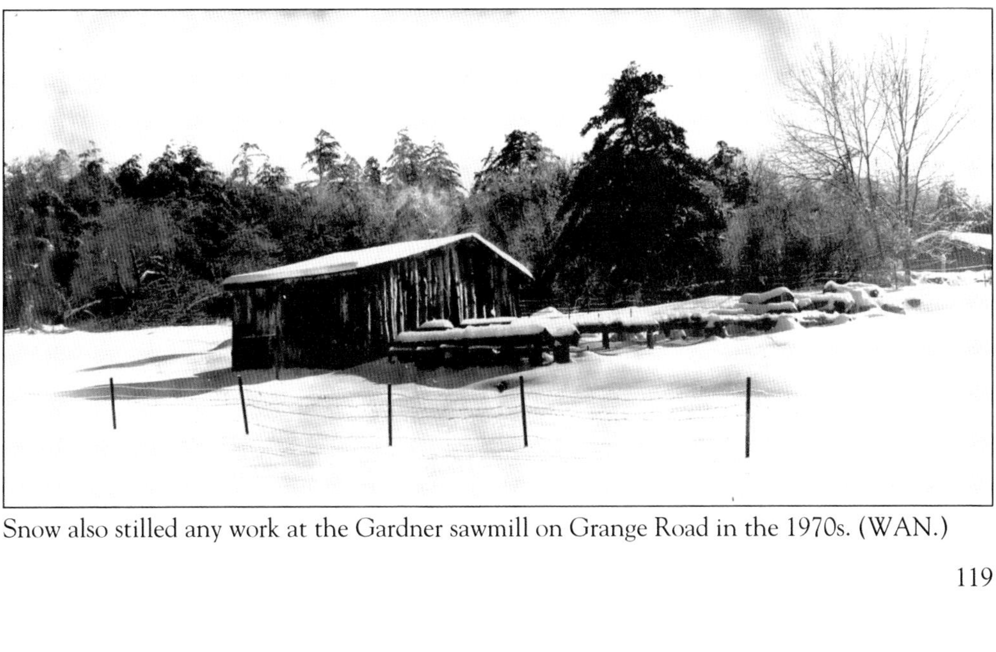

Snow also stilled any work at the Gardner sawmill on Grange Road in the 1970s. (WAN.)

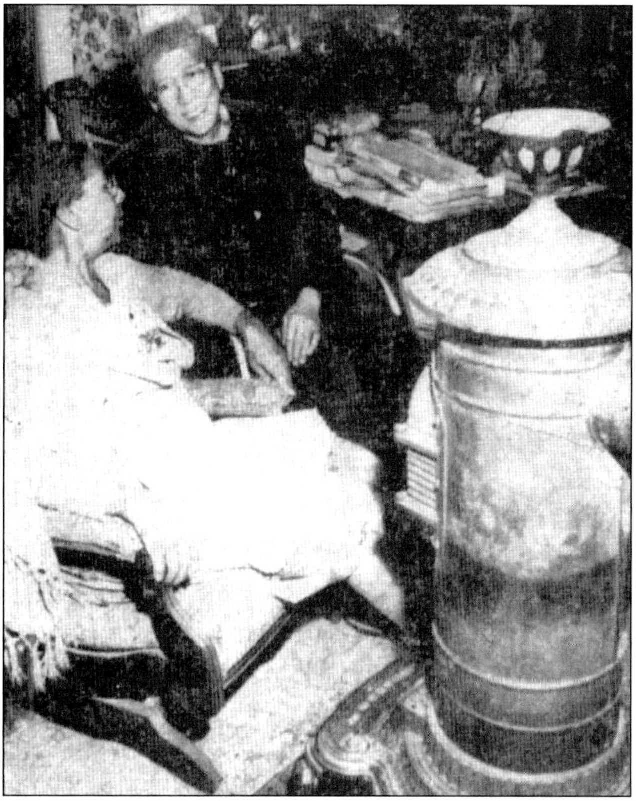

Ethel Lewis (left) and Rebekah Blackstone, the Blackstone sisters, whose great-great-grandfather was James Brayton, are shown in this 1958 photograph, taken in the Brayton house. They never had electricity or central heat, relying on kerosene lamps for light and a wood and coal stove for heating and cooking. They drew and carried water from their well, and when that went dry on occasion, they carried it from neighbors' wells across Great Road, which was then on a level with the doorway of the house.

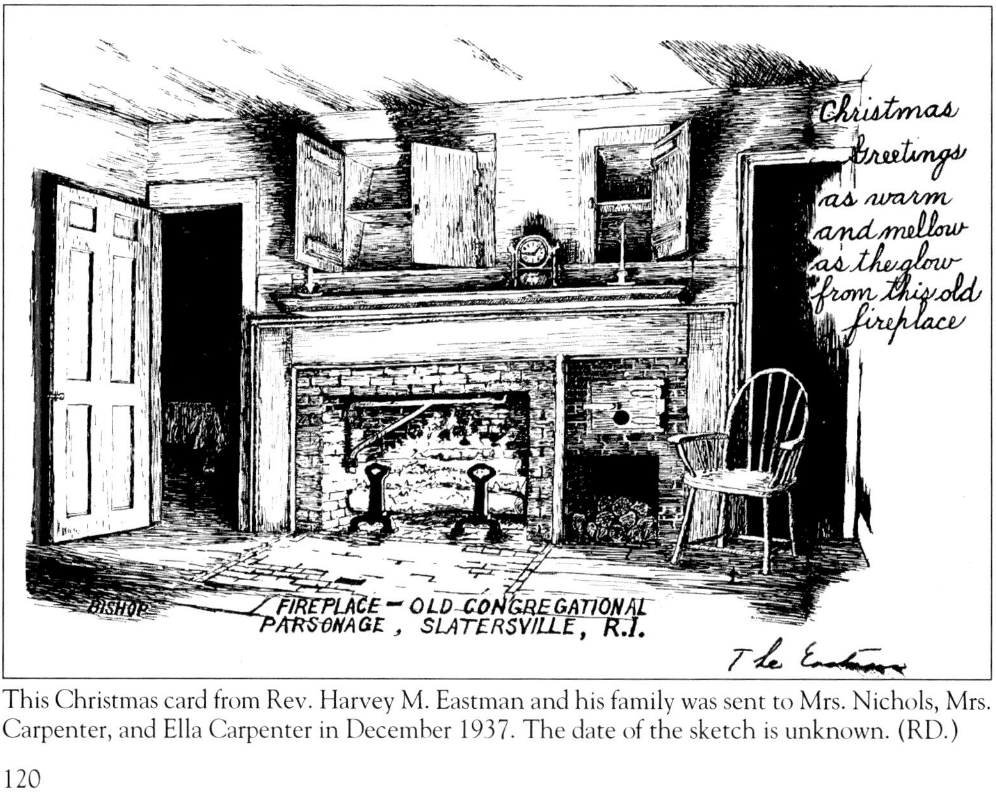

This Christmas card from Rev. Harvey M. Eastman and his family was sent to Mrs. Nichols, Mrs. Carpenter, and Ella Carpenter in December 1937. The date of the sketch is unknown. (RD.)

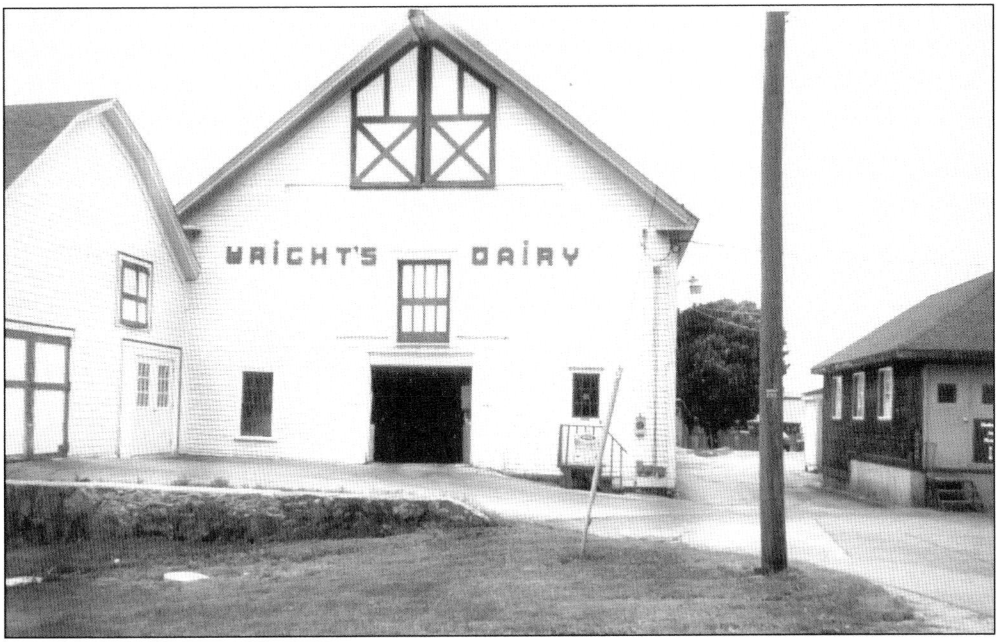

This barn at Wright's Dairy Farm is familiar to most people today and represents a century of continuous dairy farming for the Wright family. The early success of the farm was based on home delivery of milk and cream in glass bottles. In the 1970s, home delivery was discontinued, and a retail store was opened at the farm to sell milk and eggs. In 1972, home-baked pies were added, and by the 1980s, a full line of cakes, cookies, and cream pastries was sold.

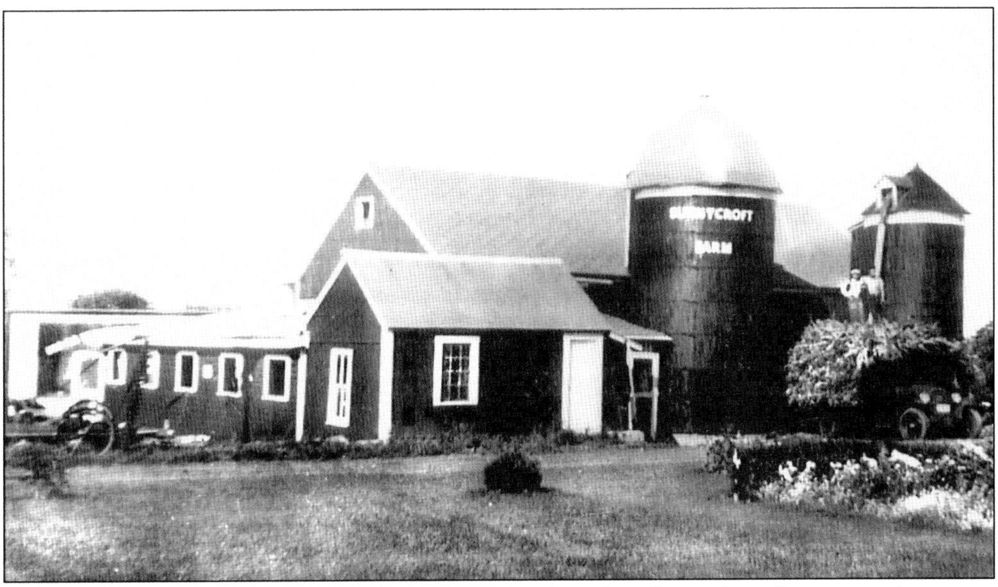

Sunnycroft Farm, seen as it appeared c. 1900, was a dairy farm located at what is now the corner of Mechanic and Central Streets in Slatersville. It was operated by Ed Schnorr Sr. (WSt.)

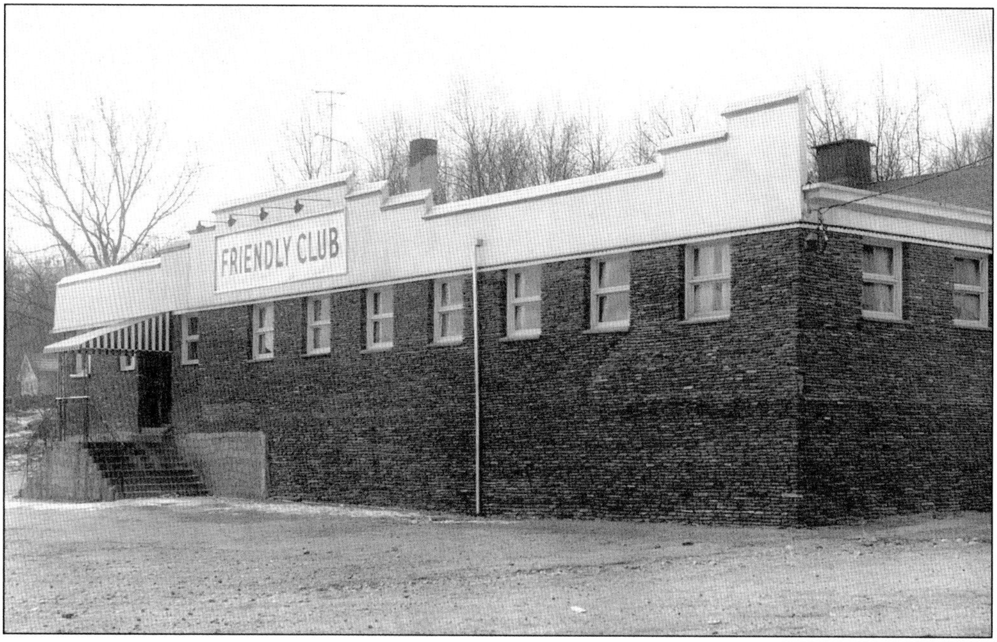

The Friendly Club succeeded the Mayfair as a restaurant on the same site at the corner of Sayles Hill Road and Route 146. It proved so popular that it was enlarged in the 1960s. (SB.)

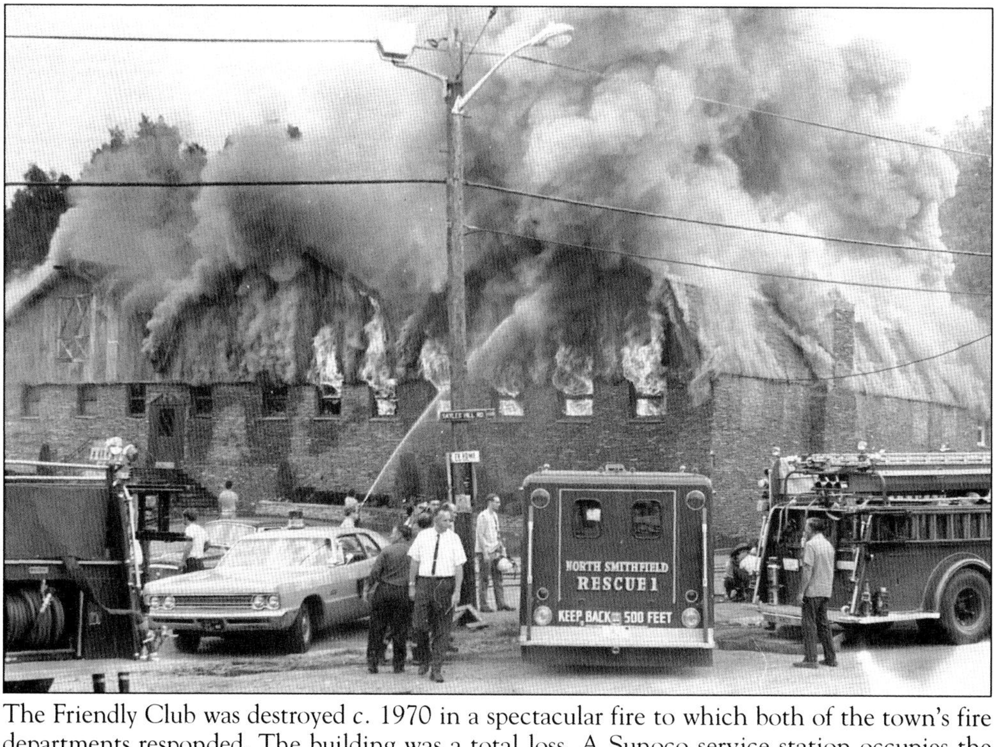

The Friendly Club was destroyed *c.* 1970 in a spectacular fire to which both of the town's fire departments responded. The building was a total loss. A Sunoco service station occupies the site today. (SB.)

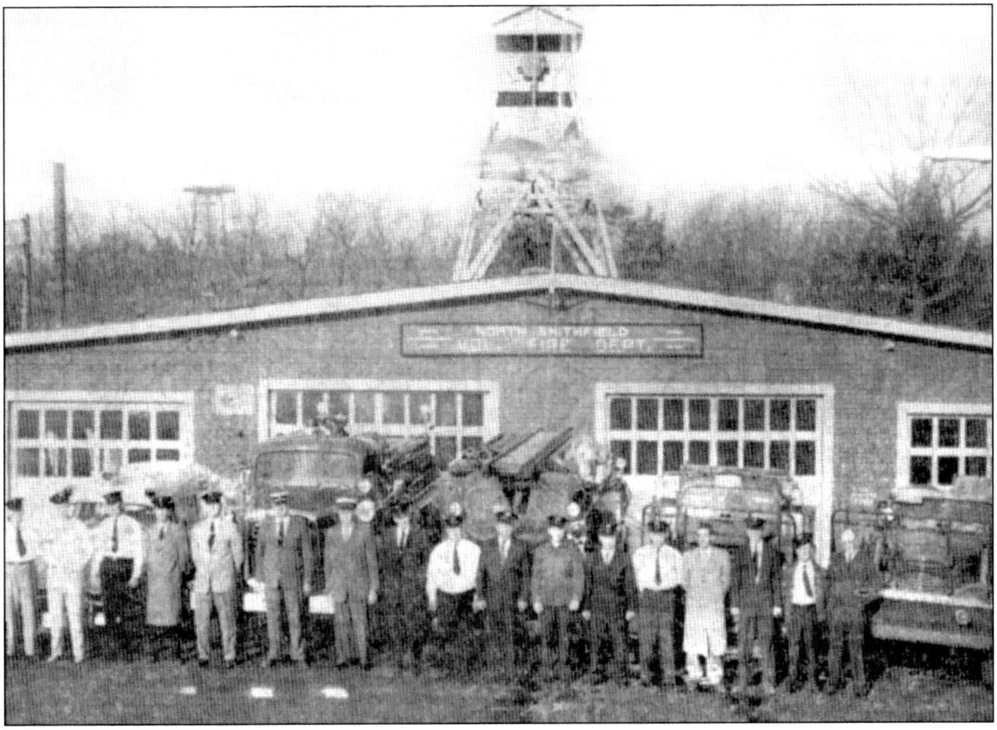

The first town fire department to be organized was the North Smithfield Fire Department, the founding members of which are pictured in front of the St. Paul Street fire station. The siren stands atop the building.

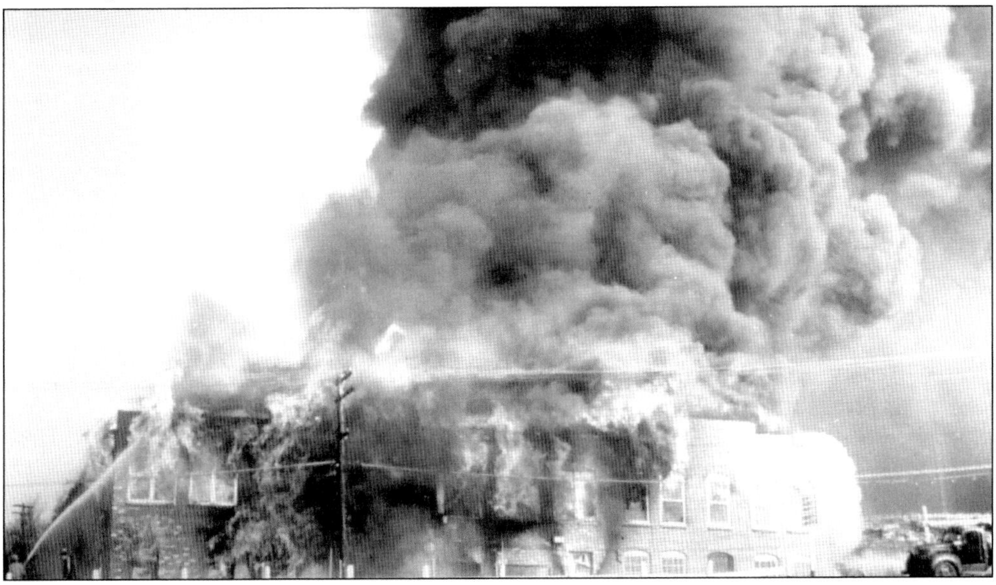

Firefighters' skills were tested at the Tondre Furniture Company fire in February 1955. The two-story brick building was lost in 25 minutes, destroying 10 looms and other textile machinery, as well as furniture. Sam Boyko rescued the pets from a pet store in the building, Lt. Eli Belrose ordered hose laid to the Branch River. Additional firemen from Woonsocker, Glendale, Nasonville, and Blackstone worked under North Smithfield Chief Earl Tabor.

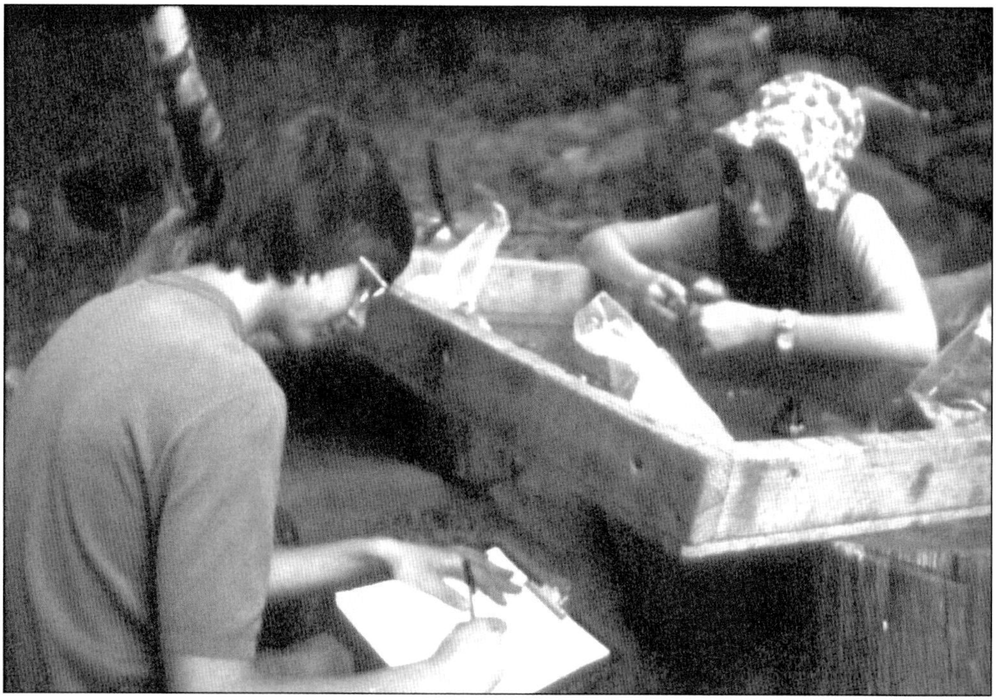

Each July between 1974 and 1976, the North Smithfield Heritage Association helped support a school project in archaeology, in which students in grades 6 through 12 excavated portions of the Jonathan Paine Farm in the woods off Rocky Hill Road under the supervision of trained archaeologists. Artifacts are stored at the North Smithfield Heritage Association headquarters. (IGN.)

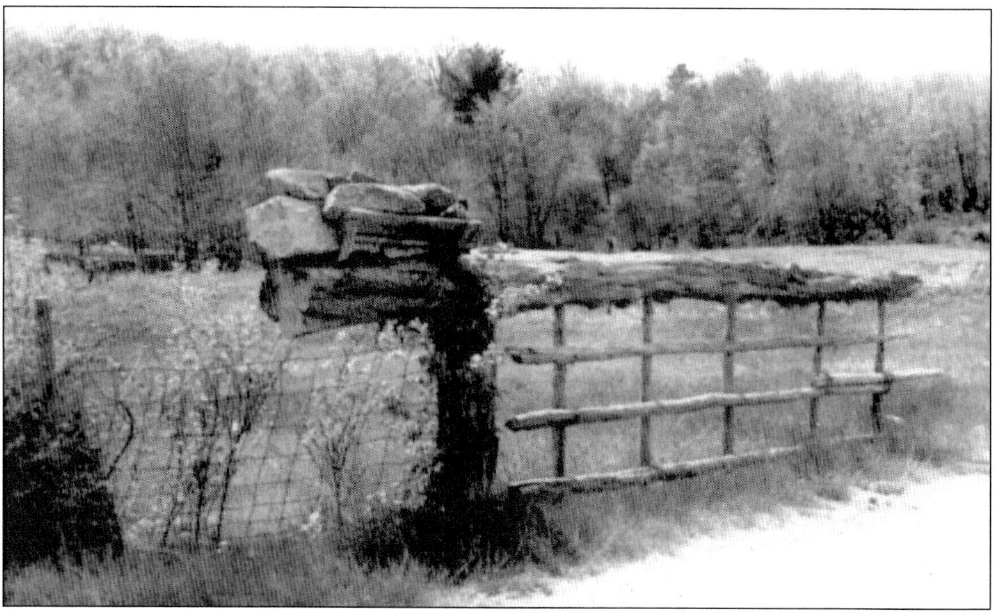

For many years, this weighted swinging gate was a feature along Providence Pike at the long drive into the Harris farm. First to have a telephone (1900) and last to have electricity (the 1950s), the Harris house dates at least to the early 19th century. (WAN.)

Ariel Mowry manned the Woonsocket Hill Fire Tower for more than 25 years, succeeding his brother Forrest, who had served for 28 years. Thus, by the time the new tower was erected in 1959, the Mowry brothers had a record of fire spotting that dated to the first tower built in 1906.

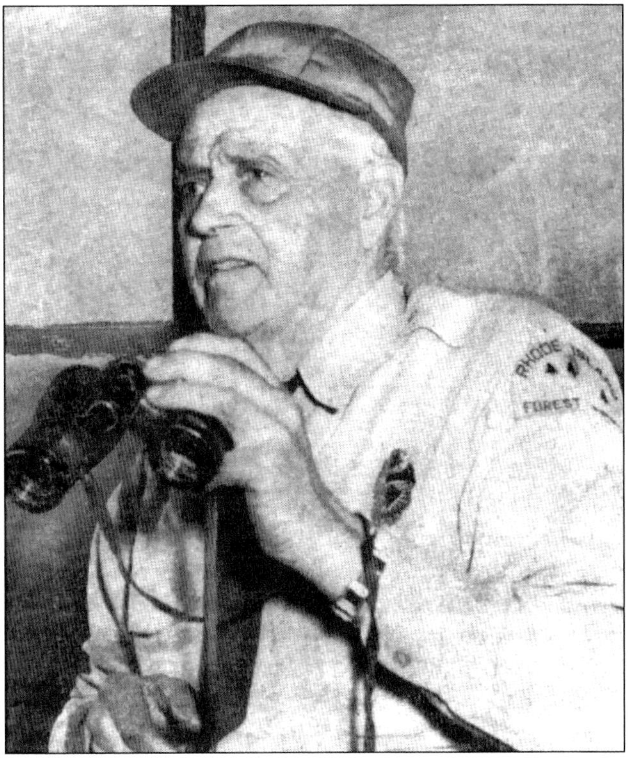

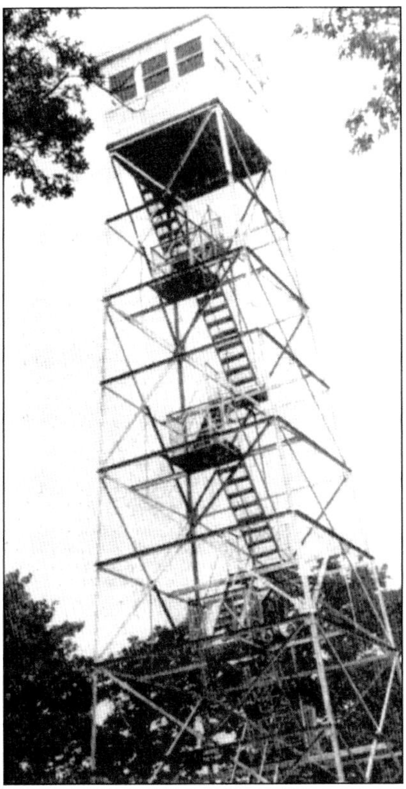

The 1959 fire tower, named for Ariel Mowry, was 65 feet high, with an 11-foot square cabin equipped with telephone, electricity, and a steam radiator. The tower commanded a view of more than 40 miles on a clear day, from the Blue Hills and Mount Wachusett to Exeter and West Greenwich.

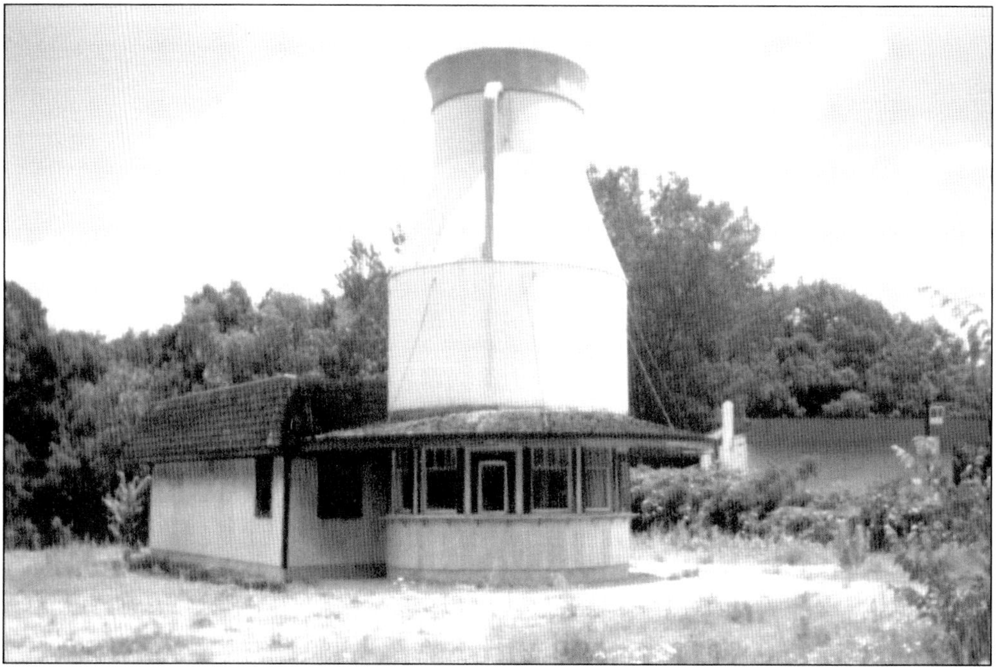

The Milk Can was a popular midcentury ice-cream spot, located on Route 146 in Lincoln. When parts of the highway were changed, the Milk Can was closed, but its unique design made it worthy of preservation. It was moved to North Smithfield but has not been reopened.

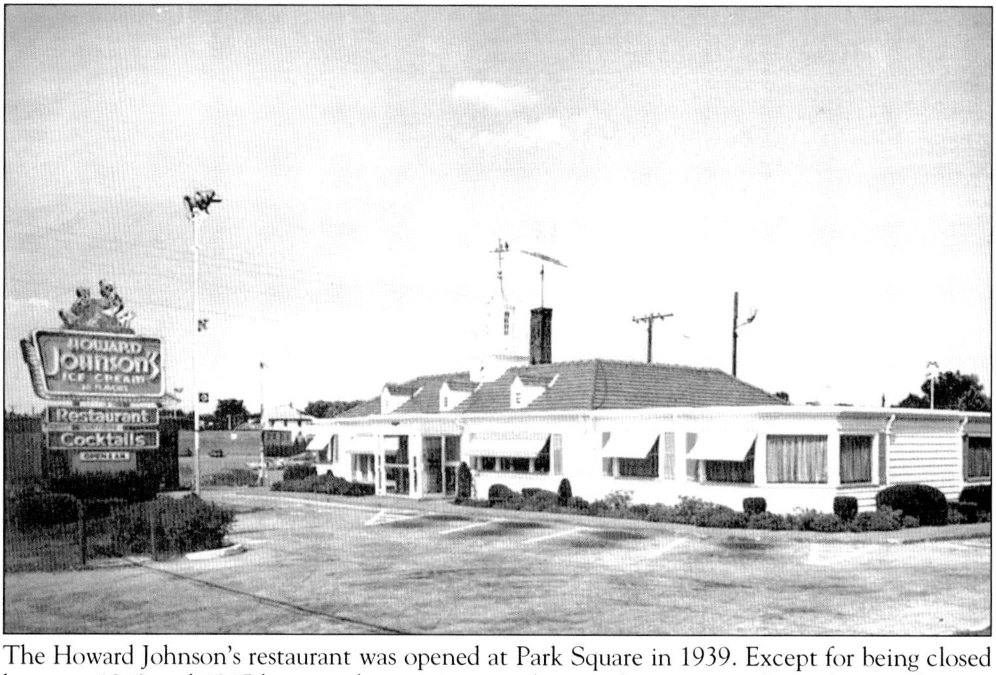

The Howard Johnson's restaurant was opened at Park Square in 1939. Except for being closed between 1942 and 1945 because the wartime gas shortage kept patrons from pleasure driving, the restaurant operated until 1988. Howard Johnson's was famous for its 28 flavors of ice cream. (HSP.)

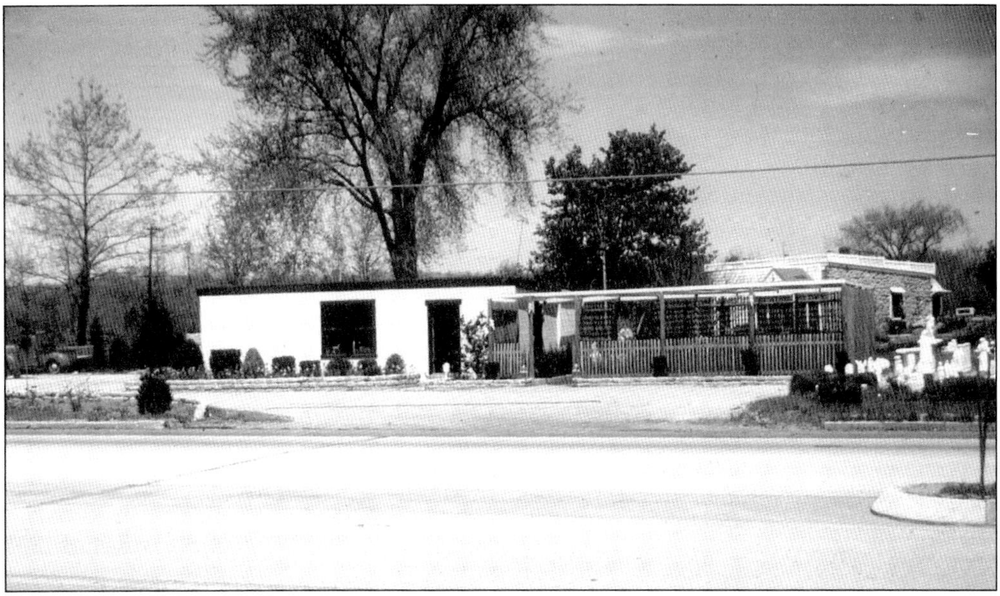

The Louisquisset Pike Nursery, near Old Smithfield Road, was started in 1934 by Oscar and Melina Boucher, who were succeeded by Glen and Garcie Robertson. Shown in the 1950s, it was a complete nursery, with shrubs and trees, as well as flowers. (GR.)

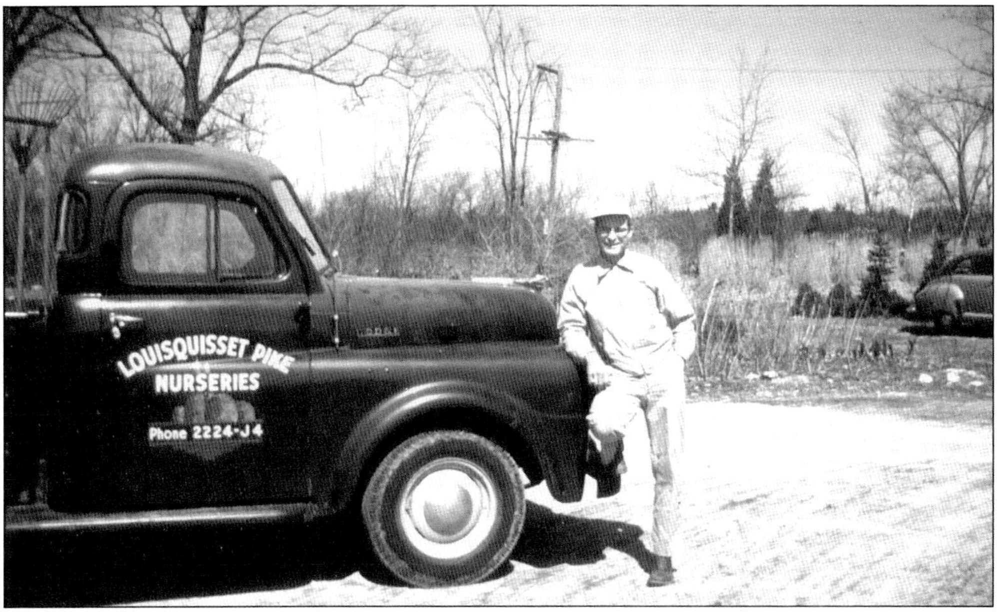

Glen Robertson poses beside his nursery truck. Although the nursery closed in 1975, vestiges can be seen in the tree and shrub growth in its former location beside Route 146A near Old Smithfield Road. (GR.)

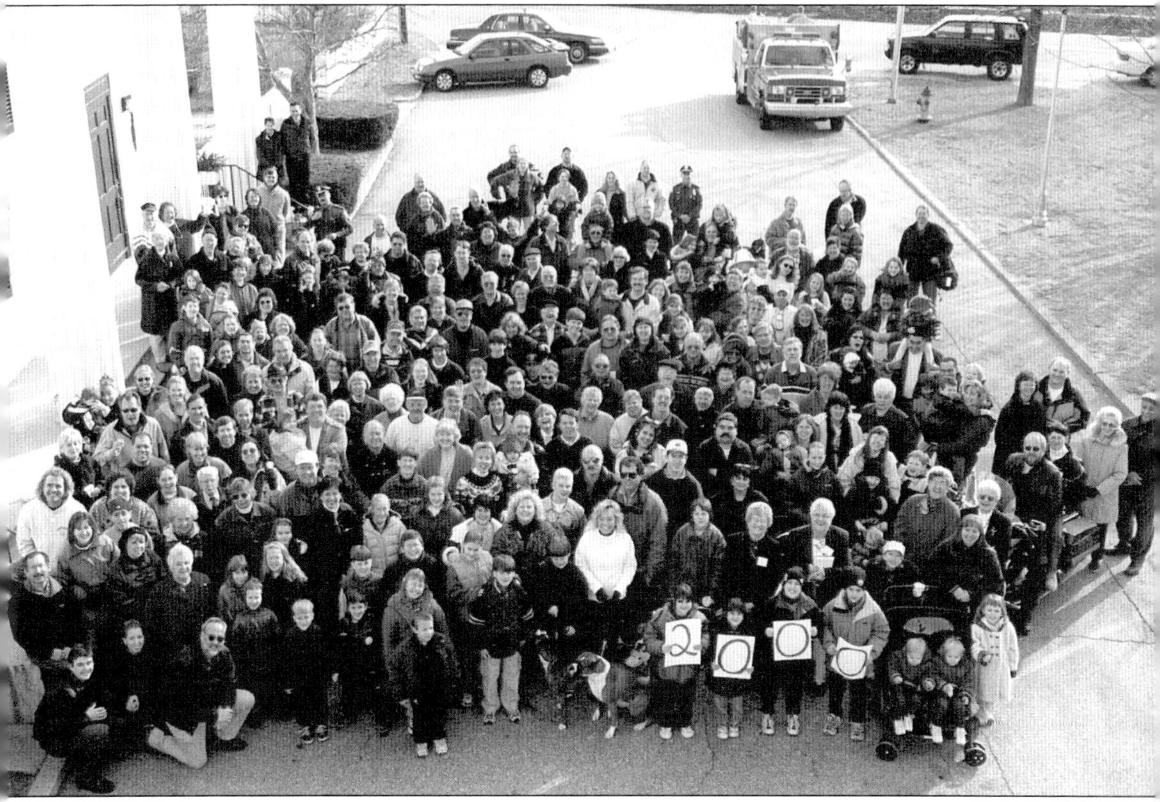

Residents of North Smithfield gather in front of the Slatersville Congregational Church for a photograph at noon on January 1, 2000. All the church bells in the Blackstone Valley rang to usher in the new millennium. Some 350 people joined the celebration.